SO-BLA-514

# KEY ISSUES IN CRIMINAL CAREER RESEARCH
New Analyses of the Cambridge Study in Delinquent Development

This book examines several contentious and understudied criminal career issues using one of the world's most important longitudinal studies, the Cambridge Study in Delinquent Development (CSDD), a longitudinal study of 411 South London boys followed in criminal records to age 40. The analysis reported in the book explores issues related to prevalence, offending frequency, specialization, onset sequences, co-offending, chronicity, career length, and trajectory estimation. The results of the study are considered in the context of development/life-course theories, and the authors outline an agenda for criminal career research generally and within the context of the CSDD specifically.

Alex R. Piquero, Ph.D., is Professor of Criminology, Law and Society and 2005 Magid Term Professor in the College of Arts and Sciences at the University of Florida, Member of the MacArthur Foundation's Research Network on Adolescent Development and Juvenile Justice and Member of the National Consortium on Violence Research.

David P. Farrington, O.B.E., is Professor of Psychological Criminology at the Institute of Criminology, Cambridge University. He is a Fellow of the British Academy, the Academy of Medical Sciences, the British Psychological Society, and the American Society of Criminology and an Honorary Life Member of the British Society of Criminology and the Division of Forensic Psychology of the British Psychological Society.

Alfred Blumstein is a University Professor and the J. Erik Jonsson Professor of Urban Systems and Operations Research, former Dean (from 1986 to 1993) at the H. John Heinz III School of Public Policy and Management of Carnegie Mellon University, and Director of the National Consortium on Violence Research.

# Cambridge Studies in Criminology

*Editors*
Alfred Blumstein *H. John Heinz School of Public Policy and Management, Carnegie Mellon University*
David Farrington, *Institute of Criminology, Cambridge University*

**Other books in the series:**

*continued after the Index*

# KEY ISSUES IN CRIMINAL CAREER RESEARCH

New Analyses of the Cambridge Study in Delinquent Development

Alex R. Piquero
*University of Florida*

David P. Farrington
*Cambridge University*

Alfred Blumstein
*Carnegie Mellon University*

CAMBRIDGE UNIVERSITY PRESS
Cambridge, New York, Melbourne, Madrid, Cape Town, Singapore, São Paulo

Cambridge University Press
32 Avenue of the Americas, New York, NY 10013-2473, USA

www.cambridge.org
Information on this title: www.cambridge.org/9780521848657

© Alex R. Piquero, David P. Farrington, Alfred Blumstein 2007

This publication is in copyright. Subject to statutory exception
and to the provisions of relevant collective licensing agreements,
no reproduction of any part may take place without
the written permission of Cambridge University Press.

First published 2007

Printed in the United States of America

*A catalog record for this publication is available from the British Library.*

*Library of Congress Cataloging in Publication data*
Piquero, Alexis Russell.
Key issues in criminal career research : new analyses of the Cambridge
Study in Delinquent Development / Alex R. Piquero, David P. Farrington,
Alfred Blumstein.
p. cm. – (Cambridge studies in criminology)
Includes bibliographical references and index.
ISBN 0-521-84865-2 (hardback) – ISBN 0-521-61309-4 (pbk.)

1. Crime and age – Longitudinal studies. 2. Crime and
age – England – London – Longitudinal studies.
3. Criminals – England – London – Longitudinal studies. 4. Juvenile
delinquents – England – London – Longitudinal studies. 5. Criminal
behavior – England – London – Longitudinal studies. 6. Criminology.
I. Farrington, David P. II. Blumstein, Alfred. III. Title. IV. Series:
Cambridge studies in criminology (Cambridge University Press)
HV6163.P57 2007
364.3609421–dc22          2006011725

ISBN 978-0-521-84865-7 hardback

ISBN 978-0-521-61309-5 paperback

Cambridge University Press has no responsibility for the persistence or accuracy of
URLs for third-party Internet Web sites referred to in this publication and does not
guarantee that any content on such Web sites is, or will remain, accurate or appropriate.

# Contents

# Foreword

In *The Great Instauration*, a work published in 1620 that heralded the coming of science as the dominant arbiter of truth, Sir Francis Bacon proclaimed that the measure of a science was how much it contributed to the alleviation of the miseries of mankind. While we sometimes debate the role that science can and should play in forming public policy, there is no doubt that the goal of science is to improve understanding to enhance control. This is very clear in the scientific study of crime where from the beginning the goal has been to understand the distribution and occurrences of crime so as to identify ways through which such behavior could be prevented and controlled. That is why understanding of the "criminal career" – its beginning, its ending, and the kinds of events that occur in between – is such an important endeavor. This is especially true for those whose criminal involvements are extreme even by the standards of those who commit serious crimes – the "career criminals" who make a career out of serious criminal behavior. This focus on the extreme criminal, in part, explains why early criminologists so easily accepted the notion that the only criminals of consequence are those who have been identified by the criminal justice system. They understood that there were other criminals and crimes that the criminal justice system did not frequently encounter, but they also understood that the crimes that most directly contributed to the miseries of mankind were those that were the focus of the criminal justice system.

While many understood the importance of preventing and controlling these extreme criminals, the early focus of criminology was on crime more generally. It was not until publication of research by Wolfgang and

Sellin in the late 1960s that criminologists understood the importance of focusing on what they called chronic delinquent offenders. As a graduate student during that time, I was fortunate to work at their research center. While my focus (as one of many students) was on the issue of age of onset, everyone understood the importance of the work of others at the center that established that in a birth cohort, 6% of the cohort accounted for 52% of the recorded delinquencies, 80% of the serious delinquencies, and a disproportionate amount of the confinements. Ten years later when I was working at the Department of Justice, I was introduced to the Attorney General as a criminologist. He asked me what were three things that I knew as a criminologist that he should know as the Attorney General. One of my responses concerned the importance of chronic offenders. While he seemed impressed with the precision of my response, he observed that while the existence of such offenders was well known, what was needed were ways to identify them before they committed so many crimes. Not much has changed since 1976 – until this book.

Wolfgang and Sellin's *Delinquency in a Birth Cohort* was different from much of criminology in its almost total absence of attention to theory. This work merged the two great elements of sociology at the University of Pennsylvania in the 1950s and 1960s—criminology and demography. The focus was on careful and complete description before explanation. Much of criminology to that point (and too much since) consisted of descriptions that reinforced poorly developed theories. Of course, the absence of explanation did not stop some from moving directly from description to control and prevention. Scales to predict repeat offenders, risk instruments to assist judges, and career offender prosecution units developed as responses to the description and estimation of the number and impact of chronic offenders. All of these efforts were well intended, and all were unlikely to succeed without a better understanding of why some offenders continued to offend more than others. The failure of these efforts even led some to suggest that there were no chronic offenders, and that if there were, their identification and control were impossible. Fortunately, some (most notably Blumstein and Farrington in their different but complementary ways) continued research that demonstrated that chronics exist, that their rate of offending (or lambda, a notation Blumstein used not only to introduce simplicity to statements about frequency but also to begin a more structured way of thinking about criminal careers) is different, and that they have characteristics that distinguish them from those who do not offend or who offend at a much lower rate. Still, the development of a theoretical understanding of the differences among these different kinds of offenders remained elusive.

The physicist Paul Dirac is quoted in Simon Singh's classic analysis of Einstein as saying that, "In science one tries to tell people, in such a way as to be understood by everyone, something that no one ever knew before them." In science there is careful description, then experimentation, then understanding (or scientific theory), and then control. This pathway requires many to contribute before the breakthrough in knowledge, hence the metaphor of standing on the shoulders of giants to advance science. Piquero, Farrington, and Blumstein have met Dirac's challenge and truly have advanced our understanding of career criminals (I cannot get out of my mind a picture of Piquero standing on Farrington standing on Blumstein). Not only do they provide the definitive analysis of the literature on career criminals and offer new insights from the Cambridge Study in Delinquency Development to the central empirical questions raised by the concept of criminal careers (e.g., age of onset, lambda, specialization, trajectories, termination), they, more importantly, begin the careful development of a theoretical model that provides the link between description and improving the conditions of "mankind." In its modern formulations, developmental criminology (or life-course criminology) has a strong descriptive and explanatory approach that complements the concept of criminal careers. As a major contributor to this literature, Piquero has demonstrated the connections between these two streams in criminological thought. In *Key Issues in Criminal Career Research*, the authors link the rich empirical literature on criminal careers with a theoretical approach that assumes the existence of a diversity of offenders and their individual criminal histories.

Scientific theory summarizes agreed-upon facts through statements about what is currently unobservable but consistent with those facts. Facts without theory are description; theory without facts is nonscientific speculation. Theory of the latter type accumulates but is not cumulative. Much of criminological theory is nonscientific, not because the authors do not value science but because the rush to theory limits the facts they consider. One study produces findings that generate a theory. In *Key Issues* we find 40 years of facts analyzed, summarized, and interpreted using a theoretical approach that fits the facts. While this does not yet provide the simple causal model that others offer as explanations of all crime, it does set us on the path for developing explanations of criminal careers that can be used to prevent and control this most troublesome form of criminal behavior.

One of the most frequently encountered criticisms of social sciences is that we state the obvious in ways that only insiders can understand. Jargon and statistical obfuscation are the most obvious manifestations of this criticism. As Dirac stated, science should be understandable to all – not its methods but certainly its findings. Piquero et al. have met this standard. Complex material is clearly presented. Useful, but not misleading, summaries are provided. The clarity of writing reflects the authors' clarity of understanding of the issues.

Charles F. Wellford
University of Maryland

# Acknowledgments

The writing of any book does not come without appreciation for the various individuals who have helped us along the way. First, we would like to thank the participants in the Cambridge Study in Delinquent Development (CSDD) for their original and current participation in the project. Without their assistance and cooperation, none of this would have been possible. Second, we are very grateful to the British Home Office for funding the CSDD and to Gwen Gundry, Lynda Morley, and Sandra Lambert for collecting criminal record data. Third, students and colleagues at Carnegie Mellon University, Cambridge University, and the University of Florida participated in seminars taught by us, read and reacted to various versions of our manuscript, and offered invaluable criticism and advice. Fourth, we would like to extend our thanks to the many colleagues and friends whose work has inspired us in our efforts to document and understand the longitudinal patterning of criminal careers. Although they are too many to mention, we would especially like to thank Robert Brame, Shawn Bushway, Avshalom Caspi, Elizabeth Cauffman, Jacqueline Cohen, Frank Cullen, Deborah Denno, Glen Elder, Jr., Mike Ezell, Delbert Elliott, Jeff Fagan, John Hagan, Peggy Giordano, David F. Greenberg, Rudy Haapanen, J. David Hawkins, Julie Horney, Daivd Huizinga, Marvin Krohn, Kenneth Land, John Laub, Marc LeBlanc, Akiva Liberman, Rolf Loeber, Shadd Maruna, Paul Mazerolle, Joan McCord, Terrie E. Moffitt, Edward P. Mulvey, Daniel S. Nagin, Wayne Osgood, Ray Paternoster, Gerald Patterson, Joan Petersilia, Lee Robins, Robert Sampson, Lyle Shannon, Ron Simons, Darrell Steffens-meier, Laurence Steinberg, Terence Thornberry, Stephen Tibbetts,

xiv                                    ACKNOWLEDGMENTS

Charles Tittle, Paul Tracy, Richard Tremblay, Christy Visher, Charles Wellford, P.O. Wikström and Marvin Wolfgang. Fifth, our editor at Cambridge University Press, Ed Parsons, and his editorial assistant, Faith Black, have been significant supporters of our project. The editorial work of Regina Paleski is also appreciated. Their keen eye for detail and useful suggestions have made this book far better than when we delivered it to them. Sixth, we would like to extend special thanks to our wives, Nicole Leeper Piquero, Sally Farrington, and Dolores Blumstein, who provided good humor and constant forgiveness as we prepared this book. Lastly, we are also grateful to the following journals and publishers for allowing us to use, in part and in revised form, materials published elsewhere, including: Lila Kazemian and David P. Farrington (2005), "Comparing the Validity of Prospective, Retrospective, and Official Onset for Different Offending Categories," *Journal of Quantitative Criminology* 21:127–147; Lila Kazemian and David P. Farrington (2006), "Exploring Residual Career Length and Residual Number of Offenses for Two Generations of Repeat Offenders," *Journal of Research in Crime and Delinquency* 43:89–113; David P. Farrington and Donald J. West (1995), "Effects of Marriage, Separation, and Children on Offending by Adult Males," in Z. S. Blau and J. Hagan (eds.), *Current Perspectives on Aging and the Life Cycle*, vol. 4: *Delinquency and Disrepute in the Life Course: Contextual and Dynamic Analyses* (Greenwich, CT: JAI Press); Alex R. Piquero, David P. Farrington, and Alfred Blumstein (2003), "The Criminal Career Paradigm," in Michael Tonry (ed.), *Crime and Justice: A Review of Research*, vol. 30 (Chicago: University of Chicago Press).

This book is dedicated to Donald J. West, founder of the Cambridge Study in Delinquent Development (CSDD).

# Introduction

"Who are YOU?" said the Caterpillar. This was not an encouraging opening for a conversation. Alice replied, rather shyly, "I – I hardly know, sir, just at present – at least I know who I WAS when I got up this morning, but I think I must have been changed several times since then." "What do you mean by that?" said the Caterpillar sternly. "Explain yourself!" "I can't explain MYSELF, I'm afraid, sir," said Alice, "because I'm not myself, you see." "I don't see," said the Caterpillar. "I'm afraid I can't put it more clearly," Alice replied very politely, "for I can't understand it myself to begin with; and being so many different sizes in a day is very confusing."
(From *Alice in Wonderland*, Chapter 5, "Advice from a Caterpillar").

Criminologists have long been interested in the longitudinal patterning of criminal activity over the life-course, or how and why criminal behavior begins, continues, and ends. Prominent qualitative and quantitative studies have sought to describe individual initiation, continuation, and cessation of criminal offending. For example, Quetelet's (1831) *Research on the Propensity for Crime at Different Ages* was one of the first large-scale studies to provide a description of the aggregate relationship between age and crime. Shaw's (1928) *The Jack-Roller* told the captivating story of Stanley's delinquency in Chicago at the turn of the century. A key "turning point" (Laub, 2004:12) was Wolfgang and colleagues' (1972) *Delinquency in a Birth Cohort*, which highlighted the fact that a small group of juvenile offenders was responsible for a disproportionate amount of crime. Undoubtedly, the Wolfgang birth cohort study stimulated the development of the criminal career paradigm that provided a framework for criminologists to ask questions regarding the onset, persistence, and desistance of criminal activity over the life-course (Piquero et al., 2003). One key outcome of the Wolfgang et al. study was the establishment of a National Academy of Sciences Panel on Criminal Careers (Blumstein et al., 1986), funded in part by the National Institute of Justice. Subsequently, the Office of Juvenile Justice and Delinquency Prevention (OJJDP) in the United States mounted three longitudinal studies, known as the Causes and Correlates studies, in Pittsburgh, Denver, and Rochester, NY (Huizinga et al., 2003; Loeber et al., 2003; Thornberry et al., 2003), to advance knowledge about the development of offending and about risk and protective factors.

One particular outgrowth of the criminal career paradigm is the developmental approach to studying criminal activity over the life-course, an approach that has become a staple within the field of criminology (Laub and Sampson, 1993; Le Blanc and Loeber, 1998; Loeber and Le Blanc, 1990; Piquero and Mazerolle, 2001; Tremblay et al., 2003). A core assumption of developmental and life-course criminology (DLC) is that changes with age in delinquency and criminal activity occur in an orderly way (Thornberry, 1997:1). Many of the DLC theories that were developed after the National Academy of Sciences Panel on Criminal Careers (Blumstein et al., 1986) were a reaction to what was perceived by many as a largely atheoretical criminal career paradigm. Thus, many of these DLC theories focused on factors influencing onset, persistence, and desistance (Farrington, 2005; Le Blanc, 1997; Loeber and Hay, 1994; Moffitt, 1993; Patterson et al., 1989; Sampson and Laub, 1993; Thornberry and Krohn, 2001).

Generally speaking, DLC is concerned with three main issues: the development of offending and antisocial behavior, risk factors at different ages, and the effects of life events on the course of development (Farrington, 2003:221). First, researchers have documented involvement and changes in criminal activity throughout adolescence and into early adulthood (Tracy et al., 1990; Tracy and Kempf-Leonard, 1996), with few studies documenting race and/or gender differences in criminal activity into adulthood (Moffitt et al., 2001; Piquero and Buka, 2002) and even fewer studies providing information on criminal activity past the early 30s (Robins, 1978). Sampson and Laub's (2003) recent follow-up of members of the original Glueck and Glueck (1950) study into their 70s is a striking counterexample. Second, researchers have paid close attention to the risk factors associated with entrance into – and continuation of – criminal activity as well as the protective factors that prevent individuals from starting offending and that help them stop offending (Farrington, 2000; Hawkins and Catalano, 1992; Loeber and Farrington, 1998). Finally, criminologists have found that some life events like marriage and steady employment can help reduce criminal activity and foster desistance (Farrington and West, 1995; Horney et al., 1995; Laub et al., 1998; Piquero et al., 2002), while other life events such as incarceration can encourage further criminal activity (Sampson and Laub, 1997) and reduce the chances of legitimate employment (Western, Kling, and Weiman, 2001).

There appear to be ten widely accepted conclusions about the development of offending (Farrington, 2003:2):

1 The age of onset of offending is most typically between ages 8 and 14, earlier with self-report data and later with official records, while the age of desistance from offending is typically between 20 and 29 (though a small subset of offenders continue well into adulthood).

2 The prevalence of offending peaks in the late teenage years: between ages 15 and 19.

3 An early age of onset predicts a relatively long criminal career duration and the commission of relatively more offenses.

4 There is marked continuity in offending and antisocial behavior from childhood to the teenage years and adulthood. In other words, there is relative stability of the ordering of people on some measure of antisocial behavior over time, and people who commit relatively many offenses during one age range have a high probability of also committing relatively many offenses during a later age range.

5 A small fraction of the population ("chronic offenders") commit a large fraction of all crimes; chronic offenders tend to have an early onset, a high individual offending frequency, and a long criminal career.

6 Offending is more versatile than specialized; violent offenders in particular appear to offend frequently in other kinds of offenses.

7 The types of acts defined as offenses are elements of a larger syndrome of antisocial behavior that includes heavy drinking, reckless driving, promiscuous sex, and so forth.

8 It appears that, as people enter adulthood, they change from group to lone offending. In fact, most offenses up to the late teenage years are committed with others, whereas most offenses from age 20 onward are committed alone.

9 The reasons given for offending up to the late teenage years are quite variable, including excitement/enjoyment, boredom, and/or emotional or utilitarian reasons. From age 20 onward, utilitarian motives become increasingly dominant.

10 Different types of offenses tend to be first committed at distinctively different ages. This sort of progression is such that shoplifting tends to be committed before burglary, burglary before robbery, and so forth. In general, diversification increases up to age 20; but after age 20, diversification decreases and specialization increases.

Still, there exist some contentious DLC issues that have not been well studied and/or have generated discrepant results. Eight issues in particular are identified here:

1 While it is clear that the prevalence of offending peaks in the late teenage years, it is less clear how the individual offending frequency (i.e., the frequency of offending among those who offend) varies with age. Some studies suggest that individual offending frequency accelerates to a peak in the late teenage years and decelerates in the 20s, whereas others suggest that individual offending frequency changes much less with age (Loeber and Snyder, 1990).

2 It is not clear whether the seriousness of offending escalates up to a certain age and then de-escalates, or whether it is much more stable with age.

3 While it is clear that an early onset of offending predicts a long career and many offenses, it is far less clear whether an early onset predicts a high individual offending frequency or a high average seriousness of offending. Nor is it clear whether early-onset offenders differ in degree or in kind from later-onset offenders or how much there are distinctly different behavioral trajectories.

4 Although chronic offenders commit more offenses than others, it is not clear whether their offenses are more serious on average or whether chronic offenders differ in degree or in kind from nonchronic offenders.

5 While it is clear that certain offenses occur on average before other types and that onset sequences can be identified, it is not clear whether these onset sequences are merely age-appropriate behavioral manifestations of some common underlying theoretical construct or if the onset of one type of behavior facilitates or acts as a stepping stone toward the onset of another. In other words, onset sequences could reflect persistent heterogeneity or state dependence (Ezell and Cohen, 2005; Nagin and Farrington, 1992a, b; Nagin and Paternoster, 1991, 2000). Similarly, little is known about onset sequences in which

childhood antisocial behavior might have some kind of influence on later offending.

6 Although there is some research that appears to indicate that offenders are more versatile than specialized, these findings have been produced largely by research using official records through age 18. Very little information has been provided about how specialization/versatility varies with age into adulthood (Piquero et al., 1999). Even less attention has been paid to the extent to which observations of specialization or versatility vary between official and self-report records (Lynam et al., 2004).

7 While much attention has been paid to the topic of desistance (Bushway et al., 2001; Giordano et al., 2002; Laub and Sampson, 2001; Laub et al., 1998; Maruna, 2001), little attention has been paid to developing estimates of career length or duration (Piquero et al., 2004) as well as residual career length (Blumstein et al., 1982; Kazemian and Farrington, 2006). Such information bears directly on policy issues regarding appropriate sentence lengths. For example, shorter residual careers would suggest shorter rather than longer sentences.

8 There has been very little research conducted on co-offending generally (Sarnecki, 2001; Warr, 2002) or on changes in co-offending over the course of a criminal career specifically (Reiss and Farrington, 1991).

Because there exists little descriptive work on the longitudinal patterning of criminal activity into adulthood (Blokland et al., 2005; Ezell and Cohen, 2005; Laub and Sampson, 2003), we focus on the first, more descriptive aspects of DLC and attempt to shed some light on the several contentious DLC issues noted above, as well as on several others not specifically identified by Farrington (2003), including how offending trajectories vary with age. A highlight of our work is that we examine these contentious issues with one of the world's most important and widely used longitudinal studies: the Cambridge Study in Delinquent Development (CSDD), a longitudinal study of 411 South London boys followed in criminal records from age 10 to age 40.

The empirical findings in this book are the results of new analyses using this classic data set, which is described in Chapter 3. Our hope is to provide descriptive information on the offending careers of over four hundred male adolescents followed into adulthood. These data are among the longest available time spans that document and describe the longitudinal patterning of criminal activity. In Chapter 2, we provide a general overview of the main findings of criminal career research, developmental and life-course criminology. Here, our task is to bring readers up to date on the current state of criminal career research, in particular to highlight some of the contentious or underresearched issues examined herein. Then, in Chapters 4 through 11, we review the difficult DLC issues and provide evidence that bear on them. Following the approach of Moffitt and colleagues' (2001) *Sex Differences in Antisocial Behaviour*, we organize each chapter as if it were a research report. Each chapter presents a brief overview of the contentious issue, what the extant research shows, and how we contribute information on it. At the end of each chapter, we list conclusions and remaining questions. The conclusions are designed to provide readers with a brief summary of what has been learned with regard to that particular issue, while the unanswered questions acknowledge that this study cannot answer all questions fully but can help stimulate and focus future research. Then, in Chapter 12 we present a summary of the findings and outline priorities for a future research agenda. Additionally, we also outline a broad sketch for the next 40 years of follow-up of the CSDD. Although the questions posed and results obtained in the ensuing chapters are designed specifically for students of criminal activity over the life-course, we try to communicate such information to a general audience as well.

CHAPTER TWO

# Overview of Criminal Careers

Researchers have long been interested in the patterning of criminal activity over the course of criminal careers (e.g., Greenberg, 1991; Rowe et al., 1990). Many years ago, Quetelet (1831) recognized that the propensity for crime varied with age. Using data on crimes committed against persons and property in France from 1826 to 1829, he found that crimes peaked in the late teens through the mid 20s. Since Quetelet's findings, many researchers have investigated the relationship between age and crime, across cultures and historical periods, and for a number of different crime types (Hirschi and Gottfredson, 1983). The relationship between age and crime has been one of the most studied issues within criminology (Farrington, 1986; Steffensmeier et al., 1989; Tittle and Grasmick, 1997).

The relationship between age and crime raises the question of the degree to which the *aggregate* pattern displayed in the age/crime curve (crime rising to a peak in the late teens and then declining more or less slowly depending on crime type) is similar to – or different from – the pattern of *individual* careers and what conclusions about individuals can be validly drawn from aggregate data. For example, how much does the observed peak of the aggregate age/crime curve reflect changes within individuals as opposed to changes in the composition of offenders? In other words, is the peak in the age/crime curve a function of active

Much of the information in this chapter is reproduced from Alex R. Piquero, David P. Farrington, and Alfred Blumstein, 2003, "The Criminal Career Paradigm." In Michael Tonry, ed., *Crime and Justice: A Review of Research*, vol. 30. Chicago: University of Chicago Press. Permission has been granted by the University of Chicago Press.

7

offenders committing more crime, or is it a function of more individuals actively offending during those peak years and fewer during the later years?

Within individuals, to what extent is the slowing of offending past the peak age a function of deceleration in continued criminal activity or stopping by some people? Across individuals, how much of the age/crime curve can be attributed to the arrival/initiation and departure/termination of different people? How about the role of co-offending? How much of the continuation of offending by lone/solo offenders is attributable to their having criminal careers of long duration, with co-offenders having shorter careers? How much of the age/crime curve for any particular crime type is a consequence of individuals persisting in offending, but switching from less serious crime types early in the career to more serious crime types as they get older? What about the relationship between past and future offending? Is there an effect of causal factors or changes in causal factors (state dependence), unobserved individual differences (persistent heterogeneity), or some combination of the two?

These questions are central to theory, as well as policy, especially those policies that are geared toward incapacitative effects of criminal sanctions, and to changes in the criminal career (e.g., rehabilitation or criminalization patterns as a result of actions by the criminal justice system). For example, if crime commission and arrest rates differ significantly among offenders and over the career, the effect of time served on overall crime will depend on who is incarcerated and for how long (Petersilia 1980:325). Addressing these and related issues requires knowledge about individual criminal careers, their initiation, their termination, and the dynamic changes between these end points (Blumstein et al., 1986).

In 1983, a Panel on Research on Criminal Careers was convened by the National Academy of Sciences at the request of the U.S. National Institute of Justice and was charged with evaluating the feasibility of analyzing the course of criminal careers, assessing the usefulness of prediction instruments in reducing crime through incapacitation, and reviewing the contribution of research on criminal careers to the development of fundamental knowledge about crime and criminals. This report outlined a basic approach for asking questions regarding the longitudinal patterning of criminal activity over the life-course, that is, the criminal career paradigm (Blumstein et al., 1986).

Since publication of the report, numerous theoretical, empirical, and policy issues have surfaced regarding the longitudinal patterning of criminal careers. One concerned the relevance of criminal career research for criminology generally and for public policy specifically. Gottfredson and Hirschi (1990) leveled a series of critiques against the criminal career approach in which they claimed that attempts to identify career criminals and other types of offenders prospectively were doomed to failure. Perhaps the most important issue they raised concerns causality. Although the criminal career paradigm necessitates a longitudinal focus in order to study the within-individual patterning of criminal activity, Gottfredson and Hirschi questioned whether longitudinal research designs could actually resolve questions of causal order. They also argued that, because correlations with offending were the same at all ages, cross-sectional designs were adequate for studying the causes of crime. They also argued that the correlates of onset, persistence, and desistance were the same.

This chapter summarizes the background and recent developments regarding the criminal career paradigm. The first section provides a brief review of this paradigm, as well as an overview of the empirical findings generated by criminal career research, with a concentration on the dimensions of criminal careers. The second section presents a discussion of selected policy implications, including the identification of career criminals and policies associated with sentence duration and time served. The final section outlines the challenges and responses to the criminal career paradigm, as well as the theories that were influenced by the criminal career paradigm.

## The Criminal Career Paradigm

At its most basic level, a criminal career is the "characterization of the longitudinal sequence of crimes committed by an individual offender" (Blumstein et al.,1986:12). This definition helps to focus researchers' attention on entry into a career when or before the first crime is committed or recorded and dropout from the career when or after the last crime is committed or recorded. The criminal career paradigm recognizes that individuals start their criminal activity at some age, engage in crime at some individual crime rate, commit a mixture of crimes, and eventually stop. Hence, the criminal career approach emphasizes the need to investigate issues related to why and when people start offending (onset), why and how they continue offending (persistence), why and if offending becomes more frequent or serious (escalation) or specialized, and why and when people stop offending (desistance). The study of criminal careers does not imply that offenders necessarily derive their livelihood exclusively or even predominantly from crime; instead, the career concept is intended only as a means of structuring the longitudinal sequence of criminal events associated with an individual in a systematic way (Blumstein et al., 1982:5). In sum, the criminal career approach focuses on within-individual changes in criminal activity over time, and this then permits aggregating this information for groups of offenders.

## Dimensions of a Criminal Career

*Participation.* The criminal career approach partitions the aggregate crime rate into two primary components: "participation," the distinction between those who commit crime and those who do not; and "frequency," the rate of offending among active offenders, commonly denoted by the Greek letter lambda, or λ (Blumstein et al., 1986:12). Participation is measured by the fraction of a population ever committing at least one crime before some age or currently active during some particular observation period. In any period active offenders include both new offenders whose first offense occurs during the observation period and persisting offenders who began criminal activity in an earlier period and continue to be active during the observation period. Importantly, the longer the average duration of offending and as offenders are followed up to older ages, the greater the contribution of persisters to measured participation in successive observation periods.

Estimates of ever-participation in criminal activity vary across reporting method (of course, they tend to be much higher with self-reports than with official records, which are a filtered subset of self-reports), the types of crimes in which participation is being measured (there is broader participation in less serious criminal activity), the level of threshold of involvement (self-report, police contact, arrest, conviction), and the characteristics and representativeness of the sample (high school students, college students, general population, offender-based, etc.). In general, ever-participation estimates are fairly similar across data sets and consistent with most criminological findings.

There is a relatively high rate of participation among males in criminal activity (Elliott et al., 1987:502). Blumstein et al. (1986) reported that about 15 percent of urban males are arrested for an index offense by age 18, and about 25 to 45 percent of urban males are arrested for a nontraffic offense by age 18. Visher and Roth's (1986) overview of several longitudinal studies employing police and court records indicates a lifetime prevalence estimate of 40 to 50 percent, with higher rates for blacks and lower rates for females. Stattin et al.'s (1989) longitudinal study of Swedish males and females revealed that by age 30, 38 percent of Swedish males and 9 percent of Swedish females were registered for a criminal offense. The cumulative prevalence of self-reported offenses is even more striking. For example, in the Cambridge study, Farrington (2003) found that 96 percent of the males reported committing at least 1 of 10 specified offenses (including burglary, theft, assault, vandalism, and drug abuse) up to age 32. Kelley et al. (1997) used self-reported data on serious violence from the three Causes and Correlates longitudinal studies and found that

39 percent of Denver males, 41 percent of Pittsburgh males, 40 percent of Rochester males, 16 percent of Denver females, and 32 percent of Rochester females reported committing at least one serious violent act by age 16.

Regardless of whether official or self-report records are used to study prevalence, three main conclusions emerge. First, male participation rates are typically higher than those for females, especially so for more serious offenses. Second, black participation rates are typically higher than those for whites, especially when participation is examined via official records as opposed to self-reports (Hindelang et al., 1981). In self-reports, blacks have also been found to report violent offending at higher mean $\lambda$ than whites (Elliott, 1994). Third, there is a strong relationship between age and participation. In particular, the probability of initiating a criminal career at a given age is highest from age 13 to 18, on the lower end for self-report estimates and on the higher end for arrest and conviction records, with few gender differences in the shape (as opposed to the magnitude) of the age-crime curve (Moffitt et al., 2001). Evidence on the probability of committing an offense at a given age is mixed, with some research indicating a consistent increase through the mid teens to a peak at ages 17–19 and then a subsequent decline, while other research indicates a decline in self-reported participation through the teens (Elliott et al., 1983; Lauritsen 1998; Thornberry 1989). Studying demographic differences in prevalence remains controversial. For example, Hindelang et al. (1981) argued that there is a race difference in the validity of self-reported delinquency measures, which leads to a serious underestimation of black males' prevalence rates in self-reports (see also Jolliffe et al., 2003).

*Key Dimensions of Active Criminal Careers.* The criminal career paradigm encompasses several dimensions of active criminal careers, including offending frequency, duration, crime type mix and seriousness, and co-offending patterns.

*Offending Frequency.* The individual offending rate, $\lambda$, reflects the frequency of offending by individuals who are engaged in crime (Blumstein et al., 1986:55). Much criminal career research has been concerned with estimating the individual offending frequency of offenders during their criminal careers (Blumstein and Cohen, 1979; Cohen, 1986; Loeber and Snyder, 1990).

Blumstein et al. (1986) summarized variations in $\lambda$ for active offenders by gender, age, and race. Regarding gender, they found surprisingly little variation in frequency across males and females (i.e., the ratios are generally 2:1 or less) for most crimes (Blumstein et al.,1986:67–68). Thus, even though they are less likely to be active in most crime types (i.e., their prevalence is less), females who are active commit crimes at frequencies similar to those of males (for an exception, see Wikström, 1990). Regarding age, Blumstein et al. reported little change with age in offense-specific frequencies for active offenders; but when all offense types were combined, there tended to be an increase during the juvenile years and a decrease during the adult years. In the Rand Inmate surveys, there appeared to be some evidence of general stability of $\lambda$ over age (Chaiken and Chaiken, 1982). The number of active crime types declined with age in adulthood in the Rand survey, but crime-specific frequencies tended to be stable (Peterson and Braiker, 1980). Finally – although research based on official records tends to indicate that there is not a strong relationship between offending frequency and demographic characteristics (i.e., race differences appear with regard to prevalence) – some recent self-report data on serious violence tend to indicate otherwise (Elliott, 1994). For example, using self-report data from the National Youth Survey, a prospective longitudinal study of a national probability sample of 1,725 youths aged 11–17 in 1976, Elliott found that nearly twice as many blacks as whites continue their violent careers into their 20s.

Spelman (1994) summarized current knowledge on offending frequencies. First, there are different values for the average offense frequencies across studies because researchers use different definitions and operationalizations of the offense rate. Second, most of the variation in offense rates can be attributed to differences in the populations sampled, especially to *where* in the criminal justice system they are sampled (e.g., one would expect $\lambda$ to be higher in a prison population than in a sample of arrestees). Third, the average offender commits around 8 crimes per year, while offenders who are incarcerated at some point in their lives commit 30–50 crimes per year when they are active, and the average member of an incoming prison cohort commits between 60 and 100 crimes per year in the year before he is incarcerated. Fourth, criminals do not commit crimes all the time; in other words, there is evidence that many offenders have long periods of time in which they commit no crimes. Fifth, the distribution of offending frequencies is highly skewed, with a few offenders committing crimes at much higher than average rates; these high-$\lambda$ offenders are obviously of great interest to criminology and to the criminal justice system.

*Duration, the Interval Between Initiation and Termination.* One aspect of the criminal career paradigm that has received a great deal of research attention is initiation, or the onset of antisocial and criminal activity

(Farrington et al., 1990). Several studies have reported higher recidivism rates among offenders with records of early criminal activity as juveniles (Blumstein et al., 1986). Although many researchers argue that individuals who begin offending early will desist later and thus have longer careers (Hamparian et al., 1978; Krohn et al., 2001), there has been much less research on the duration of criminal careers, primarily because of the difficulty involved in determining the true end of an individual's offending (Piquero, Brame, and Lynam, 2004). It is more tenable, however, to measure a *rate* of desistance for an identified group of offenders (Bushway et al., 2001). Research on desistance, or the actual termination of criminal careers, has received even less attention because of difficulties in measurement and operationalization (Laub and Sampson, 2001) in terms of knowing just when any individual's career is actually finished.

The two most common approaches for studying career termination have been through providing estimates of termination probabilities after each arrest and estimating the time between the first and last crimes committed. Blumstein et al. (1986) calculated persistence probabilities for six different data sets and found that after each subsequent event (e.g., police contact, arrest, conviction, etc.) the persistence probability increases, reaching a plateau of .7 to .9 by the fourth event across all data sets. Farrington, Lambert, and West (1998) used conviction data to calculate recidivism probabilities for the males in the Cambridge Study in Delinquent Development through age 32 and found that after the third offense the recidivism probability ranged from .8 to .9 through the 10th offense.

A number of studies have attempted to derive estimates of career duration, typically measured as career length in years. Three major studies conducted in the 1970s estimated career lengths to be between 5 and 15 years (Greenberg, 1975; Greene, 1977; Shinnar and Shinnar, 1975).

Blumstein, Cohen, and Hsieh (1982) conducted the most detailed study of criminal career duration and used data on arrests to estimate career lengths. They concluded that criminal careers are relatively short, averaging about five years for offenders who are active in index offenses as young adults. Residual careers, or the length of time still remaining in careers, increase to an expected 10 years for index offenders still active in their 30s. Offenders who begin their adult careers at age 18 or earlier have an increasing residual career length with age in their 20s (as those with short careers drop out). Then, those who are still active in their 30s have the longest residual careers. Finally, in their 40s, termination rates increase and residual careers shorten (Blumstein et al., 1982; see also Visher, 2000).

Spelman (1994) studied career lengths using data from the three-state Rand Inmate Survey and developed estimates of total career lengths of about 6 or 7 years. He showed that young and inexperienced offenders, those in the first 5 years of their career, were more likely than older offenders to drop out each year, but after 5 years the rate of dropout leveled off, rising only after the 20th year as an active offender. Farrington (2003) examined the duration of criminal careers in the Cambridge study using conviction data to age 40 and found that the average duration of criminal careers was 7.1 years. Excluding one-time offenders whose duration was counted as zero, the average duration of criminal careers was 10.4 years. Piquero, Brame, and Lynam (2004) studied the length of criminal careers using data from a sample of particularly serious offenders paroled from California Youth Authority institutions in the 1970s and found that the average career length was 17.3 years, with little difference between white (16.7 years) and nonwhite parolees (17.7 years). Finally, Laub and Sampson (2003:90) estimated that the average career length among the Glueck delinquents followed through age 70 was 25.6 years for all crimes, lower for violence (9.2 years) and higher for property offenses (13.6 years).

*Crime Type Mix and Seriousness.* The mix of different offense types among active offenders is another important criminal career dimension. The study of crime type mix includes seriousness (the tendency to commit serious crimes over the course of one's criminal career), escalation (the tendency to move toward more-serious crimes as one's career progresses), specialization (the tendency to repeat the same offense type), and crime-type switching (the pattern of switching between various types of offenses on successive crimes). All these involve study of crime-type sequences in individual criminal careers.

Diverse methodological techniques have been employed to investigate specialization. Using official records, some research provides evidence in favor of a small degree of specialization (Bursik, 1980; Rojek and Erickson, 1982; Smith and Smith, 1984), but most find that versatility is the norm throughout offending careers (Farrington et al., 1988; Nevares et al., 1990; Tracy et al., 1990; Wolfgang et al., 1972), especially at young ages. Important differences in specialization are observed between adults and juveniles: Specialization appears to be greater for adult rather than juvenile offenders (Le Blanc and Fréchette, 1989; Piquero et al., 1999). On the other hand, self-report data from the Rand studies suggest that, although there is some evidence of specialization in property crimes (Spelman, 1994), incarcerated offenders tend to report much more versatility than specialization (Chaiken and Chaiken 1982; Petersilia et al., 1978; Peterson and Braiker, 1980).

Some scholars have investigated specialization in violence. Using official records, there is very little evidence of specialization in violence in the Cambridge study (Farrington, 1989) or the Philadelphia Perinatal Cohort (Piquero, 2000a), a long-term study of 987 individuals participating in the National Collaborative Perinatal Project. These authors concluded that the commission of a violent offense in a criminal career is largely a function of offending frequency: Sooner or later, frequent offenders are likely to accumulate a violent offense in their career. Similar results have been obtained by Capaldi and Patterson (1996) with self-report data from the Oregon Youth Study. These findings do not contradict the hypothesis that different types of crime tend to be committed in no neatly ordered sequence.

Directly related to the specialization issue is the switching that occurs within and between clusters of crime types, which represent natural groupings of offense types (violence, property, other). Research indicates that adult offenders display a stronger tendency to switch among offense types within a cluster and a weaker tendency to switch to offense types outside a cluster, but the strong partitioning is not as sharp among juveniles (Blumstein et al., 1986; Cohen, 1986). Adult offenders and incarcerated juveniles are more likely to commit offenses within a cluster than to switch to offenses outside a cluster (Blumstein et al., 1988; Rojek and Erickson, 1982). Drug offenders, however, do not tend to switch to either violent or property offenses.

*Co-offending Patterns.* Another important criminal career feature is whether a person commits an offense alone or with others (Reiss, 1986). Little empirical work has been completed on co-offending, and even less information exists regarding the group criminal behavior of youths in transition to adult status or of adult offenders at different ages. Using data from the CSDD through age 32, Reiss and Farrington (1991) report that the incidence of co-offending is greatest for burglary and robbery and that juvenile offenders primarily commit their crimes with others, whereas adult offenders primarily commit their crimes alone. The decline in co-offending could be attributed to co-offenders selectively dropping out, but it seems more likely to occur because males change from a typical pattern of co-offending in their teenage years to lone offending in their 20s. In the Swedish Borlänge study, Sarnecki (1990) found that 45 percent of all youths suspected of offenses at some stage during the six-year study period could be linked in a single large network that accounted for most offenses. Recently, Sarnecki (2001) used data from all individuals aged 20 or less who were suspected of one or more offenses in Stockholm during 1991–1995 to study the extent and role of co-offending and found that 60 percent of the individuals had a co-offender at some point. Not surprisingly, he also found that males tended to co-offend primarily with other males; but among females, the proportion choosing other females was lower than the proportion of boys choosing other males as co-offenders. Conway and McCord (2002) conducted the first co-offending study designed to track patterns of violent criminal behavior over an 18-year period (1976–1994) among a random sample of four hundred urban offenders and their accomplices in Philadelphia. Using crime data collected from court records and "rap sheets," they found that nonviolent offenders who committed their first co-offense with a violent accomplice were at increased risk for subsequent serious violent crime, independent of the effects of age and gender.

## Policy Issues

The criminal career paradigm suggests three general orientations for crime control strategies: prevention, career modification, and incapacitation. Knowledge concerning the patterning of criminal careers is intimately related to these policy issues. Prevention strategies, including general deterrence, are intended to reduce the number of nonoffenders who become offenders. Career modification strategies, including individual deterrence and rehabilitation, are focused on persons already known to be criminals and seek to reduce the frequency or seriousness of their crimes. In addition, these strategies encourage the termination of ongoing criminal careers through such methods as job training and drug treatment. Incapacitative strategies focus on the crimes reduced as a result of removing offenders from society during their criminal careers. Two types of incapacitation are general (or collective) and selective, which focuses on identifying and removing the highest-frequency offenders. These three crime control strategies are reflected in specific incapacitation-oriented laws, including habitual-offender statutes, truth-in-sentencing laws, three-strikes laws, and mandatory minimum-sentencing laws.

*Crime Control Strategies.* Of all crime control strategies, the criminal career paradigm has focused the most attention on incapacitation. General (collective) incapacitation strategies aim to reduce criminal activity as a consequence of increasing the total level of incarceration, while selective incapacitation policies focus primarily on trying to select the offenders who represent the greatest risk of future offending. The former approach is consistent with the equal-treatment concerns of a low-disparity sentencing policy, while the latter focuses more on the offender than the offense. Importantly, the degree to which selective incapacitation policies can be effective depends on the ability to distinguish high- and low-risk offenders prospectively and to identify them reasonably early in their careers, before they are about to escalate or terminate criminal activity. Three related issues arise: the ability to classify individual offenders in terms of their projected criminal activity; the quality of the classification rules; and the legitimacy of basing punishment of an individual on the possibility of future crimes rather than only on the crimes already committed (and the consequent level of disparity in sentencing that is considered acceptable).

Regarding collective incapacitation, Blumstein et al. (1986) suggest that achieving a 10 percent reduction in crime may require more than doubling the existing inmate population. However, under selective incapacitation policies long prison terms would be reserved primarily for offenders identified as most likely to continue committing serious crimes at high rates. Blumstein et al. conclude that selective incapacitation policies could achieve 5 to 10 percent reductions in robbery with 10 to 20 percent increases in the population of robbers in prison, while much larger increases in prison populations would be required for collective incapacitation policies to be effective.

*Relationship to Laws.* Both collective and selective incapacitation policies are directly influenced by laws and policies that govern criminal justice decisions regarding the punishment of offenders. For example, habitual-offender statutes give special options to prosecutors for dealing with repeat offenders. Truth-in-sentencing laws are intended to increase incapacitation by requiring offenders, particularly violent offenders, to serve a substantial portion of their prison sentence, with parole eligibility and good-time credits restricted or eliminated. Three-strikes laws provide that any person convicted of three, typically violent, felony offenses must serve a lengthy prison term, usually a minimum term of 25-years-to-life. Mandatory minimum-sentence laws require a specified term to be served and prohibit offenders convicted of certain crimes from being placed on probation, while other statutes prohibit certain offenders from being considered for parole. Mandatory minimum-sentence laws can also serve as sentencing enhancement measures, requiring that offenders spend additional time in prison if they have committed particular crimes in a particular manner (e.g., committing a felony with a gun). The net effect of these laws is to increase prison populations by incarcerating certain kinds of offenders or increasing the sentence length of those offenders convicted for certain types of crimes.

## "Chronic" Offenders

Criminologists have long recognized that a small group of individuals is responsible for most criminal activity. Wolfgang et al. (1972) focused attention on the "chronic" offender by applying that label to the small group of 627 delinquents in the 1945 Philadelphia birth cohort who committed five or more (hereafter, five-plus) offenses by age 17. This group constituted just 6 percent of the full cohort of 9,945 males and 18 percent of the delinquent subset of 3,475, but it was responsible for 5,305 offenses, or 52 percent of all official delinquency, in the cohort through age 17. These chronic offenders were responsible for an even larger percentage of the more serious, violent offenses. The finding that a small subset of sample members is responsible for a majority of criminal activity is supported by data from other longitudinal data sets, including the second 1958 Philadelphia birth cohort (Tracy et al., 1990), the Puerto Rico Birth Cohort Study (Nevares et al., 1990), the Dunedin New Zealand Multidisciplinary Health Study (Moffitt et al., 2001), the Philadelphia (Piquero 2000b) and Providence (Piquero and Buka, 2002) perinatal projects, the Racine, WI, birth cohorts (Shannon, 1982), the Cambridge study (Farrington, 2003), and also by cohort studies in Sweden (Wikström, 1985), Finland (Pulkkinen, 1988), and Denmark (Guttridge et al., 1983). The finding is also replicated across gender and race (Moffitt et al., 2001; Piquero and Buka, 2002) and for both official and self-report data. Research also indicates that chronic offenders exhibit an earlier onset, a longer career duration, and more involvement in serious offenses – including violent offenses – than other offenders (Loeber and Farrington, 1998).

The five-plus cutoff advanced by Wolfgang et al. has been employed in several studies; however, because theoretical and empirical definitions of chronicity have yet to be established, questions have been raised about the extent to which similar definitions of chronicity should be used across gender (Farrington and Loeber, 1998; Piquero, 2000b), as well as the relatively arbitrary designation of five-plus offenses as characteristic of chronicity (Blumstein et al., 1985). Blumstein et al. (1985) raised other concerns with the use of five-plus as the chronicity cut point. They argued that the chronic-offender calculation, based on the full cohort, over-estimates the importance of chronic offenders because many cohort members will never be arrested. Instead, they urge that the ever-arrested subjects should be the base used to calculate the chronic-offender effect. With this base, the 627 chronics with five-plus arrests represented 18 percent of those arrested, as opposed to 6 percent of the cohort. Blumstein and colleagues also argued that the proportion of chronic offenders observed by Wolfgang et al. could have resulted from a homogeneous population of persisters. Blumstein et al. (1985) tested the hypothesis that all persisters (those with more than three arrests) could be viewed as having the same re-arrest probability. Such an assumption could not be rejected. Although those with five-plus arrests accounted for the majority of arrests among the persisters, such a result could have occurred even if all subjects with three or more arrests had identical recidivism probabilities. The implication of this analysis is that the chronic offenders who were identified retrospectively as those with five or more arrests could not have been distinguished prospectively from nonchronics with three or four arrests.

## Relevance to Incapacitation

Incapacitation effects are maximized when highest-$\lambda$, longest-duration, most-serious offenders are incarcerated. Knowledge of offenders' involvement in the various criminal career dimensions, especially the frequency of offending, has direct import for incapacitation decisions and outcomes. Prospective identification of those offenders with the highest $\lambda$, exhibiting the longest career duration and engaging in the most serious offenses, would enhance incapacitation goals. To the extent that incarceration decisions are targeted at individuals exhibiting these offending characteristics, incapacitation effects (realized by lower crime rates, shorter careers, and less serious levels of criminal activity) would be maximized.

Crime control effects through incapacitation increase with the magnitude of the individual offending frequency ($\lambda$) and with the length of incarceration, subject to the expected residual duration of the criminal careers keeping an individual in prison after his career would have ended can be designated as "wastage" (Blumstein et al., 1986). To the extent that high-$\lambda$ offenders are incapacitated during the period in which they are at highest risk of offending, more crimes will be averted by their incarceration. Incapacitation policies are more likely to be effective if they are applied during active careers and not after criminal careers have ceased or when careers are in a downswing, when offenders tend to commit crimes at rates "indistinguishable from zero" (Cohen and Canela-Cacho, 1994). Incapacitative effects will depend on the effectiveness of the criminal justice system in prospectively identifying high-rate offenders and incarcerating them during the peak crime periods of their careers.

## Policy Implications

Research on criminal careers has direct import for decision making in the criminal justice system. In this section, we address four implications of criminal career research: its role in policy and decision making about individuals, prediction of individual offending frequencies ($\lambda$), sentence duration, and research on career length and desistance and its relation to intelligent sentencing policy.

## Role of Criminal Career Research in Policy and Individual Decision Making

A principal example of the importance of criminal career research for criminal justice policy is criminal career length. Three-strikes and selective incapacitation philosophies assume that high-rate offenders will continue to offend at high rates and for long periods of time if they are not incarcerated. From an incapacitative perspective, incarceration is only effective in averting crimes when it is applied during an active criminal career. Thus, incarceration after a career ends or when it is abating is wasted for incapacitation purposes (Blumstein et al., 1982:70). By estimating residual career lengths, policy makers can better target incarceration at offenders whose expected remaining careers are longest. Incarceration policies should be based on information about the career duration distribution. The more hardcore committed offenders with the longest remaining careers are identifiable only after an offender has remained active for several years (Blumstein et al., 1982). Earlier and later in criminal careers, sanctions will be applied to many offenders who are likely to stop offending shortly anyway (Blumstein et al., 1982:71). The benefits derived from incapacitation will vary depending on an individual's crime rate and the length of his remaining criminal career. Continuing to incarcerate an offender after his/her career ends limits the usefulness of incarceration.

### Individual Prediction of λ

Rand's second inmate survey highlighted the extreme skewness of the distribution of λ for a sample of serious criminals (Chaiken and Chaiken, 1982; Visher, 1986). Naturally, the identification of a small number of inmates who reported committing several hundred crimes per year led to the search for a method to identify these offenders in advance. If high-rate offenders cannot be identified prospectively, then crime control efforts will be hampered (Visher, 1987). In this section, we highlight two related issues: the difficulty in identifying high-λ individuals and the alleviation of the concern over prediction by "stochastic selectivity."

*Difficulty in Identifying High-λ Individuals.* Although high-λ individuals emerge in the aggregate, it has been difficult to identify specific individuals in advance. Greenwood and Turner (1987) used data consisting of follow-up criminal-history information on the California inmates who were included in the original Rand survey and who had been out of prison for two years to examine the extent to which a seven-item prediction scale developed by Greenwood and Abrahamse (1982) succeeded in predicting postrelease recidivism based on self-reports of offending. The scale was not very effective in predicting postrelease criminal activity when the recidivism measure was arrest. The majority of released inmates, regardless of whether they were predicted to be low- or high-rate offenders, were re-arrested within two years. Greenwood and Turner also created a measure of the offender's annual arrest rate (i.e., the number of arrests per year of street time) for the follow-up sample and defined high-rate offenders as those inmates who had an actual annual arrest rate greater than 0.78. They found that the seven-item scale was less accurate in predicting annual arrest rates than it was in predicting re-incarceration. This frustration in prediction could reflect the possibility that the higher-$\lambda$ offenders had a lower arrest probability, thereby diminishing their difference when arrest rather than self-reports was used in the follow-up.

There are also concerns related to the false-positive prediction problem in identifying high-$\lambda$ individuals. For example, Visher (1986:204–205) reanalyzed the Rand second inmate survey and found that not only were the estimates of $\lambda$ for robbery and burglary sensitive to choices in computation (i.e., handling missing data, street time, etc.), but also that some inmates reported annual rates of 1,000 or more robberies or burglaries, thus strongly affecting the distribution of $\lambda$ and especially its mean. Finally, Visher's analysis of the Greenwood scale for predicting high-rate offenders indicated that 55 percent of the classified high-rate group (27 percent of the total sample) were false positives who did not commit crimes at high rates. In fact, the prediction scale worked better in identifying low-rate offenders. Auerhahn (1999) replicated Greenwood and Abrahamse's (1982) selective incapacitation study with a representative sample of California state prison inmates and found that the scale's overall predictive accuracy was 60 percent, indicating a great deal of error in identifying high-rate offenders. According to her calculations, a "total of 13 percent of offenders who are not high-rate are so predicted by the Greenwood/Abrahamse scale (3 percent being low-rate offenders); only 5.6 percent are so predicted using the Replication scale (1 percent low-rate offenders)" (Auerhahn, 1999:718–719).

Using longitudinal data on a sample of serious California offenders released on parole, Haapanen, (1990) tested the assumption that criminal careers are characterized by a reasonably constant rate of criminal behavior, especially among high-rate offenders. However, Haapanen found that arrest rates were not stable and declined with age. He discovered that few offenders maintained a consistent pattern of being in the lowest, middle, or highest third of the sample in terms of their rates of arrest over a four-year period (Haapanen, 1990:140). Only a small minority (28 percent over three periods and 12 percent over four periods) were in the highest third over most of the periods. Thus, the assumption that rates are stable will likely overestimate the amount of crime that could be prevented by selectively incapacitating those identified as high-rate offenders because high-rate offenders are not always high-rate. Another important finding emerging from Haapanen's analysis is that in the four years prior to incarceration offenders were accelerating in criminal activity (as measured by their arrests), suggesting that the preincarceration period may not be appropriate for establishing typical distributions of offense rates. Arrest rates tended to be much lower after release from incarceration, perhaps indicating "regression to the mean" (e.g., Maltz et al., 1980; Murray and Cox, 1979).

*Concern and Need for Prediction Alleviated by "Stochastic Selectivity."* Many analyses of the crime control potential of increasing incarceration rely on obtaining a single estimate of mean $\lambda$ from prison inmates and applying it indiscriminately to all populations of offenders (Canela-Cacho et al., 1997). This assumes that all offenders engage in the same amount ($\lambda$) of criminal behavior – regardless of whether they are in prison or jail or free in the community – and that the probability of their detection and incarceration is equal. However, measures of $\lambda$ derived from arrestee/convictee populations display a strong selection bias because individuals who have gone through the criminal justice process are unlikely to be representative of the total offender population. This selection bias could be because samples of arrestees have a higher propensity for arrest or higher offending frequencies. This is even more true of inmates. A highly heterogeneous distribution of offending frequency in the total population of offenders combined with relatively low imprisonment levels leads to substantial selectivity of high-$\lambda$ offenders among inmates and a correspondingly low mean value of $\lambda$ among those offenders who remain free (Canela-Cacho et al., 1997). "Stochastic selectivity," then, draws into prison offenders disproportionately from the high end of the $\lambda$ distribution of free offenders. Further, the lower the incarceration probability following a crime, the more selective will be the offender pool sent to incarceration and the higher will be the incapacitation effect per inmate associated with the incoming cohorts (Canela-Cacho et al., 1997). However, this is only true of high-$\lambda$ offenders who do not have a lower probability of being arrested per crime.

Using data from the second Rand inmate survey, Canela-Cacho et al. studied the issue of stochastic selectivity and found that the proportion of low-$\lambda$ burglars and robbers among free offenders was much larger than among inmates, while conversely there was a larger proportion of high-$\lambda$ burglars and robbers among resident inmates than among free offenders. Thus, selectivity occurred naturally as high-$\lambda$ offenders experienced more opportunities for incarceration through the greater number of crimes they committed (Canela-Cacho et al., 1997:142), thereby obviating the need for efforts to explicitly identify individual high-$\lambda$ offenders. An implication of this analysis is that, because some offenders tend to have low $\lambda$s, the scope for reducing crime by increasing incarceration is limited.

## Sentence Duration

Information about individual crime rates and career lengths is particularly useful for incapacitation and incarceration decisions and policies, and such knowledge can also provide useful information regarding the intelligent use of incarceration and may even provide powerful arguments against lengthy incapacitation policies. Principal among these are the decisions regarding sentence length and time served. Many current sentencing policies are based on the assumption that high-rate offenders will continue committing crimes at high rates and for long periods and thus prescribe lengthy incarceration periods. The extent to which this policy is effective, however, is contingent on the duration of a criminal career.

Much debate regarding sentence length has centered on three-strikes policies. These policies severely limit judges' discretion because they prescribe a mandatory prison sentence of (typically) 25-years-to-life following a third conviction for a prescribed set of offenses. The incapacitation effectiveness of three-strikes laws, however, depends strongly on the residual duration of criminal careers. To the extent that sentencing decisions incarcerate individuals with short residual career lengths, a three-strikes law will waste incarceration resources (Stolzenberg and D'Alessio, 1997:466).

Stolzenberg and D'Alessio (1997) used aggregate data drawn from the 10 largest cities in California to examine the impact of California's three-strikes law on serious crime rates and found that the three-strikes law did not decrease serious crime or petty theft rates below the level expected on the basis of preexisting trends. Zimring et al. (1999) obtained a sample of felony arrests (and relevant criminal records) in Los Angeles, San Francisco, and San Diego, both before and after the California law went into effect, to study the three-strikes issue. Two key findings emerged from their study. First, the mean age at arrest for those with two prior strikes and above was 34.6 years. This is particularly important because: "[O]n average the two or more strikes defendant has an almost 40 percent longer criminal adult career behind him (estimated at 16.6 years) than does the no-strikes felony defendant. All other things being equal, this means that the twenty-five-years-to-life mandatory prison sentence will prevent fewer crimes among the third-strike group than it would in the general population of felons because the group eligible for it is somewhat older" (Zimring et al., 1999:34). Second, when comparing crime trends in the three cities before and after the law, Zimring et al. found that there was no decline in the crimes committed by those targeted by the new law. In particular, the lower crime rates in 1994 and 1995 (just immediately after the three-strikes law went into effect) were evenly spread among targeted and nontargeted populations, suggesting that the decline in crime observed after the law came into effect could not be attributed to the law.

Caulkins (2001) investigated whether the use of different definitions for the first, second, and third strikes, or different sentence lengths, could make incarceration more efficient (i.e., reduce more crimes). Using data from California, he found that the broader the definition of what constituted a strike, the greater the reduction in crime but the greater the cost per crime averted. The problem with a very broad definition is that it fails to take advantage of stochastic selectivity, or the notion that high-rate offenders make up a larger proportion of third- rather than first-strike offenders (Caulkins, 2001:242). Caulkins concludes that the three-strikes law would be more effective if second- and third-strike offenders served 6- and 10-year terms instead of the 10- and 20-year terms required by the current law and if sentences were lengthened for first-strike offenders.

## Research on Career Length and Desistance

Sentencing practices involving long sentences are based on the presumption that affected offenders, if not incarcerated, will continue to commit crime at a high rate and for a long period. To the extent that this is the case, incapacitation policies will avert crimes and prevent continued careers. However, to the extent that offenders would end their careers before the expiration of a lengthy sentence, these shorter career durations will reduce the incapacitative benefits of lengthy sentences. Using data from Florida, Schmertmann et al. (1998) concluded that the aging of prison populations under three-strikes policies in that state will undermine their long-run effectiveness. In particular, they noted that the policies will cause increases in prison populations due to the addition of large numbers of older inmates who are unlikely to commit future offenses.

The key to the sentence duration issue, and why estimates of criminal career duration are so important, rests on the characteristics of the person-years – not the people – that are removed from free society as a result of such policies (Schmertmann et al., 1998:458). Such policies will be effective only to the extent that they incarcerate offenders during the stages of their criminal careers when they are committing crimes at a high rate.

Unfortunately, research on career duration and desistance is in its infancy. Knowledge on this subject will be important for furthering criminal justice policy and the cost-effective use of criminal justice resources.

## Challenge and Response to the Criminal Career Paradigm

To be sure, the criminal career paradigm and its emerging policy implications were not embraced by the entire academic community. Two criminologists in particular, Michael Gottfredson and Travis Hirschi, launched a series of critiques of the criminal career paradigm. In this section, we provide an overview of their critique, as well as the responses that followed from proponents of the criminal career paradigm.

The basis of the Gottfredson-Hirschi critique lies in their explication and interpretation of the aggregate age/crime curve. Hirschi and Gottfredson (1983) contend that the shape of the aggregate age/crime relationship is pretty much the same for all offenders, in all times and places, and is largely unaffected by life events that occur after childhood. They assert, then, that involvement in crime (and other analogous behaviors) is sufficiently stable over the life-course to obviate the necessity of collecting longitudinal data, which is a prerequisite for pursuing the criminal career paradigm. This is especially the case in their denial of the need to distinguish prevalence and frequency (because both reflect underlying propensity). They claim that prevalence and frequency vary similarly with age, but for the most part research fails to support their claim.

In their review of the criminal career concept, Gottfredson and Hirschi do not deny the fact that some offenders offend at a much higher rate than other offenders, but they argue that offenders differ in degree, not in kind; that is, offenders can be arrayed on a continuum of criminal propensity (what they term "low self-control") with individuals at the higher end of the continuum, evidencing higher criminal activity and vice versa. This is a key point because Gottfredson and Hirschi do not anticipate the existence of qualitatively distinct groups of offenders.

In a related fashion, Gottfredson and Hirschi are concerned with the proposed identification of the "career criminal" and the implied policy response of selective incapacitation. Their concern derives from the small number of chronic offenders and the limited ability of the criminal justice system to identify chronic offenders prospectively, before they reach their offending peak. In particular, they argue that by the time the criminal justice system is able to identify a career criminal, he tends no longer to be as active as he once was. That is, career criminals cannot be identified early enough in their careers to be useful for policy purposes. Thus, because Hirschi and Gottfredson believe that crime declines with age for everyone, they claim that the policy of selective incapacitation makes little sense, for career criminals would likely not be committing crimes at high rates if they were free.

As could be deduced from their arguments, Gottfredson and Hirschi (1987) are also unfriendly to the prospect of longitudinal/cohort data. Their critique in this vein is forceful and centers around five issues: (1) the longitudinal/cohort study is not justified on methodological grounds, (2) such a design has taken criminological theory in unproductive directions, (3) the study has produced illusory substantive findings, (4) it has promoted policy directions of "doubtful utility," and (5) such research designs are very expensive and entail high opportunity costs (Gottfredson and Hirschi, 1987:581). They argue instead for more emphasis on cross-sectional studies, which they claim tend to provide similar substantive conclusions to those reached by longitudinal studies but at a much smaller cost. They conclude that neither the criminal career paradigm, its constructs (prevalence, incidence, $\lambda$, etc.), nor longitudinal research has much to offer criminology.

Forcefully, Gottfredson and Hirschi (1988) question whether the concept of a "career" is valuable to the study of crime. They claim that there is no empirical support for the use of the career concept and its related terminology (p. 39). Gottfredson and Hirschi go on to critique the participation/frequency distinction and, in so doing, employ data from the Richmond Youth Project, which collected, cross-sectionally, police records and self-report data on over 2,500 males and females. They conclude that the substantive conclusions about the causes and correlates of crime do not depend on career distinctions. In fact, they show that as one moves from $\lambda$ for any kind of offending to the smaller $\lambda$ for serious offending, the correlations between demographic characteristics and criminal career offending dimensions become even smaller, largely as a result of decreasing sample size. In sum, Gottfredson and Hirschi claim that the factors associated with different criminal career parameters appear more similar than different.

Blumstein, Cohen, and Farrington (1988a) provide a response to the main critiques leveled by Gottfredson and Hirschi at the criminal career paradigm and its research agenda. They note (1988a:4) that the construct of a criminal career is not a theory of crime; instead, it is a way of structuring and organizing knowledge about certain key features of individual offending for observation and measurement and that the distinction is important because it permits different causal relationships. However, they also suggest that the criminal career concept is useful for the development and assessment of theory as it may help researchers understand the differences among offenders, especially with regard to their various criminal career parameters. Thus – unlike Gottfredson and Hirschi, who assume that as criminal propensity increases so, too, does participation, frequency, and career length – the criminal career paradigm suggests that the predictors and correlates of one criminal career parameter may differ from the predictors and correlates of another.

The key point of contention between Gottfredson and Hirschi and Blumstein et al. lies in their respective interpretations of the age/crime curve. For Gottfredson and Hirschi, the decline in the age/crime curve in early adulthood reflects decreasing offending frequency ($\lambda$) after the peak age. On the other hand, Blumstein Cohen, and Farrington claim that the decline in the aggregate arrest rate after a teenage peak does not require that offending frequency ($\lambda$) follow a similar pattern. According to Blumstein et al. (1988a:27), this is precisely where the distinction between participation and frequency becomes critical. It is possible that the decline in the aggregate age/crime curve is entirely attributable to the termination of criminal careers and that the average value of $\lambda$ could stay constant (or increase or decrease) with age for those offenders who remain active after that peak. Ultimately, of course, this is an empirical question, yet Blumstein, Cohen, and Farrington (1988a:32) suggest that participation in offending, and not frequency as Gottfredson and Hirschi suggest, is the key dimension that varies with age.

In particular, Blumstein, Cohen and Farrington (1988b:57) suggest that Gottfredson and Hirschi misunderstand key criminal career evidence, "especially the evidence of a decline in offending with age, regarding which the distinction between participation and frequency is crucial." Blumstein and colleagues claim that Gottfredson and Hirschi misinterpreted the concepts of individual crime rates, lambda ($\lambda$), and career duration and, as a result, miscalculated such estimates because of their failure to take into account the length of active criminal careers for individual offenders (Blumstein, Cohen, and Farrington, 1988b: 58–59, 62). In addition, Blumstein et al. challenge Gottfredson and Hirschi's interpretation of declines in offending with age: "[J]ust *what* is declining? ... Are still-active offenders committing crimes at lower frequencies or are increasing numbers of offenders ending their careers and ceasing to commit crimes altogether? The former is a change in λ, and the latter is a change in *participation*, and measuring these changes with age is an empirical issue." In sum, Blumstein, Cohen, and Farrington conclude that, while cross-sectional studies can only study between-subject differences, longitudinal surveys allow for the analysis of both between- and within-subject changes, and it is this latter type of analysis that frames the criminal career focus on participation, frequency, and termination. Also, within-subject changes are more relevant to issues of prevention and treatment of offending.

The debate between Gottfredson and Hirschi and Blumstein, Cohen, and Farrington bears import for policy matters and according to Osgood (2005:197), the ensuing exchange "stimulated the growth of research on crime and the life course by highlighting critical intellectual challenges and suggesting a variety of approaches for addressing them." In Gottfredson and Hirschi's view, the most important distinction should be between offenders and nonoffenders (i.e., participation). The criminal career paradigm, on the other hand, does not dispute a focus on participation, but it places emphasis on the frequency of active offenders. This focus on frequency not only reflects an interest in systematic differences in offending frequencies among active offenders, but also an interest in changes in offending frequency during active criminal careers. Both participation *and* frequency, according to the criminal career paradigm, are relevant for policy purposes because affecting both can generate payoffs in crime reduction. Blumstein et al. argue that, while longitudinal and cross-sectional research designs are useful, longitudinal data are superior to cross-sectional data in testing causal hypotheses, namely because longitudinal data permit observation of the time ordering of events observed and provide better control of extraneous variables because each person acts as his/her own control.

## Theories Influenced by the Criminal Career Paradigm

The criminal career paradigm forced criminological theorists to examine the extent to which they were able to account for the different criminal career dimensions (i.e., onset, persistence, frequency, desistance, etc.). As result of the recognition of other criminal career features and the importance of the relationship between past and future criminal activity, several life-course and developmental theories were developed that attempted to account for the patterning of criminal activity over time.

*Life-Course/Developmental Criminology*. The life-course has been defined as "pathways through the age-differentiated life span," where age differentiation "is manifested in expectations and options that impinge on decision processes and the course of events that give shape to life stages, transitions, and turning points" (Sampson and Laub, 1993:8; see also Elder, 1985). Within criminology, the life-course perspective can offer a comprehensive approach to the study of criminal activity because it considers the multitude of influences that shape offending across different time periods and contexts (Thornberry, 1997). In particular, two central concepts underlie the analysis of life-course dynamics generally and criminal activity more specifically.

The first is a trajectory, or a pathway of development, over the life span, such as in work life or criminal activity. Trajectories refer to long-term patterns of specific types of behavior. Second, and embedded within trajectories, are transitions, or specific life events (e.g., a first arrest) that evolve over shorter time spans. According to Elder (1985:32), the interlocking nature of trajectories and transitions may generate turning points or changes in the life-course. According to Sampson and Laub (1992), "The long-term view embodied by the life-course focus on trajectories implies a strong connection between childhood events and experiences in adulthood. However, the simultaneous shorter-term view also implies that transitions or turning points can modify life trajectories – they can 'redirect paths.' " As such, the life-course perspective recognizes the importance of both stability and change in human behavior.

Developmental criminology adopts this life-course view by taking into account the fact that changes in social behavior, such as delinquency and crime, are related to age in an orderly way (Patterson, 1993; Thornberry, 1997). Developmental criminology, which focuses on all sorts of antisocial and criminal activity over the life-course, studies the temporal, within-individual changes in offending over time (Le Blanc and Loeber, 1998:117) and focuses on two primary areas of study. The first concerns the development and dynamics of offending over age, while the second concerns the identification of explanatory or causal factors that predate or co-occur with the behavioral development and have an effect on its course (Le Blanc and Loeber, 1998:117).

It is important to recognize that developmental criminology departs from traditional criminological theory, which, with one principal exception (labeling theory; see Sampson and Laub, 1997) adopts a relatively nondevelopmental, or static, orientation. Thornberry (1997:2–5), for example, points out four reasons why nondevelopmental theories have led to a stagnation of knowledge regarding key criminological issues. First, static perspectives do not identify nor offer explanations for all of the key criminal career dimensions. In fact, most static theories, with the exception of Gottfredson and Hirschi and Wilson and Herrnstein, are basically state-dependent theories. Second, static theories fail to identify types of offenders based on developmental considerations. For example, perhaps some offenders start early and continue offending for long periods while others start later and desist earlier. Third, static explanations do not focus attention on either the precursors or consequences of criminal activity. For example, what factors lead to the initiation of criminal activity, and does continued criminal activity materially affect life outcomes in other, noncrime, domains, such as school and work? Fourth, static perspectives do not integrate the noncrime developmental changes that occur over the life-course as a way to understand changes in criminal activity during the same time period. For example, how do transitions in work, school, family, and interpersonal relationships relate to changes in criminal activity? In sum, developmental criminology attempts to overcome these limitations in an effort to provide a more complete understanding of criminal activity over the life-course and recognizes that there may be multiple paths to antisocial and criminal behavior (Huizinga, Esbensen, and Weiher, 1991).

Within criminology, the last decade has witnessed the infusion of scholarly work from other disciplines that have adopted a life-course perspective to the study of criminal activity. Interestingly, these theories, and the ones also constructed by criminologists, take as their starting point two key facts: the relationship between age and crime and the relationship between prior and future criminal activity. In particular, these theories have also attempted to address the following observation: Although antisocial behavior in children is one of the best predictors of antisocial behavior in adults, not all antisocial children become antisocial adults.

Moffitt's (1993) developmental taxonomy decomposes the aggregate age/crime curve into two distinct classes of offenders. The first group, designated "adolescence-limited," is hypothesized to engage in crimes solely during the adolescent period. The primary causal factors for this group include the maturity gap (i.e., adolescents are physically old enough to look like adults, but socially they are not allowed to act like adults) combined with the encouragement of peers. Moffitt anticipates that the crime repertoire of adolescence-limiteds would be restricted to mainly status and property-oriented offenses that symbolize adult social status, such as theft, smoking, vandalism, and drug use, but not violent acts. For the majority of adolescence-limiteds, their prosocial skills and attitudes allow them to recover from their delinquent experimentation and move away from their delinquent activities as they reach adulthood.

The second group of offenders in Moffitt's taxonomy, "life-course-persistent," is hypothesized to engage in antisocial activities and criminal acts throughout the life span. Composed of less than 10 percent of the population, the primary determinants of criminal activity for life-course-persistent offenders lie in the interaction between poor neuropsychological functioning and deficient home and socioeconomic environments. Unlike their adolescence-limited counterparts, life-course-persistent offenders continue their criminal involvement throughout most of their lives (i.e., they are unlikely to desist). In addition, the crime repertoire of life-course-persistent offenders is varied and includes interpersonal violence.

Thus, Moffitt's adolescence-limited offenders are likely to be influenced much more by state dependence effects, because offending among adolescence-limited offenders depends largely on life circumstances and environmental influences, such as peers. Prior criminal acts are likely to causally affect current and future offending among adolescence-limited offenders because offending is likely to further alienate parents and conventional peers. On the other hand, life-course-persistent offenders, after child socialization efforts have taken place, are likely to be a consequence of persistent heterogeneity (and to a lesser extent more dynamic processes). That is, life-course-persistent offenders are "bad apples" who exhibit significant deficits in early childhood socialization and are rarely likely to get back on track.[1]

A good deal of empirical research has tended to support some of the key hypotheses arising from Moffitt's typology (see review in Moffitt, 2006), while some studies have generated useful alterations to the theory (Nagin et al., 1995) and others challenging critical assumptions (Sampson and Laub, 2003).

Much like Moffitt's typology, Patterson and Yoerger's (1999) theory is based on a two-group model of offending that is comprised of early- and late-onset offenders. According to their perspective, early-starting offenders become involved in antisocial and criminal behaviors as a function of failed early childhood socialization due to inept parenting

---

[1] To be sure, Moffitt (1993) suggests that the life-course-persistent pathway is not entirely static. Specifically, persistent individual propensity is merely a starting point for a process of cumulative disadvantage that continues to influence the course of offending well after childhood and on into adulthood. For example, Moffitt (1993:680) outlines the beginnings of life-course-persistent causation by invoking neuropsychological risk for difficult temperamental and behavioral problems. This is followed by a second section on maintenance and elaboration over the life-course, where she puts forward the notion of snares creating cumulative disadvantage (p. 683). In the third section of life-course-persistent causation, she outlines the reasons for persistence, in which she suggests that antisocial styles become set sometime after childhood (p. 684).

practices that foster oppositional/defiant behavior. The failure of children to learn effective self- and social controls leads them to be involved in deviant peer groups, which, in turn, magnifies their offending intensity. Early-starting offenders tend to be aggressive and defiant in their interactions with others and come to be rejected by conventional peers. As a result of their social rejection, early-starting offenders tend to establish friendships with each other, thereby forming deviant peer groups that engage in criminal activities. Early starters, then, are at high risk for chronic offending and continued criminal careers as adults.

On the other hand, late-starting offenders do not suffer from failed socialization efforts. Instead, the principal cause of offending for them is their close association and interaction with deviant peer models. As a result of the aid, encouragement, and support of the peer social context, late starting youths experiment with delinquency during mid to late adolescence. However, because late-starting offenders do not suffer from inept parenting, nor are they failed socialization products, their social skills remain relatively intact and they are likely to turn away from criminal acts as adulthood approaches. Several empirical studies have tested Patterson's theory. For the most part, they confirm the key predictions regarding the effects of inept parenting, oppositional/defiant behavior, and deviant peers (see Simons et al., 1994, 1998; Patterson and Yoerger, 1999).

Loeber and his colleagues (1998, 1999) have proposed a three-pathway model that integrates both predelinquent behavior problems and delinquent acts in attempting to describe which youths are at highest risk of becoming chronic offenders. The first pathway, the "overt pathway," begins with minor aggression, followed by physical fighting and then violence. The second pathway, the "covert pathway," consists of a sequence of minor, covert behaviors followed by property damage (such as vandalism) and then serious forms of delinquency. The third pathway, the "authority-conflict pathway" prior to age 12, consists of a sequence of stubborn behaviors, including defiance and authority avoidance (such as running away). According to Loeber, individuals' development can take place on more than one pathway, with some youths progressing on all three pathways. However, the most frequent offenders are over represented among those boys in multiple pathways, especially those displaying overt and covert behavior problems. In addition, Loeber's model also allows for specialization – for example, in covert acts only – as well as escalation along pathways.

A key assumption of Loeber's model is that behavior takes place in an orderly, not random, fashion. In other words, individuals progress through lesser-order steps up through higher-order steps. The pathway model has been replicated in the youngest sample of the Pittsburgh Study, and it applied better to boys who persisted compared to those who experimented in delinquency (Loeber et al., 1998). In addition, replications have been reported by Tolan and Gorman-Smith (1998) in samples from the National Youth Survey and the Chicago Youth Development Study (see also Elliott, 1994). Finally, recent research on the pathway model in the three Causes and Correlates Study sites (Denver, Pittsburgh, and Rochester) replicated it for steps two and higher in the overt and covert pathways only (Loeber et al., 1999; but see Nagin and Tremblay, 1999).

Thus far, we have presented three specific developmental theories that allow for both static and dynamic effects. Another theory that was developed after the criminal career report is Sampson and Laub's age-graded informal social control theory. Though technically a general, nondevelopmental theory, the Sampson and Laub model allows for both static and dynamic effects on criminal activity over the life-course.

For Sampson and Laub (1993), crime can be understood as a product of both persistent individual differences and local life events. Their thesis entails three key ideas. First, delinquency in childhood and adolescence can be explained by the structural context that is mediated by informal family and school social controls. Second, they recognize that there is a substantial amount of continuity in antisocial behavior from childhood through adulthood in a variety of life domains. Third, they argue that variation in the quality of informal social bonds in adulthood with family and employment explain changes in criminality over the life-course, despite persistent individual differences in early childhood. Sampson and Laub's theory claims that, independent of persistent individual differences, informal social control mechanisms exert a causal effect on criminal activity and that the type of social control varies at different ages. Borrowing on the theory of "cumulative continuity" to explain how cumulative disadvantage connects early-childhood temper tantrums (and the like) to midlife problems such as job loss and divorce (see Caspi, Bem, and Elder, 1987; Moffitt, 1993:683–685), their theory incorporates both stability *and* change over the life-course; in fact, "change is a central part of [their] explanatory framework" (Sampson and Laub, 1993:17).

Several studies have examined Sampson and Laub's conception of stability and change and have found that both persistent individual differences (stability) *and* local life circumstances (change) are important for understanding criminal activity over the life-course. These efforts have made use of different samples, different indicators of local life circumstances, different methodologies, and different periods of the life-course (see Blokland and Nieuwbeerta, 2005; Horney, Osgood, and Marshall, 1995; Laub, Nagin, and Sampson, 1998; Piquero et al., 2002; Sampson and

Laub, 1993). Moreover, these efforts have shown that the type and quality of local life circumstances may be more important than just the presence of a particular life circumstance. For example, Laub, Nagin, and Sampson (1998) found that the quality of marriage, as opposed to marriage per se, was associated with desistance from offending in early adulthood.

Recently, Sampson and Laub (1997) have extended their age-graded theory of informal social control to incorporate a developmental conceptualization of labeling theory. In particular, this account invokes a state dependence argument in that it incorporates the causal role of prior delinquency in facilitating adult crime through a process of "cumulative disadvantage." According to Sampson and Laub, involvement in delinquent behavior has a "systematic attenuating effect on the social and institutional bonds linking adults to society (e.g., labor force attachment, marital cohesion)" (p. 144). Thus, delinquency is indirectly related to future criminal activity in that it can spark failure in school, incarceration, and weak bonds to the labor market, all of which are likely to lead to further adult crime. This cycle occurs because severe sanctions, which ultimately end up labeling offenders, limit the opportunities available to individuals to follow a conventional lifestyle. It is also important to note that the cumulative continuity of disadvantage is the result of both persistent individual differences and the dynamic process where childhood antisocial behavior and adolescent delinquency foster adult crime through the weakening of adult social bonds (Sampson and Laub, 1997:145).

The process of cumulative disadvantage is believed to be linked to the four social control institutions of the family, school, peers, and state sanctions. For Sampson and Laub (1997), interactional continuity begins with the family. They argue that child behaviors tend to influence parents just as much as parent behaviors influence children, and it is likely that a child's negative behavior not only will be punished by parents, but further actions may be influenced by parental labels placed on their children and their child's subsequent adoption of the label. The school also occupies a key place in Sampson and Laub's cumulative-disadvantage theory. For example, teachers may react to a child's unruly behavior by retreating from a teacher–student relationship that is designed to foster intellectual and personal growth. To the extent that this rejection "undermines the attachment of the child to the school and, ultimately, the child's performance in the school," it may lead to further disruptive and delinquent behavior. Another key aspect of their theory revolves around peers. Children who are rejected by their peers tend to be more aggressive, and for some children peer rejection fosters association with deviant peers, many of whom share the same aggressive characteristics. The final aspect of cumulative disadvantage for Sampson and Laub is the criminal justice and institutional reaction. Their argument here involves the negative structural consequences of criminal offending and the resulting official sanctions that limit noncriminal opportunities. According to Sampson and Laub (1997:147), adolescent delinquency and its negative consequences (e.g., arrest, trial, incarceration, etc.) "increasingly 'mortgage' one's future, especially later life chances molded by schooling and employment." Thus, the stigma associated with arrest and especially incarceration tend to limit good job prospects and, as a result, job stability. Given that job stability is virtually a prerequisite for lasting interpersonal relationships, arrest and incarcerations are likely to reduce an offender's marriage premium. In sum, Sampson and Laub claim that official (and severe) reactions to primary deviance tend to create problems of adjustment that are likely to foster additional crime in the form of secondary deviance.

In a preliminary test of this thesis, Sampson and Laub (1997) examined the role of job stability at ages 17 to 25 and 25 to 32 as an intervening link between incarceration and adult crime. After controlling for a number of theoretically relevant variables, including arrest frequency, alcohol use, and persistent unobserved heterogeneity, Sampson and Laub found that, compared to delinquents with a shorter incarceration history, boys who were incarcerated for a longer period of time had trouble securing stable jobs as they entered young adulthood.

The theories outlined in this section all share a common theme in that they are designed to assess within-individual change in both criminal activity and the factors associated with criminal activity over the lifecourse. Yet, they differ in important respects. Compared to the static general theories of crime that assume that there is a general cause and one pathway to crime for all offenders and that once this causal process has occurred change is highly unlikely (see Gottfredson and Hirschi, 1990; Wilson and Herrnstein, 1985), a dynamic general theory, such as the one postulated by Sampson and Laub, maintains the assumption of general causality but allows for the possibility that life circumstances can materially alter an individual's criminal trajectory, above and beyond persistent individual differences. That is, Sampson and Laub's model allows for both persistent heterogeneity and state dependence effects. Developmental theories, such as those advanced by Moffitt, Patterson, and Loeber, are quite complex in that they assume that causality is not general and that different causal processes explain different offender types. Moreover, this causal process may emphasize persistent heterogeneity, as in Moffitt's life-course-persisters and Patterson's early-starting-offenders, or a state dependent effect, as in the dynamic accounts found among Moffitt's adolescence-limited offenders and Patterson's late-start-offenders.

Table 2.1. *General, Developmental, Life-Course Classification Scheme*

|          | General                                        | Developmental                                                              |
|----------|------------------------------------------------|----------------------------------------------------------------------------|
| Static   | Gottfredson and Hirschi; Wilson and Herrnstein | Moffitt's Life-Course-Persistent Offender; Patterson's Early-Starting Offender; |
| Dynamic  | Sampson and Laub                               | Moffitt's Adolescence-Limited Offender; Patterson's Late-Starting Offender  |

Empirical research has attempted to adjudicate between these theoretical models, and thus far the evidence tends to favor a middle-ground position, such as the one advanced by Sampson and Laub (see Paternoster et al., 1997). However, recent evidence tends to suggest that local life circumstances operate in somewhat different ways across distinct offender groups (see Chung et al., 2002; Piquero et al., 2002).

An important point concerns the relationship between static (persistent heterogeneity)/dynamic (state dependence) and general/developmental theories. Paternoster et al. (1997) presented a useful classification on this front, reproduced here as Table 2.1. As can be seen, developmental theories can be compared against purely static/general theories and can be viewed along a continuum of parsimony. For example, static/general theories are the most parsimonious in emphasizing a purely persistent heterogeneity explanation, followed by dynamic/general theories that emphasize a combined persistent heterogeneity/state dependence explanation. These are followed by developmental/static theories and then – the least parsimonious – dynamic/developmental theories, which emphasize a mixture of persistent heterogeneity/state-dependent explanations across offender types. In sum, the sometimes competing explanations of persistent heterogeneity and state dependence are not necessarily incompatible; sometimes one is stronger, sometimes another, but they are not necessarily mutually inconsistent with one another.[2]

---

[2] One could also infer from Moffitt (1993:680–684) that the life-course-persistent pathway is a mixture of static and dynamic processes (where static processes create the starting point for a process of cumulative disadvantage that continues to influence offending over the life-course). Thus, some may read Moffitt's life-course-persistent pathway as a developmental theory reflecting both static and dynamic processes.

The purpose of this book is to contribute to the knowledge base regarding criminal careers by analyzing in depth the offending careers of one particular cohort: the Cambridge Study in Delinquent Development (CSDD), a sample of 411 South London males who have been followed in criminal records from age 10 to age 40. In so doing, we anticipate contributing to the areas of research identified in this chapter by carefully analyzing their offending careers.

# Overview of CSDD Data

We use data from a classic, large-scale, longitudinal study to examine the patterning of criminal activity: the Cambridge Study in Delinquent Development. We provide a description of (1) the sample, (2) measures of offending, (3) attrition, and (4) the social context in which the data were first collected.

## Cambridge Study in Delinquent Development

### Description of the Sample

The Cambridge Study in Delinquent Development (CSDD) is a prospective longitudinal survey of the development of antisocial and offending behavior in 411 South London boys, mostly born in 1953. The study began in 1961, and for the first 20 years it was directed by Donald West; in 1969, David Farrington joined the team and has been the director of the study since 1981. The original aim of the study was (1) to describe the development of delinquent and criminal behavior in inner-city males, (2) to investigate how well it could be predicted in advance, and (3) to explain why juvenile delinquency began, why it did or did not continue into adult crime, and why adult crime often ended as men reached their 20s. The

Much of the information in this chapter is reproduced from David P. Farrington and Donald J. West, 1995, "Effects of Marriage Separation, and Children on Offending by Adult Males." In Z. S. Blou and J. Hagan, eds., *Current Perspectives on Aging and the Life Cycle*, vol 4: *Delinquency and Disrepute in the Life Course: Contextual and Dynamic Analyses*. Greenwich, CT: JAI Press. Permission has been granted by Elsevier. Material also was reproduced from David P. Farrington, 2003, "Key Results from the First Forty years of the Cambridge Study in Delinquent Development." In T.P. Thornberry and M.D. Krohn, eds., *Taking Stock of Delinquency: An Overview of Findings from Contemporary Longitudinal Studies*. Boston: Kluwer. Permission has been granted by Springer.

main focus was on continuity and discontinuity in behavioral development, on the effects of risk factors and life events on development, and on predicting future behavior. Major results of the CSDD can be found in four books (West, 1969, 1982; West and Farrington, 1973, 1977) and in more than 100 papers by Farrington (2003b).

At the time they were first contacted in 1961–2, the boys were all living in a working-class area of South London (see Farrington and West, 1995). The vast majority of the sample was chosen by taking all of the boys who were then aged eight or nine and on the registers of six state primary schools within a one mile radius of an established research office. In addition to 399 boys from these six schools, 12 boys from a local school for the educationally subnormal were included in the sample, to make it more representative of the population of boys in the area. Hence, the boys were not a probability sample drawn from a population, but rather a complete population of boys of that age in that area at that time.

Most of the boys (357, or 87 percent) were white in appearance and of British origin, in the sense that they were being brought up by parents who had themselves been brought up in England, Scotland, or Wales. Of the remaining 54 boys, 12 were black, having at least one parent of West Indian (usually) or African origin. Of the remaining 42 boys of non-British origin, 14 had at least one parent from the North or South of Ireland, 12 had a parent from Cyprus, and 16 had at least one parent from another country (Australia, France, Germany, Malta, Poland, Portugal, Spain, or Sweden). On the bases of their fathers' occupations when they were aged eight, 94 percent of the boys could be described as working-class (categories III, IV, or V on the Registrar General's scale, describing skilled, semiskilled, or unskilled manual workers), in comparison with the national figure of 78 percent at that time. The majority of the boys were living in two-parent families, with both a father and a mother figure; at age eight or nine, only 6 percent of the boys had no operative father and only 1 percent had no operative mother. This was, therefore, a traditional white, urban, working-class sample of British origin.

The boys in the CSDD were interviewed when they were aged 8–9, 10–11, 14–15, and again at ages 16, 18, 21 (at a research office), and at about 25 and 32 in their homes by young male social science graduates. A ninth interview was conducted at age 48, but it has not yet been analyzed. In addition to interviews with and tests of the boys, interviews with their parents were carried out by female psychiatric social workers who visited their homes. These took place about once a year from when the boy was about 8 years old until he was aged 14–15 and was in his last year of compulsory education. The boys' teachers also completed questionnaires when the boys were aged about 8, 10, 12, and 14.

## Measures of Offending

At each wave, searches were carried out in the central Criminal Record Office in London to locate findings of guilt of the boys; of their biological mothers, fathers, brothers, and sisters; of their wives or female partners; and of people who offended with them (their co-offenders). Because (at least until the 1970s) conviction in London was very likely after arrest, the requirement of conviction in London does not represent a major distinction from the arrest data that are the more commonly available official record data in the United States (Blumstein et al., 1985:194). The minimum age of criminal responsibility in England is 10. Juveniles between the 10th and 14th birthday are referred to as "children," and those between the 14th and 17th birthday (the minimum age for adult court at that time) are "young persons" (Blumstein et al., 1985:196). The Criminal Record Office/National Identification Bureau contains records of all relatively serious offenses committed in Great Britain or Ireland. Convictions were counted only if they were for offenses normally recorded in the Criminal Record Office, thereby excluding such minor crimes as common assault, traffic infractions, and drunkenness. The most common offenses included were thefts, burglaries, and unauthorized taking of vehicles, although there were also quite a few offenses of violence, vandalism, fraud, and drug abuse. In the case of 18 males who had emigrated outside Great Britain or Ireland by age 32, applications were made to search their criminal records in the eight countries where they had settled, and searches were actually carried out in five countries. Because most males did not emigrate until their 20s and they had rarely been convicted in England, it is likely that the criminal records are quite complete. The latest search of conviction records took place in the summer of 1994, when most of the males were age 40.

The recorded age of offending is the age at which an offense was committed, not the age on conviction. There can be delays of several months or even a year or more between offenses and convictions, making conviction ages different from offending ages. Offenses are defined as acts leading to convictions. One court appearance can be for several different offenses, and it is sometimes a matter of chance whether two different offenses lead to two different court appearances or to only one. An analysis based only on recorded offenses would overestimate the number of separate offending events, because one event can lead to two recorded offenses (e.g., when an apprehended burglar is convicted of both burglary and of going equipped to steal). In order to yield the closest approximation to the number of offending events, offenses are only counted herein if they are committed on different days. Where two offenses were committed on the same day, only the most serious was counted. And while this occasionally led to the underreporting of separate offending events on the same day, most court appearances arose from only one offending day.

We also use a subset of self-reported delinquency for further analyses. We compare prospective and retrospective ages of onset using both official and self-reported offending (e.g., Brame et al., 2004; Maxfield et al., 2000). Specifically, the self-reported delinquency information for eight crime types was collected for ages 15–18, 19–21, 22–24, and 27–32.

## Attrition

Generally, the attrition rate has been unusually low for such a long-term survey, and because our focus concerns the conviction records, attrition is essentially nonexistent. The only types of "missing data" in the conviction records concern individuals who are not at risk of conviction because they were either incapacitated or they died. In the CSDD, 10 of the 411 subjects died by the age of 40, while only 6.8 percent, or 28 of the 411 men, were incarcerated at some point before the age of 40. The mean time served was 1.5 years. In some of the analyses, all individuals contribute information when they are alive, i.e., they are censored after the death age. Our initial exploration showed that incarceration did little to alter patterns of offending, and we believe this was largely due to the relatively infrequent use of incarceration and the small amount of time off the street among those who were incarcerated.

## Comparisons to Other Data Sources

The CSDD provides information about the development of offending and antisocial behavior in an inner-city, working-class British white male sample born about 1953. How far the same results would be obtained with females, black or Asian children, suburban or rural children, middle- or upper-class children, children born more recently, or children born in other countries are important considerations. Generally speaking, substantive results obtained with the CSDD are similar to those obtained with comparable male samples from Sweden (Farrington and Wikström, 1994), Finland (Pulkkinen, 1988), and from other Western industrialized countries (Farrington, 2003; Farrington and Loeber, 1999).

## Context of the Research: 1960s South London

It is useful to sketch a portrait of the area from which the 411 South London boys came, written in the early 1990s (Farrington and West,

1995). The large majority (399 of 411) of the boys came from the six primary schools that were within a mile of the researchers' office in a Cambridge University Settlement, an organization originally set up to do good works for poor people in the area. The boys' homes were spread about in an oblong-shaped area, roughly 1.75 miles long and 1.5 miles across at its widest point. It was a traditional English, urban, working-class neighborhood with an incidence of officially reported juvenile delinquency slightly higher than the national average but much higher than in the privileged areas called "leafy suburbs." In the early 1960s, when the study began, the great majority of the local population consisted of white families, most of whom had lived in the area for many years, often for several generations (West, 1969).

The proximity to many renowned institutions (under two miles from the Houses of Parliament, under a mile from the Institute of Psychiatry, and close to the headquarters of the Labour Party) only served to highlight the general dreariness of the immediate environment. It was a heavily built-up area crossed by busy arterial roads with shops and crossed by main railway lines linking the capital with the southern counties. The side streets accommodated a good deal of light industry in addition to housing a quite dense population. At the north end of the area, a large, grim, prisonlike Victorian building served as a local-authority residential facility for the homeless where, according to a psychiatric survey, many of the inmates were chronically mentally disordered and/or alcoholic. The sight of these scruffy social derelicts sitting about on outdoor walls and benches was disliked by some of the boys' mothers, who were concerned for the safety of their young children. Also at the north end of the area, the surroundings of a local road junction, notorious just after World War II as a haunt of youthful gangs carrying bicycle chains as weapons, were being transformed (in the early 1960s) into a large shopping center surrounded by tall government offices.

Nevertheless, the signs of relative deprivation were obvious. The food and goods in the local shops were of the cheapest kind, and a general air of shoddiness prevailed, unhelped by a clutter of television aerials and elderly cars. At the south end of the area was one of the busiest of the London magistrates' courts, where some celebrated leaders of criminal mobs had appeared. More cheerful was the thriving local street market, open six days a week (and still going strong). A trip down this "lane" in search of bargains and gossip was a regular feature of the housewives' lives. There was no lack of public houses (bars), open evenings and lunchtimes, selling vast quantities of English beers, mostly in rather grim and barren premises but a popular venue for working-class social life. The male tradition of turning over the bulk of wages to "the wife," but keeping

OVERVIEW OF CSDD DATA

back an undisclosed but substantial proportion for spending in the pub and the betting shop, was still prevalent in the 1960s.

When the study began, a rehousing program was in full swing, but some depressing, barracklike tenement blocks, built at the turn of the century, were still in use. They were generally surrounded by an asphalt compound, with stone stairways leading to entrance doors ranged along communal balconies so that residents had to pass each other's windows to gain access. Even older were the streets of damp, decaying terraced houses built for workers in Victorian times with outside lavatories and no indoor bathrooms. These were being systematically purchased and demolished by the local authority to make way for the erection of publicly owned estates, some of them tower blocks of the kind since reviled for their noisiness, lack of decent privacy or facilities for children, and vulnerability to vandalism and crime, others relatively spacious and equipped with the latest technological comforts, such as underfloor heating. Residents' accounts of living in one of the better and more imaginative new estates, still not completed when the research began, have been published by Parker (1983). Initially, however, a third of the CSDD sample were still living in accommodations with no bathroom in the early 1960s. Owner occupation was beyond the aspirations of all but a few, and some families, especially those with many children, were too poor to pay the rents demanded by the housing department for the new places, so they hung on in the worst and most rundown streets that still awaited demolition.

On the other hand, external signs of gross poverty, prevalent before the war, such as the sight of barefoot and undernourished children with ragged clothes, had disappeared, and there was virtually full employment for any healthy and willing adult. The print trade, based in this part of London for centuries, provided jobs for the more enterprising of the boys' fathers, while others were stallholders or dock workers. The mothers who worked were mostly part-time office cleaners, traveling to the City of London in the early hours to perform their tasks.

Within this overall picture of a working-class ethos devoid of middle-class cultural interests and educational values, there was noticeable variation in personal standards, with some families living in squalor, others struggling to keep up appearances under difficult conditions, and yet others appearing to be comfortably off with a profusion of household appliances and modern furnishings. Even the most deprived managed to have a television set. Lavish spending on funerals was traditional – paid for, one imagines, with the help of insurance. Few parents visualized their sons going on to higher education. Many were content for them to take up unskilled jobs like their fathers and brothers, but others wanted them to become apprenticed to a trade. Even the relatively affluent, however, had no aspirations to take on the responsibility of a mortgage to own their own house.

There were no private schools in the neighborhood, and the local state-supported primary schools attended by the boys were in keeping with the character of their surroundings: forbidding-looking Victorian structures encircled by concrete play areas. One of the schools was set among rows of grim-looking nineteenth-century terraces lacking any open spaces. Another was close to a major new housing development that was gradually engulfing the neighboring streets. Another was close to a confluence of major roads and local shops and served nearby families from both old Victorian mansion blocks and a newly built housing estate. All the schools were coeducational, and classes of 40 children were quite usual. Academic aspirations being low and the neighborhood uninviting, the schools were unattractive to ambitious teachers. Standards of literacy among the pupils, as measured by tests on the sample, were significantly below the London average for 10-year-olds. As a possible reflection of nutritional as well as intellectual deficits, our boys were also significantly below the national average in height for their age.

The schools differed in their regimes, one having a particularly authoritarian and somewhat aloof head teacher who believed in segregating pupils of similar age into separate streams according to academic achievement, or lack of it, and another having a more paternalistic head teacher who disagreed with such arrangements and tried to promote good relations with the parents. No evidence was found that these differences, marked as they were, had any significant long-term impact on delinquency potential.

Recreational facilities for children were limited. Soccer and swimming were promoted by some of the schools, but the activities of local youth clubs were generally somewhat regimented or run by religious organizations and so did not appeal to many of the boys.

The passage of time has brought changes, not all for the better. The old "rag and bone" yards served by horses and carts collecting scrap metal have disappeared. The shops are still lacking in higher-quality merchandise. In keeping with national trends, the local cinema has gone, and a McDonald's restaurant has sprung up. Signs of gentrification have appeared in some streets, with old houses refurbished, new and well-designed doors and windows installed, and middle-class enclaves established. The derelict areas from past demolitions are covered with grass now and are often used as children's playgrounds, but they are contaminated with dog dirt; the inhabitants of some of the worst estates feel the need to keep large dogs for protection.

The contrasts between relatively comfortable and dilapidated dwellings are very evident. Economic recession and high unemployment, weighing most heavily on the poorer and less educated sections of the population, have doubtless contributed to this contrast. Some estates look neat and pleasant, while others are run down, defaced with graffiti and the passageways littered with rubbish and smelling of urine. As one resident of the tower blocks on the estate Tony Parker called "Providence" explained to him (1983:26), there had been a great deterioration since the buildings were first put up in landscaped surroundings; Foreign visitors used to come to admire the design, but ugly blocks had been built close by and filled with transient problem families, mostly blacks. The stairwell windows were all smashed, obscene graffiti were everywhere, the garage area was choked with garbage, and wild kids from these places were invading the towers, now bereft of a residential caretaker, and wreaking havoc in the elevators and passages.

It its true that there has been a very visible influx of Afro-Caribbean people into the area, which is not far from Brixton, the scene of racial disturbances in the early 1990s. Black youths are particularly prone to poverty, unemployment, and social alienation in this area. Involvement of children with prohibited drugs, a relative rarity when the study began, is now an established feature of the local youth crime picture. The grim-looking school buildings remain, but their interiors have been refurbished and look more cheerful and childrens' art work is prominently displayed, enlivened by the contrasting styles of the different ethnic groups that are now a settled feature of the area. Unfortunately, with the nationwide concern about child abuse and a much publicized abduction and sexual murder of a local schoolboy by a pedophile "ring" in the early 1990s, the schools have had to become more security conscious.

# How Do Prevalence and Individual Offending Frequency Vary with Age?

What does the longitudinal patterning of criminal activity over age look like? Such basic questions have been studied in the criminal career literature, sometimes resulting in different conclusions.

Prevalence provides a measure of how many individuals participate in a crime type in any period. The shape of the age-crime curve for prevalence is generally agreed upon by most criminologists as data typically provide similar conclusions regarding trends in shape (though self-report records sometimes show an earlier peak for some crime types and a later peak for others). Both official and self-report records suggest that the prevalence of offending increases to a peak in the teenage years, at about ages 15–19, and then declines in the 20s (Blumstein et al., 1986; Elliott et al., 1989; Farrington, 1986; Piquero et al., 2003; Wolfgang et al., 1987). Prevalence curves typically form the basis of many conclusions regarding the aggregate age/crime relationship.

On the other hand, estimates of individual offending frequency, though generally minimally studied, tend to vary considerably – often because the definition of individual offense frequency varies. Some researchers prefer to simply plot the number of offenses (frequency) engaged in by sample members over time or over a particular time period, while other researchers argue that individual offending frequency should be defined by the amount of crime engaged in over a particular time period among those offenders who are active (i.e., offending) during that time period.

The evidence on individual offending frequency is mixed. Early studies reviewed by Farrington (1986) suggested that individual offending frequency did not vary systematically with age, in official records or self-reports. However, more-recent evidence using offender and community samples suggests that individual offending frequency may vary with age in the same way as the prevalence curve does. For example, Loeber and Snyder (1990), using a sample of juvenile court careers in Arizona, found that individual offending frequency increased from age 9 to age 16. In the three Office of Juvenile Justice and Delinquency Prevention (OJJDP) studies, it increased between ages 10 and 14 according to self-reports (Kelley et al., 1997). In official records from London and Stockholm, Farrington and Wikström (1994) concluded that individual offending frequency stayed constant with age in London but increased to a peak at age 15 (and then decreased) in Stockholm. Using data from the Seattle Social Development Project, Farrington et al. (2003) found that individual offending frequency increased with age and was much higher in self-reports, but stayed constant in court referrals. Still other scholars report decreasing offending frequencies with age (Hirschi and Gottfredson, 1983). Generally, then, there is mixed evidence on this topic, with some research showing that individual offending frequency does not change with age (Farrington, 1998; Loeber and Snyder, 1990). Recently, Sampson and Laub (2003:569) examined the frequency of offending among the Glueck delinquent sample of white males from Cambridge, MA, from ages 7 to 70 and found that, after selecting men who had one or more arrests at ages 7–16, 17–24, 25–31, 32–39, 40–49, and 50–59, the frequency of all crimes eventually declined with age. Among these 46 men, property crimes peaked around age 17, violent crimes in the late 20s, and alcohol/drug crimes in the middle/late 30s.

In this chapter, we begin with very basic descriptive information about criminal offending through age 40 in the CSDD. Such preliminary depictions of the data are important because they enhance our understanding of the involvement by sample members in delinquency and criminal activity over time. Such rudimentary descriptive pieces of information provide us with the bare minimum for understanding more in-depth criminal career patterns to be studied later in this book.

First, estimates of participation, or prevalence (i.e., the distinction between those who engage in crime and those who do not), will be presented for each age. Information on prevalence or participation is useful because it shows the relative size of the delinquent population across demographic groups, as well as over time. Second, estimates of individual offending frequency will be presented. This is important because little is known about how individual offending frequency among active offenders varies over the life-course generally and for violence in particular. Many studies show that offending frequency declines with age, but those studies usually fail to account for the termination of individual careers, so the decline is a combination of some people dropping out from active participation and the more ambiguous "slowing down" of those still active. We hope to be able to clarify that distinction. Additionally, we also present a breakdown of the types of offenses committed at different ages in the CSDD through age 40.

Thus, after presenting aggregate age/crime curves, we provide data on how an individual's offending frequency varies with age and differentiate the decline in λ, the offending rate among active offenders, from termination. This chapter will provide basic descriptive data on λ over time among active offenders and will present some of the first-ever depictions of this information for a large sample from childhood to adulthood.

## Methods

### Measures

Information on offending was obtained through the use of conviction records from age 10 through age 40. Prevalence estimates were obtained by coding each individual as having offended or not at each age, 10–40 inclusive. Individual offending frequency estimates are presented two ways. The first includes the full sample of individuals (i.e., offenders and nonoffenders) and simply presents the mean number of convictions. The second presents the mean number of convictions between ages 10 and 40 for active offenders only; that is, convictions in each particular age period are presented only for active offenders (excluding offenders inactive during that period). For this final analysis, we calculate individual offending frequency among active offenders, or lambda (λ), for total convictions as well as for violent convictions.

## Results

The prevalence of offending, measured through convictions in the CSDD, varies with age in the same way as many of the prevalence estimates observed in extant criminal career research. For example, as shown in Figure 4.1, the early to middle teenage years witness a steady increase in prevalence from 2 percent to just over 10 percent at the peak age of 17 (10.7 percent). Then, after this peak at age 17, prevalence decreases in early adulthood to age 23, at which point it remains quite stable until the

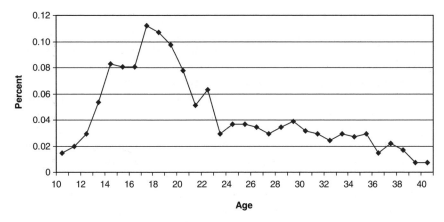

**Figure 4.1.** Prevalence of Conviction at Different Ages

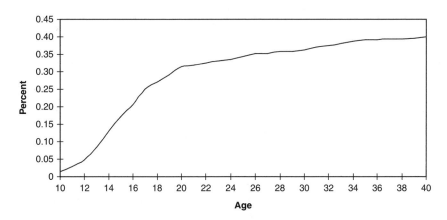

**Figure 4.2.** Cumulative Prevalence of Convictions

mid 30s, at which point prevalence drops at the end of the 30s to just three men incurring a conviction at age 40 (0.7 percent).

Figure 4.2 presents information on the cumulative prevalence of convictions through age 40 in the CSDD. The cumulative prevalence refers to the fraction of the population who by a certain age are ever convicted of a crime. The cumulative prevalence tells us what proportion of the population has ever been convicted in the CSDD. As can be seen, the cumulative prevalence rises rapidly until about age 18 and then grows to an asymptotic at age 40. For example, the cumulative prevalence at age

15 is 17.3 percent; at age 20, it is 31.4 percent; at age 25, it is 34.3 percent; at age 30, it is 36.3 percent; at age 35, it is 39.2 percent; and at age 40, it is 39.9 percent. Although it is possible that the cumulative prevalence could increase into the 40s and 50s, late-adult onset (post age 40) is exceedingly rare. Suffice it to say, then, that the age-40 cumulative prevalence of almost 40 percent is probably very close to the maximum for the CSDD males.

This cumulative prevalence estimate can be considered as middle of the road with regard to other criminal career studies (Blumstein and Graddy, 1982; Christensen, 1967). For example, about a third of Philadelphia males had a police contact by age 18 (Wolfgang et al., 1972), while the Racine cohorts show that almost 70 percent of the subjects had been in contact with the police by their 30s (though the Racine data contain many more trivial offenses, including status offenses) (Shannon, 1988). In the Project Metropolitan Stockholm study, the cumulative prevalence at age 30 was about 20 percent (Andersson, 1990).

Table 4.1 shows types of offenses committed at different ages. The most common offenses in the CSDD were burglary, theft or taking vehicles, other theft, and shoplifting. There was also a fair degree of violent offending in these data. Additionally, for the most part there appears to be no detectable tendency for some crime types to increase over time any more than any other crime type. In fact, most crime types appear to be decreasing with age, especially after age 20, except disqualified driving. And this table similarly shows that the total number of convictions peaks at ages 17–20 and then declines throughout the rest of the observation period.

As a point of reference, we present an abridged version of this table in Table 4.2 that contains the number of persons convicted and the sum of offenses per conviction by type of crime (for 18 different crime types) and age in the CSDD for four distinct time periods (<17, 17–24, 25–32, and 33–40) so as to be comparable with a similar table presented by Sampson and Laub (1993:56, Table 3.3b). With a few exceptions, the pattern here is such that, much like Sampson and Laub's analysis of the Boston-area males, participation peaks either in the <17 or the 17–24 category and declines into the 25–32 and 33–40 age periods. When examining only the aggregate totals, it can be seen that both the number of persons convicted and the sum total number of convictions peak in the age period 17–24 (249 persons and 342 convictions).[1]

---

[1] The number of persons convicted in different columns (i.e., in each age period) of Table 4.2 need not represent unique individuals because the same person could have been convicted in multiple periods.

Table 4.1. *Types of Offenses at Different Ages (760 Convictions)*

| Offense | Age Range | | | | | | Total |
|---|---|---|---|---|---|---|---|
| | 10–16 | 17–20 | 21–25 | 26–30 | 31–35 | 36–40 | |
| Theft from shops | 20 | 7 | 7 | 4 | 9 | 8 | 55 |
| Theft from motor vehicles | 18 | 11 | 5 | 3 | 1 | 0 | 38 |
| Theft of motor vehicles | 7 | 5 | 5 | 0 | 1 | 0 | 18 |
| Take and drive motor vehicles | 30 | 39 | 11 | 9 | 1 | 0 | 90 |
| Theft of cycle | 8 | 0 | 0 | 1 | 0 | 0 | 9 |
| Theft from machines | 9 | 4 | 1 | 3 | 0 | 0 | 17 |
| Theft from work | 1 | 13 | 2 | 2 | 2 | 2 | 22 |
| Other theft | 21 | 24 | 13 | 4 | 1 | 2 | 65 |
| Burglary | 54 | 38 | 18 | 10 | 4 | 3 | 127 |
| Fraud | 4 | 14 | 13 | 9 | 8 | 2 | 50 |
| Receiving | 6 | 11 | 6 | 7 | 5 | 0 | 35 |
| Equipment to steal | 14 | 10 | 3 | 3 | 0 | 0 | 30 |
| Robbery | 3 | 6 | 4 | 4 | 0 | 1 | 18 |
| Assault | 4 | 14 | 10 | 9 | 8 | 6 | 51 |
| Wound | 0 | 0 | 1 | 0 | 0 | 0 | 1 |
| Threats | 5 | 8 | 6 | 5 | 4 | 1 | 29 |
| Weapon | 3 | 9 | 2 | 3 | 0 | 1 | 18 |
| Sex offense versus female | 5 | 0 | 0 | 0 | 1 | 2 | 8 |
| Sex offense versus male | 0 | 1 | 0 | 0 | 1 | 1 | 3 |
| Drug | 0 | 10 | 5 | 2 | 2 | 1 | 20 |
| Arson | 1 | 0 | 1 | 0 | 0 | 0 | 2 |
| Damage | 1 | 11 | 2 | 3 | 8 | 2 | 27 |
| Disqualified driving | 0 | 7 | 5 | 7 | 8 | 0 | 27 |
| Total | 214 | 242 | 120 | 88 | 64 | 32 | 760 |

In the next set of graphs, we present information on individual offending frequency for the CSDD sample. Recall that by age 40 the CSDD men accumulated 760 convictions. Figure 4.3 presents the conviction rate estimates from age 10 to age 40. Importantly, this graph includes all individuals in the sample and simply presents a count of the number of convictions over the course of the observation period. As can be seen here, the conviction rate peaks at ages 17 (69 convictions) and 18 (67 convictions) and then begins to decline with the emergence of adulthood. Between ages 24 and 30, the offending rate remains quite

Table 4.2. *Number of Persons and Sum of Offenses Convicted by Type of Crime and Age in CSDD*

| Age →<br>Crime ↓ | <17 | | 17–24 | | 25–32 | | 33–40 | | Total |
|---|---|---|---|---|---|---|---|---|---|
| | N | Sum | N | Sum | N | Sum | N | Sum | SUM |
| Violent | 7 | 9 | 27 | 35 | 21 | 24 | 11 | 13 | 81 |
| Robbery | 3 | 3 | 4 | 9 | 3 | 5 | 1 | 1 | 18 |
| Burglary | 30 | 54 | 33 | 54 | 13 | 13 | 2 | 6 | 127 |
| Drug | 0 | 0 | 9 | 14 | 4 | 5 | 1 | 1 | 20 |
| Shoplifting | 16 | 20 | 10 | 13 | 9 | 9 | 6 | 13 | 55 |
| Theft from MV | 12 | 18 | 15 | 16 | 4 | 4 | 0 | 0 | 38 |
| Theft of MV | 31 | 37 | 35 | 59 | 8 | 11 | 1 | 1 | 108 |
| Theft – work | 1 | 1 | 14 | 14 | 2 | 3 | 4 | 4 | 22 |
| Theft of cycle | 8 | 8 | 0 | 0 | 1 | 1 | 0 | 0 | 9 |
| Theft from machines | 7 | 9 | 3 | 5 | 2 | 3 | 0 | 0 | 17 |
| Other theft | 16 | 21 | 31 | 37 | 5 | 5 | 2 | 2 | 65 |
| Other fraud | 4 | 4 | 12 | 22 | 9 | 15 | 7 | 9 | 50 |
| Receive stolen prop. | 6 | 6 | 16 | 17 | 6 | 7 | 5 | 5 | 35 |
| Suspicion | 11 | 14 | 11 | 12 | 4 | 4 | 0 | 0 | 30 |
| Vandalism | 2 | 2 | 11 | 11 | 9 | 9 | 5 | 7 | 29 |
| Disqualified driving | 0 | 0 | 7 | 12 | 9 | 11 | 4 | 4 | 27 |
| Weapons | 3 | 3 | 10 | 11 | 3 | 3 | 1 | 1 | 18 |
| Sex offense | 4 | 5 | 1 | 1 | 0 | 0 | 5 | 5 | 11 |
| Total | 161 | 214 | 249 | 342 | 112 | 132 | 55 | 72 | 760 |

*Note:* At ages 17–24, there were six dead males. At ages 25–32, there were eight dead males. At ages 33–40, there were ten dead males.

stable, but small (under 20 convictions at each age) until another drop in the late 30s. By age 40, the offending rate is very small (three men were convicted of one crime each).

Thus far, the results indicate that prevalence and offending rate reveal very similar patterns, with a peak in late adolescence followed by a drop into adulthood.

Figure 4.4 presents another graphical presentation of individual offending frequency (λ), but this time it alters the calculation of offending to include only active offenders, that is, defined here as "active" for the period between their first and last recorded offenses (convictions).[2] To

---

[2] We recognize that the λ issue has been – and likely will continue to be – a contentious one in criminology (see Gottfredson and Hirschi, 1990:240–248). Yet, we believe that the extent to

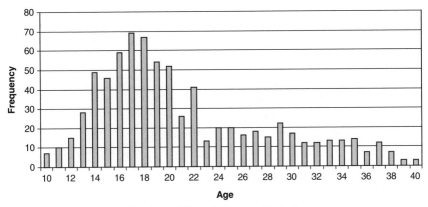

**Figure 4.3.** Aggregate Number of Convictions at Each Age

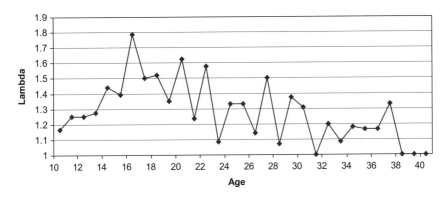

**Figure 4.4.** Individual Offending Frequency (λ)

obtain λ of actives at each age, we took the total number of offenses at each age divided by the number of offenders at each age. So, the average active λ at age 12, for example, would be given by the total number of offenses committed by the set of active age-12 offenders (15 offenses) divided by the total number of age-12 offenders (12 offenders), generating a λ equal to 1.25.

As can be seen from Figure 4.4, λ peaks at age 16 at 1.78. This rate remains fairly stable, hovering around 1.50 through age 22, then declines

which λ varies (or does not vary) over the life-course is still unclear. For Gottfredson and Hirschi (1990) and Sampson and Laub (2003), the λ curve is similar to the prevalence curve, rising to a peak in late adolescence/early adulthood and then exhibiting the classic decline throughout adulthood. For Blumstein et al. (1986, 1988a, 1988b), this decline does not necessarily have to take place (though it certainly may), and it is instructive to examine λ patterns among active offenders and types of crime (with a specific focus on violence).

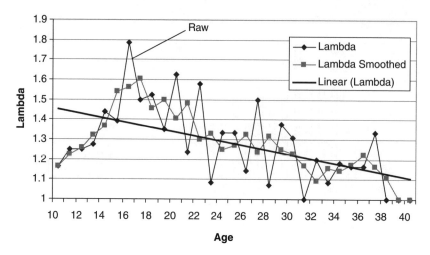

**Figure 4.4a.** Smoothed Figure 4.4

steadily until the late 20s. There appears to be a flattening during that period and into the mid 30s, an increase after that to a new peak at age 37, and then a decline to a level of 1.0 for the last three periods, when the number of offenders and the number of offenses is the same. At age 38, there were eight offenders and eight offenses (i.e., one offense per offender), while at ages 39 and 40 there were three offenders and three offenses (i.e., one offense per offender). Thus, in general, there seems to be a reasonably steady decline in the number of convictions per year by those convicted using the CSDD data to study all crimes in the age range 10–40.

Figure 4.4a presents the same information, except that we smooth the λ estimates using three point-smoothing techniques, so that $f_{sm}(a) = [f(a-1) + f(a) + f(a+1)]/3$, with the first and last values left unaltered. The lower trend is the smoothed figure, while the higher trend is the raw figure. The smoothed curve is easier to describe and interpret than the raw curve because it avoids all those sharp ups and downs (it still has ups and downs, but they are more gentle). Also, the smoothed curve is similar to the prevalence curve, with a peak at age 18. We also added a linear trend line for comparison.

Because the data may be being spread too thin over the age range studied, and because there are so few offenders and convictions during the mid to late 30s, we decided to recalculate and re-plot λ, this time using six categorical age bands (10–15, 16–20, 21–25, 26–30, 31–35, and 36–40). Figure 4.5 displays λ for total convictions over these six age bands. As can be seen, λ increases from age 10 to 15 (2.18) and then to its peak at ages 16–20 (2.86), at which point it drops but remains steady

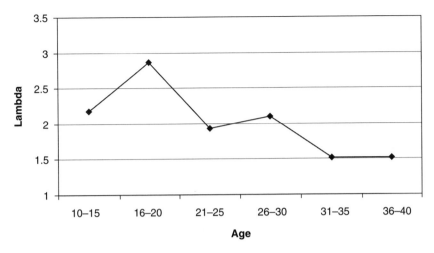

**Figure 4.5.** Individual Offending Frequency (λ) Across Age Groups

around 2.0 between ages 21 and 30. After age 31 and through age 40, λ remains flat and stable at 1.52. In sum, λ exhibits an early increase followed by a steady decline over time.

In the final set of analyses in this chapter, we investigate whether the λ estimates varied according to crime type, with the specific focus on violence. Because violent offenders and offending were rare (only 81 violent convictions) in the CSDD and because at a number of individual ages there were no violent convictions, we present this information using the six age bands presented in Figure 4.5 (i.e., 10–15, 16–20, 21–25, 26–30, 31–35, and 36–40) and calculate the violence λ.

Figure 4.6 presents these λ estimates for violence. Although there is a difference in scale (because of the rarity of violence), the λ estimates follow a reasonably similar pattern to total offenses. Bounded by 1.0 at ages 10–15, the violence λ increases to a peak at ages 16–20 (1.529), declines to 1.133 at ages 21–25, and remains stable through age 40 (ranging between 1.076 at ages 26–30 to 1.2 at ages 31–35 to 1.166 at ages 36–40). Although not large in absolute value, this specific finding may be a feature of convictions only because it is rare to have more than one conviction for violence in an age range.

## Continuity in Offending

To close the discussion on offending prevalence and frequency, we assess this question in the context of continuity in offending. To examine

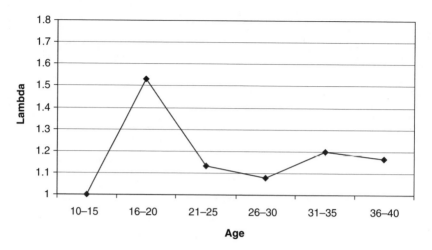

**Figure 4.6.** Individual Offending Frequency ($\lambda$) – Violence Only

continuity, we assess offending between different age periods, from 10–15 through 36–40. The results of this analysis may be found in Table 4.3.

In the CSDD data, 46 of the 69 recorded offenders at 10–15 were offenders at 16–20 (66.66 percent), whereas 58 out of 340 nonoffenders at 10–15 were offenders at 16–20 (17.05 percent).[3] The odds ratio for this comparison is the odds of offending at 16–20 for those who were offenders at 10–15 (46/23) divided by the odds of offending at 16–20 for those who were nonoffenders at 10–15 (58/282), which comes to 9.72. Roughly speaking, being an offender at 10–15 increased the risk of offending at 16–20 by over nine times. The odds ratio measures the strength of the relationship, or the degree of continuity.

Table 4.3 shows that there was considerable continuity in offending among the South London males. It might be expected that odds ratios for adjacent age ranges would be greater than those for nonadjacent age ranges, but this was not invariably true in London, although two adjacent comparisons (16–20 versus 21–25 and 31–35 versus 36–40) yielded two of the highest odds ratios. It might also be expected that the two most widely separated age ranges (10–15 versus 36–40) would yield the lowest odds ratio, and this was true. However, even in this case the odds ratio (4.16) indicated strong continuity in offending over this long time period. At the same time, caution should be taken when interpreting this table, especially for the age 36–40 group, because of the very small number of individual offenses here.

---

[3] Two males who died prior to age 20 were excluded from this comparison.

Table 4.3. *Continuity in Offending Between Different Age Ranges*

| Age 1 | Age 2 | R2/R1 | R2/NR1 | Odds Ratio |
|-------|-------|-------|--------|-----------|
| 10–15 | 16–20 | 66.66 | 17.05 | 9.72 |
| 10–15 | 21–25 | 50.74 | 8.28 | 11.44 |
| 10–15 | 26–30 | 32.83 | 5.93 | 7.74 |
| 10–15 | 31–35 | 26.86 | 7.14 | 4.77 |
| 10–15 | 36–40 | 13.43 | 3.59 | 4.16 |
| 16–20 | 21–25 | 41.58 | 6.57 | 10.11 |
| 16–20 | 26–30 | 30.00 | 3.94 | 10.45 |
| 16–20 | 31–35 | 25.00 | 5.61 | 5.64 |
| 16–20 | 36–40 | 12.12 | 2.98 | 4.49 |
| 21–25 | 26–30 | 33.87 | 6.14 | 7.87 |
| 21–25 | 31–35 | 32.25 | 6.45 | 6.91 |
| 21–25 | 36–40 | 14.75 | 3.52 | 4.8 |
| 26–30 | 31–35 | 38.09 | 7.2 | 7.98 |
| 26–30 | 36–40 | 26.82 | 2.77 | 13.07 |
| 31–35 | 36–40 | 26.19 | 2.78 | 12.67 |

*Notes:* R2/R1 = percentage at age 2 out of those recorded at age 1. R2/NR1 = percentage recorded at age 2 out of those not recorded at age 1. All odds ratios, $p < .05$.

## Comment: Do Prevalence and Individual Offending Frequency Track Each Other?

We set out in this chapter to provide basic evidence regarding the longitudinal patterning of prevalence, cumulative prevalence, the aggregate offending rate, and $\lambda$, or the individual offending frequency ($\lambda$) among active offenders so as to provide basic descriptive information regarding the natural history of offending for the CSDD males and so that our results could be compared with existing criminal career studies.

In the CSDD data, and much like extant research, the prevalence of offending (measured via convictions) peaked at age 17 (11.19 percent), at which point it began the commonly observed decline into adulthood. In fact, by age 40 the prevalence of offending was less than 1 percent. Cumulative prevalence in the CSDD was observed to expand rapidly throughout the early to mid teenage years, at which point it continued increasing, but at a much slower pace. By age 40, 39.9 percent of the Cambridge males had incurred at least one conviction. The aggregate offending rate closely tracked prevalence in the CSDD, peaking also at age 17 (69 offenses). When we considered $\lambda$, or the offending frequency among active offenders, the peak was at age 16 ($\lambda = 1.787$ offenses), but it remained reasonably steady thereafter, only to begin a slow, steady decline after age 22. Finally, when we considered the violence λ in the CSDD, we found that, although it was much lower due to the rarity of violence among the South London males, it followed the λ for all crimes quite closely, except that it was virtually flat (a little over 1.0) from age 21 onward.[4]

In short, the conviction rate was highest between ages 16 and 18, where the males' individual offending frequency peaked and where we observed 195 convictions, or 25.65 percent of all 760 convictions in the data by age 40. At that age, there were only three convictions, one each committed by three different men. Also, the fact that prevalence and individual offending frequency paralleled one another in terms of shape provides support for Gottfredson and Hirschi's position that these two criminal career parameters reveal substantively similar trends, at least for convictions in the CSDD.[5] Calculations for total crime λ indicated that it peaked in the late teens and began a slow, steady decline through adulthood, while calculations for violence λ indicated a similar peak in late adolescence, but a much flatter, more stable trend between ages 21 and 40. Regarding continuity in offending between different age periods, we found that there was appreciable continuity in offending in the CSDD. Although it was the case that continuity was strongest in adjacent age periods, continuity was still observed between even the most widely separated age ranges.

## Take-Home Messages

1 Prevalence increases to a peak at age 17 in the CSDD conviction data and then declines.
2 Cumulative prevalence increases rapidly during the mid to late teenage years, stabilizing at 40 percent by age 40 in the CSDD conviction data.
3 The aggregate offending rate closely tracks the prevalence curve in the CSDD conviction data.
4 λ estimates for total convictions increase to a peak at age 16 and range above 1.2 in the first 20 years, only to begin a slow, steady decline between ages 21 and 40.

[4] Of course, it is important to recognize that λ cannot go below 1.0.
[5] Some caution should be exercised here because of the small number of cases available for some of these analyses.

5 $\lambda$ estimates for violence increase to a peak between ages 16 and 20, slowly decline in early adulthood, and remain flat and stable through age 40.

6 There is appreciable continuity in offending among the South London males. Although continuity is most pronounced in adjacent age ranges, it is also observed when comparing offending between the two most widely separated age ranges (10–15/36–40).

## Unanswered Questions

1 Does studying overall offending mask variation in type of offending (i.e., serious or violent offending)?

2 Would different results be obtained using self-reports rather than convictions?

3 How do serious offending patterns over the life-course with regard to prevalence, cumulative prevalence, and individual frequency vary across race and sex?

4 What do $\lambda$ estimates look like throughout the entire life-course, across crime type, for males and females, and for whites and nonwhites?

CHAPTER FIVE

# How Does Onset Age Relate to Individual Offending Frequency?

Do those males experiencing an early onset of offending commit more crimes over time than their later-onset counterparts? This is a question that is central to several contemporary developmentally based criminological theories. For example, it may be that both individual offending frequency and offense seriousness increase with age and peak at a higher level for early-starters. That is what some developmental theorists would argue (see Loeber and Hay, 1994; Moffitt, 1993), presumably because early onset is an indicator of a more severe tendency toward delinquency and criminal activity.

In official and self-report records, early onset predicts a relatively large number of offenses in total (Farrington et al., 1990; Le Blanc and Fréchette, 1989). Using official records, several studies show that individual offending frequency is approximately constant after onset (Farrington et al., 1998:101; Hamparian et al., 1978:60l; Tarling, 1993:57). Across individuals, Tolan and Thomas (1995) and Krohn et al. (2001) showed that the frequency of offending in self-reports was greatest for those with the earliest ages of onset. Recently, Farrington et al. (2003), using data from the Seattle Social Development Project, investigated how strongly an early age of onset predicts a large number of offenses (in total and per year) in self-reports compared with court referrals. Their findings indicated that an early age of onset predicted a large number of offenses in both self-reports and court referrals. However, an early onset (ages 11–12) predicted a high frequency of offending after onset in court referrals but not in self-reports, possibly because of the reluctance to refer youths aged 11–12 (in grades 5–6) to court after offending; those who

60

were referred may have been a relatively extreme group with a high frequency or seriousness of offending (Farrington et al., 2003:933, 949). Unfortunately, the data used in the Farrington et al. study were limited because it only went up through age 17, thus missing the important transition into adulthood.

As shown, only a few studies have examined how onset age relates to offending frequency among active offenders with age, and no research has linked these two criminal career dimensions (onset age and individual offense frequency) together into adulthood. Thus, it is not clear what an early age of onset predicts. It could predict a high individual offending frequency, a high average seriousness of offending, or a longer criminal career. It is widely accepted that onset age is an important predictor of the future career, but it is not yet clear just what aspects of the future career it most strongly predicts. In addition, we do not know the extent to which knowledge of frequency, in addition to onset, predicts seriousness nor the extent to which knowledge of seriousness, in addition to onset, predicts frequency. In fact, there has been generally little research on the seriousness of offending over time and how it is related to onset age, though one would expect all three of these criminal career parameters – individual offending frequency, offense seriousness, and onset age – to be related (Blumstein et al., 1986; Moffitt, 1994).

## Methods

### Data Analysis Approach

In this chapter, we provide basic data on the relationships between onset age, individual offending frequency, and offense seriousness (violence) with age, using convictions in the CSDD. To do so, we rely on simple descriptive plots and mean analysis.

## Results

Figure 5.1 presents information on the age at first conviction. It shows that the large majority of offenders (73 per cent) incurred their first conviction prior to age 20. Additionally, although the mean age at first conviction is 18.12 (median age = 16), which may seem somewhat older than many American-based criminal career studies, two points should be made. First, many American studies are limited to the juvenile career and so are censored at age 18; that will invariably make onset appear earlier because it omits onset at later ages. Second, some men in South London were first convicted as adults, even in their 30s, which has the effect of

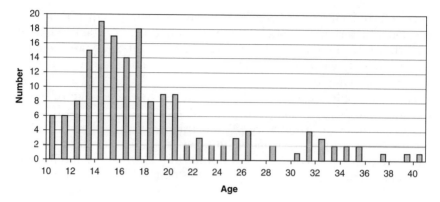

**Figure 5.1.** Age at First Conviction

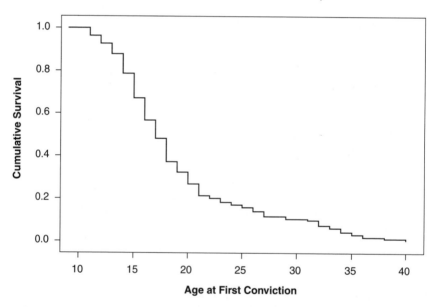

**Figure 5.2.** Survival Function for Age at First Conviction

stretching out the mean. Because of this skew, it is useful to also inspect the median and mode of the age at first conviction, which in the CSDD turn out to be 16 (8.5 per cent of the cases) and 14 (11.6 per cent of the cases) years of age, respectively – ages that resemble many onset-age findings around the world. The median is particularly useful here because it avoids the distortion of a few very high onset-age values.[1]

A useful approach to analyzing onset is hazard/survival analysis, the results of which are provided in Table 5.1. As can be seen, age 14 corresponds to the age at which there is the highest number of individuals (n = 19) incurring an onset (i.e., first conviction). However, the hazard rate is higher at age 17 (hazard = .257) than it is at age 14 (hazard = .159). The relatively high onset rate at age 17 could have been caused by the fact that juveniles legally became adults at age 17 at this time, and police could well have become more willing to arrest a 17-year-old than a 16-year-old for the same action. The lower inhibitions that the police had against arresting adults (in comparison with juveniles) could have caused the increased onset rate at 17 among the South London males.[2] Figure 5.2 presents the cumulative survival function for the age at first conviction. This figure clearly shows how the proportion of the sample "surviving" (i.e., not experiencing an onset) declines over time and that most convictions occur during the mid adolescent years.

Table 5.2 presents a description of the total number of convictions (including the initial conviction) incurred until age 40 by age of onset. As can be seen, those individuals exhibiting an early age at first conviction are more likely than those exhibiting a later age at first conviction to accumulate many convictions through age 40. In fact, the six males who were first convicted at age 10 had, on average, 12 convictions by age 40, while the eight males who were first convicted at age 18 had, on average, 2.5 convictions by age 40. Figure 5.3 presents this information in graphical format: As age at first conviction increases, the total number of convictions decreases. In part, this is because early starters have more time to accumulate convictions. But it also reflects a clear tendency for more offending.

If we were to use what has become a standard age of onset cutoff, age 14 (Patterson et al., 1992; Tibbetts and Piquero, 1999), we can compare the mean number of convictions incurred by those who exhibit an early onset (<14) compared to those who exhibit a later onset (14+). The 35 males (8.5 per cent of the total sample of 411 males, 21.3 per cent of the 164 total offenders) who had early onset accumulated an average of 8.77 convictions, while the 129 males with later onset (31.4 per cent of the total sample, 78.65 per cent of the total 164 offenders) accumulated an average

---

[1] It is useful to note here that in many longitudinal data sets onset information is gleaned from self-report records, which tend to evince an earlier onset age by two to three years when compared to official records (see also Farrington et al., 2003; Moffitt et al., 2001).

[2] We use the term "arrest" here only as a heuristic. Our data are in the form of conviction, but in the United Kingdom, at that time, virtually all arrests resulted in convictions.

Table 5.1. *Hazard of Onset Age (Among Those Ever Convicted, N = 164)*

| Age | Number Ever Convicted | Number of Events | Proportion Terminating | Proportion Surviving | Cumulative Proportion Surviving at End | Cumulative Probability Density | Hazard Rate |
|---|---|---|---|---|---|---|---|
| .0 | 164 | 0 | .000 | 1.000 | 1.000 | .000 | .000 |
| 1.0 | 164 | 0 | .000 | 1.000 | 1.000 | .000 | .000 |
| 2.0 | 164 | 0 | .000 | 1.000 | 1.000 | .000 | .000 |
| 3.0 | 164 | 0 | .000 | 1.000 | 1.000 | .000 | .000 |
| 4.0 | 164 | 0 | .000 | 1.000 | 1.000 | .000 | .000 |
| 5.0 | 164 | 0 | .000 | 1.000 | 1.000 | .000 | .000 |
| 6.0 | 164 | 0 | .000 | 1.000 | 1.000 | .000 | .000 |
| 7.0 | 164 | 0 | .000 | 1.000 | 1.000 | .000 | .000 |
| 8.0 | 164 | 0 | .000 | 1.000 | 1.000 | .000 | .000 |
| 9.0 | 164 | 0 | .000 | 1.000 | 1.000 | .000 | .000 |
| 10.0 | 164 | 6 | .036 | .963 | .963 | .036 | .037 |
| 11.0 | 158 | 6 | .038 | .962 | .926 | .036 | .038 |
| 12.0 | 152 | 8 | .052 | .947 | .878 | .048 | .054 |
| 13.0 | 144 | 15 | .104 | .895 | .786 | .091 | .109 |
| 14.0 | 129 | 19 | .147 | .852 | .670 | .115 | .159 |
| 15.0 | 110 | 17 | .154 | .845 | .567 | .103 | .167 |
| 16.0 | 93 | 14 | .150 | .849 | .481 | .085 | .162 |
| 17.0 | 79 | 18 | .227 | .772 | .372 | .109 | .257 |
| 18.0 | 61 | 8 | .131 | .868 | .323 | .048 | .140 |
| 19.0 | 53 | 9 | .169 | .830 | .268 | .054 | .185 |
| 20.0 | 44 | 9 | .204 | .795 | .213 | .054 | .227 |

| Age | number ever convicted | events | proportion terminating | proportion surviving | cumulative proportion surviving at end | cumulative probability density | hazard rate |
|---|---|---|---|---|---|---|---|
| 21.0 | 35 | 2 | .057 | .942 | .201 | .012 | .058 |
| 22.0 | 33 | 3 | .090 | .909 | .182 | .018 | .095 |
| 23.0 | 30 | 2 | .066 | .933 | .170 | .012 | .069 |
| 24.0 | 28 | 2 | .071 | .928 | .158 | .012 | .074 |
| 25.0 | 26 | 3 | .115 | .884 | .140 | .018 | .122 |
| 26.0 | 23 | 4 | .173 | .826 | .115 | .024 | .190 |
| 27.0 | 19 | 0 | .000 | 1.000 | .115 | .000 | .000 |
| 28.0 | 19 | 2 | .105 | .894 | .103 | .012 | .111 |
| 29.0 | 17 | 0 | .000 | 1.000 | .103 | .000 | .000 |
| 30.0 | 17 | 1 | .058 | .941 | .097 | .006 | .060 |
| 31.0 | 16 | 4 | .250 | .750 | .073 | .024 | .285 |
| 32.0 | 12 | 2 | .166 | .833 | .061 | .012 | .181 |
| 33.0 | 10 | 3 | .300 | .700 | .042 | .018 | .352 |
| 34.0 | 7 | 2 | .285 | .714 | .030 | .012 | .333 |
| 35.0 | 5 | 2 | .400 | .600 | .018 | .012 | .500 |
| 36.0 | 3 | 0 | .000 | 1.000 | .018 | .000 | .000 |
| 37.0 | 3 | 1 | .333 | .666 | .012 | .006 | .400 |
| 38.0 | 2 | 0 | .000 | 1.000 | .012 | .000 | .000 |
| 39.0 | 2 | 1 | .500 | .500 | .006 | .006 | .666 |
| 40.0 | 1 | 1 | 1.000 | .000 | .000 | ** | ** |

*Notes:* (1) "Age" reflects the age in years for each window of observation; (2) "number ever convicted" refers to the number of individuals exposed to the risk of onset during the interval; (3) "events" refers to the number of individuals who "onset" during that period; (4) "proportion terminating" refers to the proportion of the sample who were terminated (onsetted) in that interval; (5) "proportion surviving" refers to the proportion of individuals surviving in that interval (i.e., those who did not onset); (6) "cumulative proportion surviving at end" refers to the cumulative proportion of the sample surviving at each age through the end of the observation period; (7) "cumulative probability density" refers to the cumulative probability density; and (8) "hazard rate" refers to the hazard rate of onset, or the instantaneous failure rate among survivors at time t.

Table 5.2. *Total Number of Convictions by Onset Age*

| Age at First Conviction | Number of Offenders | Mean Number of Convictions |
|---|---|---|
| 10 | 6 | 12.33 |
| 11 | 6 | 11.50 |
| 12 | 8 | 6.62 |
| 13 | 15 | 7.40 |
| 14 | 19 | 4.63 |
| 15 | 17 | 7.88 |
| 16 | 14 | 4.21 |
| 17 | 18 | 3.27 |
| 18 | 8 | 2.50 |
| 19 | 9 | 2.00 |
| 20 | 9 | 2.11 |
| 21–40 | 35 | 1.60 |

*Note:* Because of small cell sizes, information from ages 21–40 is grouped.

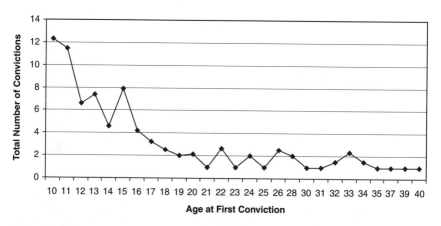

**Figure 5.3.** Relationship between Age at First Conviction and Total Number of Convictions

of 3.51 convictions (t = −4.44, p < .05). Further, Table 5.3 presents the mean total number of convictions at six different age bands (10–15, 16–20, 21–25, 26–30, 31–35, 36–40) for the early- and late-onset groups. As can be seen, at each age band those incurring an onset prior to age 14 (the early-onset group) exhibited a higher mean number of convictions in

Table 5.3. *Mean Number of Convictions by Onset Group and Age Band*

| | Age Band | | | | | |
| --- | --- | --- | --- | --- | --- | --- |
| Onset group | 10–15 | 16–20 | 21–25 | 26–30 | 31–35 | 36–40 |
| Late onset (14+) | .36 | 1.52 | .61 | .54 | .33 | .18 |
| Early onset (<14) | 3.08 | 2.91 | 1.27 | .60 | .66 | .27 |
| T-values | 6.52* | 2.42* | 2.07* | 0.27 | 1.30 | 0.66 |

*p < .05

each age range, though the comparisons were only statistically significant for the 10–15, 16–20, and 21–25 age bands, likely because of low cell sizes from the 26–30 age band upward. What is also interesting in this table is that, while the late-onset group peaks at an average of 1.52 convictions at ages 16–20, the early-onset group, while also peaking at ages 16–20 (average of 2.91 convictions), is still accumulating a fairly high rate of convictions five years later in the 21–25 age band (average of 1.27 convictions). In short, an early age of onset predicts a large number of offenses in the CSDD conviction records.[3]

But what about the relationship between onset age and serious offending, measured here as violence, among the South London males? Do those with an early onset accumulate violent offenses throughout their careers? To examine this question, we examine how onset age and violent offending relate in the CSDD data.

First, we plot in Figure 5.4 the total number of violent convictions by age at first conviction. Here, violent convictions seem to be confined to those exhibiting an early onset of offending. In fact, the number of violent convictions is quite small during the onset age period from 18 until 39, when one individual, who experienced his first conviction at age 39, was convicted for a violent offense.

Table 5.4 presents a tabular representation of the relationship between onset age (continuously) and both the percentage of individuals becoming violent/career and the average number of violent convictions. Given the low incidence of violence (both in terms of relative number of violent offenders and total number of violent convictions in the CSDD data), it is

---

[3] If we were to examine the relationship between onset age (in brackets, including 10–12, 13–16, 17–20, 21–25, 26–30, 31–35, 36–40) and offense frequency (in brackets, including 10–15, 16–20, 21–25, 26–30, 31–35, 36–40), we would be led to substantively similar conclusions. That is, those males exhibiting an earlier onset of offending engage in many more crimes, on average, in the periods following onset. Nevertheless, the offending frequency appears to decline with age regardless of onset age.

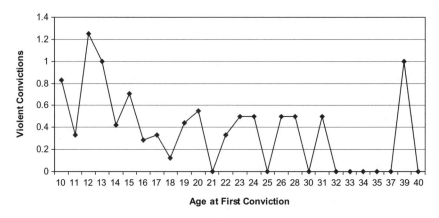

**Figure 5.4.** Relationship between Age at First Conviction and Total Number of Violent Convictions

not a surprise that with the continuous onset age indicator there is no significant relationship between onset age and violence. Nevertheless, it can be seen that violence is concentrated among offenders with an earlier onset age.

Because of the thin spread in the data after age 21 or so, we collapsed Table 5.4 into Table 5.5 across four onset age groups, 10–13, 14–16, 17–20, and 21+, and reanalyzed the percentage of being a violent offender and the mean number of violent convictions. As can be seen from Table 5.5, individuals who experienced an onset in the age-10-to-13 group had a higher percentage of being a violent offender at some stage and incurred a higher average number of violent convictions. In general, this trend was linear (i.e., earlier onset = more violence), but the relationship was only significant between the onset age groups and the average number of violent convictions.

To better examine this relationship, we use the dichotomous onset age measure described earlier and present information on violent offending for early (<14) and late (14+) onset offenders (see Table 5.6). As can be seen, although early-onset offenders are more likely than late-onset offenders to be violent and accumulate a higher mean number of violent convictions, only the latter relationship between onset group and the average number of violent convictions attains significance (t = 1.93, p < .05).

Finally, we investigate the relationship between onset age (in age ranges) and age at last conviction, career length, total offenses, $\lambda$, and a variety index of the number of different crime types (out of 18) the individual was convicted of. We anticipate that those individuals exhibiting an

Table 5.4. *The Relationship Between Onset Age and Violence*

| Age at First Conviction | N | Percentage Becoming Violent/Career | Mean Number of Violent Convictions |
|---|---|---|---|
| 10 | 6 | 33 | .83 |
| 11 | 6 | 33 | .33 |
| 12 | 8 | 50 | 1.25 |
| 13 | 15 | 46 | 1.00 |
| 14 | 19 | 26 | .42 |
| 15 | 17 | 41 | .70 |
| 16 | 14 | 14 | .28 |
| 17 | 18 | 33 | .33 |
| 18 | 8 | 12 | .12 |
| 19 | 9 | 44 | .44 |
| 20 | 9 | 33 | .55 |
| 21 | 2 | 00 | .00 |
| 22 | 3 | 33 | .33 |
| 23 | 2 | 50 | .50 |
| 24 | 2 | 50 | .50 |
| 25 | 3 | 00 | .00 |
| 26 | 4 | 50 | .50 |
| 28 | 2 | 50 | .50 |
| 30 | 1 | 00 | .00 |
| 31 | 4 | 50 | .50 |
| 32 | 2 | 00 | .00 |
| 33 | 3 | 00 | .00 |
| 34 | 2 | 00 | .00 |
| 35 | 2 | 00 | .00 |
| 37 | 1 | 00 | .00 |
| 39 | 1 | 100 | 1.00 |
| 40 | 1 | 00 | .00 |
| Total | 164 | 31.7 | 0.493 |

earlier as opposed to later onset will tend to have longer criminal careers and commit many more offenses. The results confirm these hypotheses.

As shown in Table 5.7, individuals who experience an earlier onset tend to have much longer criminal careers than individuals who experience a later onset and to also have engaged in many more – and more kinds of – offenses throughout their careers. These results are statistically significant ($p < .05$), with the earliest-onset age group evincing the highest risk. For example, individuals who incurred a first conviction

Table 5.5. *The Relationship Between Early Onset (Age Bands) and Violence*

| Onset Age Bands | N | Percentage of Violent Offender (%) | Mean Number of Violent Convictions |
|---|---|---|---|
| 10–13 | 35 | 42.86 | 0.914 |
| 14–16 | 50 | 28.00 | 0.480 |
| 17–20 | 44 | 31.82 | 0.363 |
| 21+ | 35 | 25.71 | 0.257 |
| Total | 164 | 31.71 | 0.493 |
| F-Value | | 0.963 | 3.207* |

*p < .05

Table 5.6. *The Relationship Between Early and Late Onset and Violence*

| Onset Group | N | Percentage of Violent Offender (%) | Mean Number of Violent Convictions |
|---|---|---|---|
| Late | 129 | 28.68 | 0.37 |
| Early | 35 | 42.86 | 0.91 |
| Chi-square/(df = 1) | | 2.55+ | |
| T-value | | | 1.93* |

+p < .12; *p < .05

between the ages of 10 and 13 had career lengths, on average, of over 11 years, while individuals who incurred a first conviction at age 21 or later had career lengths, on average, of less than 2 years. Similarly, those who onset at ages 10–13 incur, on average, almost 9 offenses throughout their careers, while those who onset at age 21 or later accumulated only about 1.6 offenses by age 40. The greater number of offenses committed by early-onset offenders appears to be a function of a higher frequency of offending during their careers.[4] With regard to age at last conviction, the data indicate that those who onset at ages 10–13 had their last conviction, on average, at about age 24, while those who onset at ages 21 or later had

---

[4] But mean $\lambda$ seems to be constant (see Table 5.7).

Table 5.7. *Relationship Between Onset Age and Career Length (Offenders Only)*

| Onset Age | N | Career Length (Mean) | Age at Last Conviction (Mean) | Number of Offenses (Mean) | Individual λ (Mean) | Variety Index (Mean) |
|---|---|---|---|---|---|---|
| 10–13 | 35 | 11.58 | 24.10 | 8.77 | 0.89 | 4.80 |
| 14–16 | 50 | 10.36 | 25.80 | 5.62 | 0.66 | 3.54 |
| 17–20 | 44 | 4.27 | 22.95 | 2.63 | 1.09 | 2.27 |
| 21+ | 35 | 1.61 | 30.81 | 1.60 | 0.83 | 1.37 |
| Total | 164 | 7.12 | 25.74 | 4.63 | 0.84 | 3.00 |
| F-value | | 18.43* | 8.32* | 20.26* | 1.87 | 19.99* |

*p < .05

their last conviction, on average, at about age 30. This result was also statistically significant (p < .05). The comparison of onset age group and λ failed to indicate a significant difference; however, the two onset age groups with the highest λ were ages 17–20 (1.09) and 10–13 (0.89).[5]

Finally, we present the relationship between the variety index and the age at first conviction. Based on extant research (Gottfredson and Hirschi, 1995; Moffitt, 1994), we suspect an inverse relationship such that individuals with a first conviction at an earlier age will tend to have engaged in many more different kinds of offenses than those experiencing a first conviction at a later age. Figure 5.5 confirms this expectation. Here, it can be seen that those individuals whose age at first conviction was between ages 10 and 15 tended to engage in many more different crime types than individuals whose age at first conviction was after age 15. Those individuals tended to engage in four or fewer different crime types. In short, individuals experiencing a first conviction prior to age 15 were convicted of over twice as many different offenses as individuals who experienced their first conviction after age 15.

## Comment: How Does Onset Age Relate to Individual Offending Frequency?

Although most researchers recognize the importance of (early) onset age as a harbinger of undesirable things to come, few longitudinal studies have investigated the extent to which onset age relates to individual

---

[5] Of course, it is important to note that λ did not vary significantly with onset age grouping.

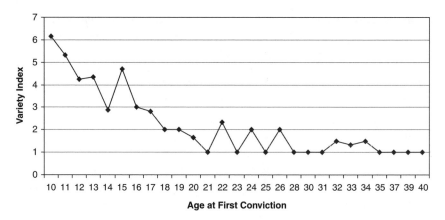

**Figure 5.5.** Relationship between Age at First Conviction and Variety Index

offending frequency over the life-course and whether onset age relates specifically to serious offending.

The median age at first conviction in the CSDD data was about 16 years old. A subsequent hazard rate analysis of onset also corroborated this estimate. Additionally, as many previous studies have indicated, those individuals who exhibit an early onset also tend to acquire a higher number of convictions than their counterparts who onset later.

When we focused on the relationship between onset age and the seriousness of offending (violence), we found that those individuals who were early-onset were more likely than late-onset offenders to be involved in violence through age 40. In a supplemental logistic regression analysis predicting violence, however, we found that while the total number of convictions was a significant predictor of violence, onset age was not, therefore implying again that onset age operates through the frequency of offending. That is, those who exhibit an early onset have a higher probability of being a violent offender because they accumulate a higher number of convictions. Further, among those with a higher number of convictions, violence is a likely result.

Finally, we examined how onset age related to other criminal career parameters, including career length, age at last conviction, the number of convictions, the variety index, and $\lambda$. Those analyses indicated that, as would be expected, individuals who incurred an early onset were more likely to also exhibit longer criminal careers, to have accumulated many more offenses than those individuals who incurred onset later, and to have been convicted of many different kinds of offenses. Additionally, although $\lambda$ was higher for those with an early onset, $\lambda$ remained fairly constant regardless of onset age.

## Take-Home Messages

1 Both the mode and the hazard indicated that age 14 was the peak age of onset, while the median age at first conviction was age 16.

2 Those individuals who exhibited an early onset (<14 years of age) tended to accumulate many more convictions over the life-course than those who exhibited a later onset (14+ years of age).

3 Individual offending frequency was quite high in the years immediately following early onset and remained fairly stable immediately thereafter.

4 Violence was more likely among those individuals who exhibited an early onset, but the total number of convictions incurred by the males was a better predictor of violence than was onset age.

5 Onset age was significantly associated with career length, total convictions, and the variety index. That is, those individuals who exhibited an early onset were more likely to have longer criminal careers, accumulate more offenses, and be convicted of many more different types of offenses than their late-onset counterparts. However, the relationship between onset age and $\lambda$ at the individual level did not necessarily indicate a linear trend, as those individuals who onset between 17 and 20 evinced the highest mean $\lambda$. Still, there was a lack of a relationship between onset age and $\lambda$.

## Unanswered Question

1 Is early onset a mere reflection of criminal propensity such that those individuals with an early onset have "more" criminal propensity, or do early-onset offenders merely have more time and opportunity to accumulate more, and more serious, offenses?

# How Does Specialization/Versatility Vary with Age?

The notion of specialization in offending has had a long history in criminology, and researchers have devoted considerable attention to it. Research questions have included: Do some offenders disproportionately commit some particular types of crime, such as violence, during their offending careers? Are patterns of specialization, if they do exist, concentrated in the juvenile years, or do offenders become more specialized at older ages (Cohen, 1986; Piquero et al., 1999). Or is it the case that offenders tend to engage in a diversity of criminal acts, be they violent, nonviolent, and/or drug related and that such diverse patterns of offending continue throughout one's criminal career?

Extant criminological theory also sees the specialization issue as important. For example, some theories, such as Gottfredson and Hirschi's general theory of crime, anticipate very little specialized offending in the career, while other theories, such as Moffitt's developmental taxonomy, hypothesize some level of specialization for one type of offender (i.e., adolescence-limited) but more generalist patterns for another type (i.e., life-course-persister). The issue of specialization is also important for policy reasons (Farrington et al., 1988). For example, if offending were more specialized, then knowledge about earlier types of offenses in one's career would help officials to predict later offense types and help criminal and/or juvenile justice/adult decision-making efforts.

Much research has been brought to bear on the issue of specialization/versatility. Three findings stand out from this line of research. First, most studies indicate that offenders, especially frequent offenders, engage in a varied array of criminal acts throughout their offending careers and that there is but a small degree of specialization in a few select crime types (Farrington et al., 1988). This implies that there are both few offending specialists and only minor specialization in a few select crime types. Second, offenders tend to concentrate their offending activities within larger categories of offenses, and most offenders tend to switch within categories (Cohen, 1986), but the most active and frequent offenders switch both within and across categories. Third, what little specialization exists tends to occur past adolescence and tends to increase as the career progresses (Blumstein et al., 1986; Piquero et al., 1999).

Although the research presented above suggests that offenders tend to be more versatile with only limited indication of specialization, this tentative conclusion is based on results produced largely by research using official records through age 18. In fact, few researchers have followed subjects in a longitudinal fashion well into adulthood. In this chapter, we examine how specialization varies with age into adulthood. In our study, we use an approach that invokes the binomial probability over the offender's career (Farrington, 1989; Piquero, 2000a).

## Methods

### Measures

By age 40, 164 of the 411 South London men (39.9 percent) had been convicted, and these men accounted for 760 total convictions, with theft of a motor vehicle (14.21 percent) and burglary (16.71 percent) being the most common types. Of the 411 men, 52 (12.7 percent) had at least one violent conviction by the age of 40, and there were a total of 81 violent convictions. Violent convictions included assault ($n = 51$), threatening behavior ($n = 29$), and wounding ($n = 1$). The fraction of convictions that were for violence was obtained by dividing the number of violent convictions (81) by the total number of convictions (760), or .1065. The fraction of nonviolent convictions was $1 - .1065$, or .8935.

### Data Analysis Approach

We begin our investigation of specialization in violence with the assumption that violent offenses are committed at random in criminal careers (Farrington, 1998:429; see also Farrington, 1989, 1991; Piquero, 2000a). Here, we employ the binomial distribution to examine how the probability of committing a violent offense increases as the total number

Table 6.1. *Cambridge Specialization Analysis*

| Number of Offenses Committed | Number of Offenders | Number of Nonviolent Offenders | Number of Violent Offenders | Expected Nonviolent Offenders | Expected Nonviolent Percentage | Expected Violent Offenders | Expected Violent Percentage |
|---|---|---|---|---|---|---|---|
| 1 | 52 | 45 | 7 | 46.462 | 0.893 | 5.538 | 0.106 |
| 2 | 34 | 25 | 9 | 27.143 | 0.798 | 6.856 | 0.201 |
| 3 | 14 | 10 | 4 | 9.986 | 0.713 | 4.013 | 0.286 |
| 4 | 11 | 6 | 5 | 7.010 | 0.637 | 3.989 | 0.362 |
| 5 | 9 | 4 | 5 | 5.125 | 0.569 | 3.874 | 0.430 |
| 6 | 7 | 5 | 2 | 3.561 | 0.508 | 3.438 | 0.491 |
| 7 | 4 | 2 | 2 | 1.818 | 0.454 | 2.181 | 0.545 |
| 8 | 3 | 1 | 2 | 1.218 | 0.406 | 1.781 | 0.593 |
| 9 | 6 | 4 | 2 | 2.177 | 0.362 | 3.822 | 0.637 |
| 10 | 5 | 2 | 3 | 1.621 | 0.324 | 3.378 | 0.675 |
| 11 | 1 | 1 | 0 | 0.289 | 0.289 | 0.710 | 0.710 |
| 12 | 5 | 4 | 1 | 1.294 | 0.258 | 3.705 | 0.741 |
| 14 | 1 | 0 | 1 | 0.231 | 0.231 | 0.768 | 0.768 |
| 16 | 2 | 1 | 1 | 0.413 | 0.206 | 1.586 | 0.793 |
| 17 | 2 | 0 | 2 | 0.369 | 0.184 | 1.630 | 0.815 |
| 18 | 1 | 0 | 1 | 0.165 | 0.165 | 0.834 | 0.834 |
| 19 | 2 | 1 | 1 | 0.294 | 0.147 | 1.705 | 0.852 |
| 20 | 3 | 1 | 2 | 0.395 | 0.131 | 2.604 | 0.868 |
| 22 | 2 | 0 | 2 | 0.235 | 0.117 | 1.764 | 0.882 |
| Total | 164 | 112 | 52 | 109.815 | 0.669 | 54.184 | 0.330 |

*Note*: No individual was convicted for 13, 15, or 21 crimes.

of offenses increases. If offenders specialize in violence, the actual number of violent offenders should be significantly fewer than expected, and each one should commit more violent offenses (on average) than expected. On the other hand, if there were complete generality in offending, the probability of committing a violent offense would increase with the number of offenses committed.

## Results

More precisely, for the group of offenders who commit $n$ offenses, we can expect .1065 in violent offenses if violence were distributed randomly. If different types of offenses were committed at random (probabilistically), it might be expected that 10.65 percent of the 52 offenders who committed only one offense would commit a violent offense. Table 6.1 shows that the observed number of one-time offenders (7) whose offense was violent was somewhat close to the expected value of 5.538. For the next offense category of two offenses, it was expected that 20.16 percent (i.e., a proportion equal to $(1-[.8935]^2)$ of the 34 offenders who committed two offenses would commit at least one violent offense. The actual number of violent offenders, 9, is close to the expected number of violent offenders, 6.856. For the third offense category, it might be similarly expected that 28.66 percent (i.e., a proportion equal to $1 - [.8935]^3$) of the 14 offenders who committed three offenses would commit at least one violent offense. The actual number of violent offenders, 4, is virtually identical to the expected number of violent offenders, 4.013. As one proceeds along the offense-number categories, it can be observed that the predicted number of violent offenders is very close to the actual number of violent offenders.

Assuming complete generality in offending, it might be expected that 33.03 percent (n = 54.184) of the 164 offenders would commit at least one violent offense – quite close to the actual figure of 31.70 percent (52 violent offenders/164 total offenders). Had there been a tendency to specialize in violent offending, the number of violent offenders would have been significantly fewer than expected, and each one would have committed more violent offenses, on average, than expected. A chi-square goodness-of-fit test showed that the actual numbers were not significantly different from the expected numbers ($\chi^2_{(18)} = 6.745$, p > .05).[1] Thus,

---

[1] The value for $\chi^2$ is given by $\sum(O_i-E_i)^2/E_i$, where $O_i$ is the observed number of violent offenders and $E_i$ is the expected number of violent offenders. The degrees of freedom are given by $c-1$, where $c$ is the number of categories. Some readers may observe that an expected value of at least one or more in each category is needed. In an effort to determine if the small number of expected violent offenders in the present analysis beginning at offense category 10 biased the test, we created a category 10 + that took all of the offenders

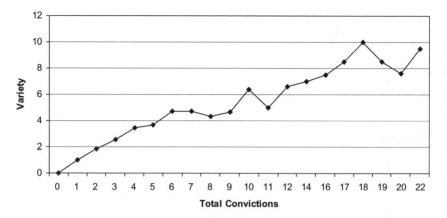

**Figure 6.1.** Relationship Between Total Number of Convictions and Variety of Offending Index

there appears to be no detectable tendency for offenders to specialize in violence in the CSDD data.

In the results presented in the text, we did not include robbery in the violence category because of that crime type's vagueness (i.e., it is a property crime from the offender's perspective, even though it may be seen as a violent crime from the victim's perspective). There were nine men who committed 18 robberies through age 40 in the CSDD. Four of these individuals did not commit any of the three other violent offenses. When we re-estimated all of the specialization-in-violence models with robbery included as a violent offense, we reached the same substantive conclusion: There was no detectable tendency to specialize in violence in the CSDD.

As an alternative view of the versatility issue, we present two graphical representations of the relationship between the total number of 18 different types of offenses (variety) and (1) total convictions and (2) the age at first conviction. Given the findings thus far, we would expect that individuals who engage in a larger number of different crime types (i.e., exhibit variety throughout their offending careers) will also have many more total convictions than their low-variety offending counterparts, as well as exhibit an earlier age at first conviction. The results of these two investigations can be found in Figure 6.1 (average variety at

at or above 10 and combined them into one category. This alternative goodness-of-fit test yielded results that were similar to those obtained with the unaltered conviction distribution – that is, because the actual number of violent offenders is not significantly different from the expected number of violent offenders, it can be concluded that there is no detectable tendency for offenders to specialize in violence.

each number of convictions) and previously in Chapter 5 (Figure 5.5; variety and age at first conviction), respectively.

Figure 6.1 displays how much variation exists in the types of offenses compared to the total number of convictions. The figure clearly shows that the average number of different offenses (variety) increases as a function of the total number of convictions, and it is likely that a conviction for a violent offense will be among those large numbers of convictions. For example, individuals who have 14 convictions have been convicted of seven different crime types, on average.

There are a few other findings in Figure 6.1 that are worth mentioning. For example, the number of different offense types increases fairly linearly with the number of convictions for fewer than 10 convictions, but it does seem to saturate for a large number of convictions. Not all offenses are equally likely, and the total number of offense types is constrained to 18, whereas the number of convictions is not. Specifically, for individuals who have been convicted for a very high number of offenses, the growth in the number of different offenses slows and seems to reach a plateau of 10 different crime types. Out of 18 different crime types, then, the maximum number attained by any individual was 10.

One other analysis was undertaken to examine the relationship between variety and violence specifically. We examined the mean number of different crime types (i.e., the mean on the variety index) for those individuals who were convicted of at least one violent offense by age 40. On average, these 52 men were convicted of 4.346 different offenses compared to the nonviolent men, who were convicted of 0.743 different offenses by age 40 ($t = 9.362$, $p < .05$).

Thus far, we have shown that the number of offenses and whether an individual is a violent offender are closely related. As a further investigation of this issue, we conducted a logistic regression assessing whether the offender had a violent conviction (or not) by age 40 using three variables: the total number of convictions through age 40, whether the individual ever had a co-offender throughout his offending career, and whether the offender exhibited an early onset. Given the pattern of results thus far, we suspect that the strongest predictor of whether or not an individual was a violent offender would be the total number of convictions by age 40. In other words, we expect that the number of offenses will be the single largest determinant of violent offending and that it should dwarf all other influences. As can be seen in Table 6.2, that hypothesis is correct. Indeed, the total number of convictions is by far the best predictor of whether an individual becomes a violent offender, and it is the only significant predictor in the model.

Table 6.2. *Logistic Regression Predicting Violent Offending*

| Variable | B | SE(B) | Wald | Exp(B) |
|----------|-----|-------|------|--------|
| Early onset | −.102 | .474 | 0.046 | 0.903 |
| Co-offender | −.064 | .440 | 0.021 | 0.938 |
| Total number of convictions | .145 | .042 | 12.133* | 1.156 |
| Constant | −1.416 | 0.355 | 15.878 | |
| Model chi-square/df | 17.428/3 | | | |

*p > .05

## Comment: Is There Specialization in Violence?

A key focus of criminal careers/life-course research has been the study of whether offenders specialize in their offending activities (Blumstein et al., 1986; Wolfgang et al., 1972). This line of research has tended to find that offenders exhibit little evidence of specialization in specific types of offenses (i.e., auto theft, burglary, etc.), but tend to concentrate their offending within a particular domain of crime (i.e., nonviolent more so than violent) (see Cohen, 1986; Piquero et al., 2003).

Following this line of work, we began this chapter by asking a simple question: Do offenders specialize in violence? Given the interest in violence as a specific, policy-related outcome, we focused on whether the males in the CSDD were likely to be specialists in the large category of violence. We took a life-course approach by examining the type and volume of offenses throughout individuals' careers and employed a methodological approach that did not impose any undue constraints on the data (such as the Forward Specialization Coefficient, or FSC; see Farrington et al., 1988). Though the data were censored at age 40 for the CSDD, we believe that we have provided important information on specialization past the late teens/early 20s, where many specialization studies end.

Although violence was more rare than common, the analyses indicated that the 164 male offenders (from the full cohort of 411) did not specialize in violence. We must conclude, then, that there is little specialization in violence and that violent offenders are simply frequent offenders who happen to commit a violent offense during their career (i.e., they commit more offenses, thus with increasing numbers they are more likely to accumulate a violent conviction). This casts doubt on efforts to target "the violent offender"; rather, theoretical and policy efforts should spend more time studying the frequent offender, as this offender commits a greater volume of crime and is likely to engage in a violent crime sooner or later during his career.

## Take-Home Messages

1 Convictions in the CSDD indicate no evidence of specialization in violence for the South London males.
2 The number of offenses is the strongest predictor of whether an individual is a violent offender.

## Unanswered Questions

1 What about sex differences in specialization?
2 What about specialization in certain other types of offenses found within larger categories?

CHAPTER SEVEN

# Comparing the Validity of Prospective, Retrospective, and Official Onset for Different Offending Categories

This chapter aims to compare prospective (proximate) onset ages with retrospective (distant) and official onset ages for different offense types. The key question addressed here is how much retrospective and official onset ages agree with prospective ages, which are assumed to be the most accurate.

Age of onset, the age at which offending behavior begins, is a central concept in criminal career research. Some studies have explored the predictors of onset (Farrington and Hawkins, 1991; Farrington et al., 1990; Nagin and Farrington, 1992a), whereas others have focused on the impact of early onset on later features of criminal careers (see Chapter 5). Age of onset is one of the best predictors of the length and intensity of the criminal career (Blumstein et al., 1985; Farrington, 1973; Farrington and Hawkins, 1991; Farrington et al., 1990, 1998, 2003; Le Blanc and Fréchette, 1989; Loeber and Le Blanc, 1990). Research has also shown that a later onset can have a considerable favorable impact on the later criminal career (Farrington et al., 1990).

Farrington (1989) showed that the age-crime curve differed from one offense type to another. This suggests that the age of onset may vary from one offense category to another, although this aspect of criminal career research has been somewhat neglected (see Jolliffe et al., 2003; Le Blanc and Fréchette, 1989). Farrington et al. (1990) also emphasized the

This chapter draws heavily from Lila Kazemian and David P. Farrington, 2005, "Comparing the Validity of Prospective, Retrospective, and Official Onset for Different Offending Categories." *Journal of Quantitative Criminology* 21:127–147. Reprinted by permission of Springer-Verlag, New York.

relevance of measuring the time intervals between onset of different types of offenses to identify specific onset sequences, such as transitions from minor to more serious offenses (see Farrington et al., 1990; Le Blanc and Fréchette, 1989).

Le Blanc and Fréchette (1989) provided information on the age of onset of various offense types up to age 21. Their results showed that petty larceny (age 8.33), shoplifting (11.35), and vandalism (11.68) had the lowest average ages of onset, whereas fraud (19.79) and homicide (19.89) had the latest mean onsets. Burglary (14.22), motor vehicle theft (15.24), and aggravated theft (16.64) appeared in mid adolescence; these results suggested a gradual progression from minor offenses to more serious forms of offending. Similarly, Svensson (2002) identified offense types committed at onset that predicted a high risk of persistent criminal offending (i.e., strategic offenses; see Wikström et al., 1995) and those that predicted a low risk. Thus, it appears clear that obtaining valid information about the onset of different types of offending is essential for criminal career research.

Studies comparing self-reported and official ages of onset have been scarce. Farrington (1989) showed that the first self-reported offense generally occurred before the first conviction (also see Farrington et al., 2003). Le Blanc and Fréchette's (1989) results showed that up until the early 20s the sample of delinquent males in the Montreal Two Sample Longitudinal Study (MTSLS) had an average age of onset of 10.8 years in self-reports and 14.6 years in official records. The authors concluded that "there is a gap of about 3 years between the commission of the first offense and the appearance of the adolescent in the justice system and of 4 years between the first offense and the first official sanction by a court" (p. 79). Loeber et al. (2003) found similar results: The average age of onset for self-reported serious delinquency was 11.9 years old, while the first court contact for an index offense occurred at an average age of 14.5 years. Moffitt et al. (2001) also argued that estimates of age of onset vary according to the type of data used. The authors compared the ages at first arrest, first conviction, and first self-reported offense and found that "investigations that rely on official data to study crime careers will ascertain age of onset approximately 3 to 5 years after it has happened" (p. 83).

Additionally, few studies have compared prospective and retrospective measures of offending, and even fewer of these have focused on age of onset. It has been argued that prospective longitudinal studies are costly and unnecessary and that cross-sectional or retrospective studies are an equally valid method of measurement (see Gottfredson and Hirschi, 1990). However, results found in the few studies that have explored the concurrent validity between prospective and retrospective onset did not support this assumption. Using self-report data from the National Youth

Survey, Menard and Elliott (1990) found that the degree of concurrence between prospective and retrospective onset ages was rather low (approximately 25 percent).

Henry et al. (1994) also explored the concurrent validity between prospective and retrospective measures of offending. The authors assessed the test-retest stability of ages of onset reported in interviews at 13 and 18. Their analyses revealed an overall agreement rate of 58 percent between both interviews. At age 18, 14 percent of their respondents admitted to shoplifting, but reported a later onset than they had at age 13. Also, 28 percent of initial shoplifters denied the act in the second interview. The authors found that, in addition to the 97 initial shoplifters, 146 new respondents reported (at age 18) having shoplifted before age 13; it is likely that these respondents remembered their onset as earlier than it actually was. In the first interview, respondents were not asked the specific age at which they had started offending, but rather whether they had ever engaged in each act. In the subsequent interview, they were questioned about their participation in these offenses before age 13. Henry et al. (1994) concluded that offenders generally remembered committing a given offense, but not the specific age at which they committed it for the first time. It seemed that "[e]ven when retrospective reports correlated significantly with prospective data, the absolute level of agreement between the two sources was quite poor" (p. 100).

Using data from the Seattle Social Development project, Jolliffe et al. (2003) also found little agreement between prospective and retrospective ages of onset. Their results showed that average retrospective onset ages were lower than prospective onset ages. They also found that vandalism had the lowest (24 percent) concordance rate between prospective and retrospective ages of onset, whereas marijuana use, vehicle theft, and drug selling had the highest (36 percent, 32 percent, and 32 percent, respectively). In short, the few studies that have compared prospective and retrospective onset ages have generally highlighted the limitations of retrospective data.

The main objective in this chapter is to contrast prospective ages of onset with retrospective and official ages of onset for different offense types. Maxfield et al. (2000:92) argued that projects that have sought to assess the validity of self-reports were generally based on samples of adolescents, and "Few studies have examined these issues with adult samples or have traced youth longitudinally into adulthood." The analyses carried out here assess the validity of self-reports between early adolescence and mid adulthood.

In comparisons between prospective and retrospective ages of onset, it is likely that the degree of concurrent validity will be higher for more serious offenses; offenders may be more likely to remember the specific details of such incidents in contrast to acts of petty theft or other forms of minor offending. In comparisons between self-reported and official ages of onset, it is also likely that the degree of concurrent validity will be lowest for minor forms of offending and highest for more serious offenses. Serious offenses are more likely to lead to convictions, and thus the self-reported age at first offense is more likely to agree with the age at first conviction.

## Methods

### Measures

Data from the CSDD were analyzed from interviews completed at ages 14, 16, 18, and 32. These ages were selected for two main reasons: The entire initial sample was interviewed (as opposed to subsamples at ages 21 and 25), and measures of self-reported offending were available. The initial self-report questionnaire at age 14 included 38 offense types (see West and Farrington, 1973). Farrington (1989) combined these offenses and created 10 categories, 6 of which were used in this study: burglary, shoplifting, theft of vehicles, theft from vehicles, theft from machines (parking meters, telephone boxes, etc.), and vandalism. Analyses were limited to these categories for the simple reason that age-of-onset information was available at all ages only for these six offenses. Because several offenses could make up a given category, age of onset was computed when respondents committed at least one of the acts included in the group.

Prospective onset covers offending behavior up to age 18 (based on interviews at 14, 16, and 18). In cases where the age of onset reported in the first interview differed from the age of onset reported in a later interview, the first age reported was considered to be the prospective age of onset. For instance, if the age of onset reported at age 18 was different from the age of onset reported at age 14, the information collected at age 14 was considered to be the valid age of onset. This rule was based on the assumption that self-reported information is likely to be more accurate when the time lag between the offense and the interview is shorter; this is particularly true in cases where precise information is required, such as age of onset (see Henry et al., 1994). Retrospective onset here refers to the age of onset reported in the age-32 interview. Because the focus is on comparisons between prospective (up to age 18) and retrospective (age 32) self-reported ages of onset, long-term retrospective reports are being studied; these comparisons were of course limited to individuals who had reported an onset in both prospective and retrospective reports.

Official onset refers to the age at first conviction, from age 10 to 40. The main question explored in this study relates to the degree of agreement between prospective measures of onset (which are presumed to be the most accurate) and retrospective and official measures.

Jolliffe et al. (2003: 5–6) explained: "All self-reports of delinquency are retrospective to some extent, in that they provide information about offending during a prior time period." Our definition of "prospective onset" could have been problematic if the offenses generally occurred many years prior to the interview. However, the distribution of onset ages at each interview revealed that this was not the case. For most offenses, both average and median onset ages reported at the age-14 interview generally occurred within a relatively short time period before (two or three years at the most); the same was true for onset ages reported at age 16. Because minor offenses (e.g., shoplifting and vandalism) tend to onset earlier, they displayed slightly longer time lags between the time of the offense and the interview, with average and median onset ages ranging from three to five years. The main difficulty would occur if individuals reported at the age-18 interview an onset having occurred many years prior to the interview. However, the males were only asked about offenses committed in the past three years in this interview, so these measures of onset can be regarded as prospective.

Comparisons between the prospective age of onset (up to age 18) and retrospective and official ages of onset for each of the six offenses mentioned above are provided. When onset age was available for both sources, the degree of agreement between them was assessed. Paired-sample t-tests were also performed in cases where age of onset was available for both sources, to assess whether statistically significant differences were observed between the two sources of onset age.

## Results

### Comparison of Prospective (Proximate) and Retrospective (Distant) Ages of Onset

Two important issues will be addressed in this section, namely how age of onset varies over different measurement methods and offense types. Comparisons between prospective and retrospective ages of onset are presented in Table 7.1. Average ages of onset are presented for cases where the offenses were admitted prospectively but denied[1] retrospectively, denied prospectively but reported retrospectively, or admitted

---

[1] One could also conceive of denials as omissions.

Table 7.1. Comparison of Average Prospective and Retrospective Ages of Onset

| | Burglary | Shoplifting | Theft of Vehicles | Theft from Vehicles | Theft from Machines | Vandalism | Total |
|---|---|---|---|---|---|---|---|
| Prospective admission, retrospective denial[a] | 14.1 (n=41, 48%) | 12.1 (n=81, 35%) | 15.2 (n=49, 49%) | 14.8 (n=43, 54%) | 14.5 (n=86, 63%) | 11.2 (n=243, 75%) | 10.6 (n=300, 87%) |
| Prospective denial, retrospective admission[b] | 15.9 (n=21, 71%) | 11.4 (n=44, 93%) | 19.5 (n=25, 48%) | 18.2 (n=22, 68%) | 16 (n=25, 76%) | 11.8 (n=6, 100%) | 14.8 (n=111, 76%) |
| Both prospective and retrospective admissions (t-test) | n=44 | n=151 | n=51* | n=37 | n=50 | n=80* | n=210 |
| Average prospective onset age | 14.4 | 11.7 | 15.3 | 14 | 14.6 | 11 | 11.6 |
| Average retrospective onset age | 14.6 | 11.3 | 16.6 | 15.1 | 14.5 | 12.2 | 11.6 |
| Prospective = retrospective | 8 (18%) | 17 (11%) | 14 (27%) | 4 (11%) | 10 (20%) | 9 (11%) | |
| Prospective > retrospective | 25 (57%) | 80 (53%) | 13 (26%) | 14 (38%) | 19 (38%) | 26 (33%) | |
| Prospective < retrospective | 11 (25%) | 54 (36%) | 24 (47%) | 19 (51%) | 21 (42%) | 45 (56%) | |

*p<.05

[a]Percentages in this row refer to denial rates at age 32, which are based on the total number of males who reported an onset in prospective reports and who were interviewed at age 32.

[b]Percentages in this row refer to the proportion of cases where the age of onset reported at age 32 was below 18, despite denial in prospective accounts (up to age 18).

Note: When respondents have reported more than one offense, average ages of onset in the total columns are based on the average age on first offense.

in both prospective and retrospective reports. In the third case, mean ages of onset are presented for each source, and the extent of the differences between prospective and retrospective onset ages is assessed (i.e., the number of cases where both sources are the same and where prospective onset is either greater or less than retrospective onset).

Table 7.1 shows that denial rates were high. Overall, 87 percent of the males denied at least one offense at age 32 that they had admitted to in prospective reports. With the exception of shoplifting, denial rates were highest for minor forms of offending (vandalism and theft from machines) and lowest for more serious offenses (burglary and theft of vehicles). Respondents may have denied minor acts if they felt that they were trivial and not worth mentioning or may have forgotten them. The results observed for shoplifting may be a result of the fact that respondents continued to engage in acts of shoplifting long after they had stopped committing vandalism and theft from machines and perhaps thought it would be more difficult to conceal these acts. Nonetheless, respondents were generally more reluctant to report (or be forgetful of) minor offenses than more serious forms of crime.

Prospective admissions and retrospective denials were far more common than the reverse (prospective denial and retrospective admission); this is true for all offense types. It is also interesting to point out that in cases where the act was admitted only in retrospective reports, most offenses (with the exception of theft of vehicles and theft from vehicles) had an average retrospective age of onset that occurred before 18 (roughly ranging from 11 to 16 years old). Because prospective reports included offending behavior up to age 18, it appears that some offenders either tended to conceal their offending behavior in prospective accounts or retrospectively remembered initiating these acts earlier than they actually did. These results may be a consequence of retrospective bias; in retrospect, offenders tended to forget the age at which they initiated offending. Overall, 76 percent of individuals who admitted to offending at age 32 (only) reported an onset earlier than age 18 in retrospective accounts; this proportion was highest for vandalism (100 percent) and shoplifting (93 percent). However, these figures are based on small sample sizes.

When both prospective and retrospective accounts of onset were available, average retrospective ages tended to be slightly higher than prospective ages of onset, which suggests that offenders retrospectively tended to overestimate the age at which they initiated their offending behavior. However, prospective and retrospective ages were significantly different only for vandalism and theft of vehicles.

Table 7.1 reveals that minor offenses such as shoplifting and vandalism always had the earliest onsets, regardless of whether results were available for only prospective, only retrospective, or both prospective and retro-spective accounts. In contrast, theft of vehicles always had the latest onset, for all accounts; these results suggest a progression in onset sequences, from minor to serious forms of offending.[2] When both prospective and retrospective ages of onset were available, a limited proportion of subjects tended to report the same onset age in both periods (from 11 percent to 27 percent). The agreement rate between prospective and retrospective reports was lowest for vandalism, shoplifting, and theft from vehicles (all 11 percent) and highest for theft of vehicles (27 percent). This result may be attributed to the fact that theft of vehicles is one of the more serious forms of offending (and is more recent), and hence offenders were more likely to remember the specific details of these events.

What can possibly cause these low agreement rates? It is possible that individuals with heavy substance use habits were more likely to forget the specifics of offenses that occurred in the past. This issue was addressed by using drug and alcohol consumption variables measured at age 32. The males were asked about the frequency of their drug use (cannabis, heroin, cocaine, amphetamines, magic mushrooms, barbiturates/downers, LSD, and amylnitrite) in the past five years and their weekly alcohol con-sumption. Most males (81 percent) had not consumed any drugs in the previous five years. Only 22 percent of males were regarded as heavy drinkers (consumption of more than 40 units of alcohol per week). Overall, 25 percent of males had serious drug or alcohol consumption problems. Chi-square tests were carried out to explore the association between serious substance use and the degree of discrepancy between prospective and retrospective ages of onset. Results showed that most males (69 percent) with heavy substance use habits (drugs or alcohol) were likely to report different onset ages in retrospect, in contrast to the 47 percent of res-pondents who did not have serious substance use habits. This difference was statistically significant ($x^2 = 13.89$, df $= 1$, p $< .05$). Thus, the limita-tions associated with the use of retrospective reports appear to be even more significant with samples of individuals displaying problems of substance use.

## Comparison of Prospective and Official Ages of Onset

Table 7.2 compares prospective and official ages of onset, and the results are presented according to the same logic used in Table 7.1 (prospective admission only, conviction only, and both prospective admission and

---

[2] Of course, theft of vehicles typically requires some skill (to drive), which typically occurs at older ages.

Table 7.2. *Comparison of Average Prospective and Official Ages of Onset*

| | Burglary | Shoplifting | Theft of Vehicles | Theft from Vehicles | Theft from Machines | Vandalism | Total |
|---|---|---|---|---|---|---|---|
| Prospective admission, no conviction | 14.1 (n=43) | 11.8 (n=214) | 15.2 (n=58) | 14.6 (n=66) | 14.6 (n=134) | 11.2 (n=319) | 10.7 (n=356) |
| Prospective denial, with conviction | 22.8 (n=17) | 24.9 (n=10) | 22.1 (n=18) | 21.5 (n=11) | 22.3 (n=6) | 26 (n=2) | 13.9 (n=44) |
| Both prospective admission and conviction (t-test) | **n=50***** | **n=32***** | **n=49***** | **n=24**** | **n=13*** | **n=27***** | n=103 |
| Average prospective onset age | 14.2 | 12.5 | 15.2 | 14 | 14 | 10.7 | 11.9 |
| Average official onset age | 17.8 | 20.4 | 16.8 | 18.4 | 18.8 | 22.7 | 16.9 |
| Prospective = official | 10 (20%) | 2 (6%) | 19 (39%) | 4 (17%) | 2 (15%) | 0 | |
| Prospective > official | 7 (14%) | 2 (6%) | 6 (12%) | 5 (21%) | 1 (8%) | 0 | |
| Prospective < official | 33 (66%) | 28 (88%) | 24 (49%) | 15 (62%) | 10 (77%) | 27 (100%) | |

***$p < .001$;  **$p < .01$;  *$p < .05$

*Note:* When respondents have reported or been convicted for more than one offense, average ages of onset in the total columns are based on the average age of first offense.

conviction). It was common for respondents to report offenses for which they were never convicted, but the opposite was rarely true: Relatively few respondents had been convicted for offenses that were not admitted in self-reports up to age 18.

In cases where there were both a prospective report of onset and a conviction, the average age at first conviction was always higher than the age of onset reported prospectively; this was true for all forms of offending and particularly so for vandalism, shoplifting, and theft from machines. The t-test results revealed that these differences were significant for all offending categories. In general, it was rather uncommon for official onset to occur before prospective onset (ranging from 0 percent to 21 percent of all respondents). Concordance rates between prospective and official ages of onset were low; they were highest for theft of vehicles (39 percent) and burglary (20 percent) and lowest for vandalism (0 percent) and shoplifting (6 percent). This suggests that the level of agreement between self-reports and official measures of offending increases with the seriousness of the offense.[3]

Minor forms of offending had the earliest average onset ages in prospective reports, but they tended to be convicted at later ages in comparison to other offending categories. Furthermore, in cases where offenders admitted to the acts in prospective reports and were also convicted for them, vandalism and shoplifting had the greatest discrepancies between prospective and official ages of onset. These high discrepancies could reflect the time lag that occurred between the first minor shoplifting or vandalism offenses in early adolescence (i.e., stealing sweets, damaging school buildings, etc.), which were highly unlikely to lead to arrest or were likely to be ignored even if detected. The more serious acts (stealing from shops and stores, breaking windows, etc.) appeared later, in adolescence or adulthood. Theft of vehicles and burglary had the earliest official ages of onset and showed less prominent discrepancies between prospective and official ages of onset. Discrepancies between prospective and official ages of onset appeared to be more pronounced for minor forms of offending than for more serious offenses. Thus, self-reported and official onset sequences seem to be distinguished by opposite patterns. Comparisons between prospective and retrospective self-reports suggested a progression in onset sequences, from minor to more serious forms of offending, whereas official records may suggest a serious-to-minor onset sequence or may be an artifact of reporting convictions.

[3] More generally, it should be recognized that the concordance rates will not necessarily be the same because it often takes several (self-reported) offenses, which tend to have a low probability of detection, before a conviction occurs. Additionally, more-minor offenses, such as vandalism, often are ignored even if detected.

**Onset Sequences**

Table 7.3 shows self-reported onset sequences, and Table 7.4 shows official onset sequences. Each table gives, for individuals who have committed two types of offenses at different ages, the percentage who committed each offense first (excluding cases where the onset age was the same for both offenses). To our knowledge, these particular comparisons of both self-reported and official onset sequences for specific forms of offending have not been explored in previous criminal career research.

Table 7.3 shows that, according to self-reports, shoplifting and vandalism most frequently began before the other four types of offending (ranging from 85 percent to 95 percent for the former and 77 percent to 92 percent for the latter). In contrast, it was less common (from 5 percent to 38 percent) for theft of vehicles to begin before other types of offenses. Where respondents admitted either shoplifting, vandalism, or theft of vehicles, almost all cases of shoplifting (95 percent) and vandalism (92 percent) occurred before the incident of vehicle theft. Similarly, most cases of shoplifting (85 percent) and vandalism (77 percent) occurred before burglary. These results reveal a minor-to-serious onset sequence in self-reported offending.

In Table 7.4, the figures are not as easily interpretable, because the number of respondents who were convicted for both offenses is generally limited. Respondents were most likely to be convicted for theft of vehicles and burglary before any other type of offense (ranging from 47 percent to 80 percent for the former and from 47 percent to 60 percent for the latter). Also, convictions for vandalism often tended to occur before convictions for shoplifting (71 percent).

The results in Tables 7.3 and 7.4 support the assumption that self-reported and official offending indicate different onset sequences. One plausible explanation for this result relates to the differential treatment of offenders by the criminal justice system. At younger ages, when they are still strangers to the system, males are more likely to be convicted only if they commit relatively serious offenses. At older ages or once individuals have penetrated the justice system, they may be granted less leniency and may be more likely to be convicted for any offense, regardless of how minor.

## Comment: Prospective, Retrospective, and Official Onset for Different Conviction Types

This chapter aimed to compare prospective age of onset with retrospective and official ages of onset for different types of offenses. Comparisons between prospective and retrospective onset ages revealed

Table 7.3. *Self-Reported Onset Sequences of Specific Forms of Offending*

| reported subsequently / reported first | Vandalism | Shoplifting | Theft from Machines | Theft from Vehicles | Theft of Vehicles | Burglary |
|---|---|---|---|---|---|---|
| Vandalism | — | 59% (127/216) | 86% (122/141) | 84% (86/102) | 92% (106/115) | 77% (69/90) |
| Shoplifting | 41% (89/216) | — | 86% (107/125) | 85% (76/89) | 95% (96/101) | 85% (67/79) |
| Theft from machines | 14% (19/141) | 14% (18/125) | — | 69% (44/64) | 68% (51/75) | 55% (36/65) |
| Theft from vehicles | 16% (16/102) | 15% (13/89) | 31% (20/64) | — | 62% (34/55) | 50% (27/54) |
| Theft of vehicles | 8% (9/115) | 5% (5/101) | 32% (24/75) | 38% (21/55) | — | 30% (17/57) |
| Burglary | 23% (21/90) | 15% (12/79) | 45% (29/65) | 50% (27/54) | 70% (40/57) | — |

*Note:* This table only includes cases where different ages of onset are admitted for two given offenses.

Table 7.4. Official Onset Sequences of Specific Forms of Offending

| convicted first \ convicted subsequently | Vandalism | Shoplifting | Theft from Machines | Theft from Vehicles | Theft of Vehicles | Burglary |
|---|---|---|---|---|---|---|
| Vandalism | — | 71% (5/7) | 0% (0/1) | 40% (2/5) | 20% (2/10) | 40% (4/10) |
| Shoplifting | 29% (2/7) | — | 50% (1/2) | 50% (5/10) | 33% (4/12) | 53% (10/19) |
| Theft from machines | 100% (1/1) | 50% (1/2) | — | 50% (3/6) | 50% (4/8) | 44% (4/9) |
| Theft from vehicles | 60% (3/5) | 50% (5/10) | 50% (3/6) | — | 38% (6/16) | 48% (10/21) |
| Theft of vehicles | 80% (8/10) | 67% (8/12) | 50% (4/8) | 62% (10/16) | — | 47% (14/30) |
| Burglary | 60% (6/10) | 47% (9/19) | 56% (5/9) | 52% (11/21) | 53% (16/30) | — |

This table only includes cases where first convictions for two given offenses occur at different ages.

that in retrospect offenders rarely remembered the exact age at which they initiated offending. Agreement rates between prospective and retrospective ages of onset were generally low, particularly for minor forms of offending and in cases where respondents had heavy substance use habits. In general, retrospective reports tended to overestimate the age of onset compared with prospective reports. Denial rates were quite high, and, with the exception of shoplifting, there was a negative association between offense seriousness and denial rates.

Comparisons between prospective and official ages of onset also revealed very low agreement rates, lowest for minor offenses and highest for more serious forms of offending. Offenders may remember more accurately the specific details of more serious forms of offending. The age at first conviction was almost always higher than the age of onset admitted to in prospective reports, and discrepancies between the two were more pronounced for minor offenses. Finally, self-reported and official onset sequences displayed opposite patterns (a minor-to-serious onset sequence for the former and a serious-to-minor sequence for the latter).

## Take-Home Messages

1 For those who admitted (reported) both, average prospective onset tended to occur earlier than average retrospective onset. This suggests that, retrospectively, offenders had a tendency to overestimate the age at which they committed their first offense.

2 Results indicated that the agreement rate between prospective and retrospective reports was lowest for minor offenses (vandalism, shoplifting, and theft from vehicles) and highest for theft of vehicles.

3 Agreement rates between prospective and official ages of onset were highest for serious forms of offending. This result suggests that official onset may not be appropriate for minor offenses, due to the criminal justice system's tolerance of and low priority given to these crimes.

4 In comparisons with official records, most offenses never led to a conviction, which is consistent with results from past studies.

5 Also in agreement with past research, the official onset of offending tended to occur later than the self-reported onset. This was especially the case for minor offending, such as shoplifting and vandalism. Furthermore, the agreement rates between self-reported and official ages of onset were closer for the more serious offenses.

6 Many respondents tended to deny (omit) acts that they had reported at an earlier age, particularly minor types of offending.
7 Results demonstrate the limitations of retrospective data and support the importance of prospective longitudinal studies. Retrospective data cannot substitute for prospective reports of offending. More specifically, retrospective accounts seem to be particularly inappropriate for research requiring detailed information on offending (e.g., about age of onset), as offenders are unlikely to remember these specificities after long periods of time. Because many parameters used in criminal career research require precise information (age of onset, frequency, age of desistance, etc.), retrospective data may not be well suited for this type of research.

## Unanswered Questions

1 The present study did not include violent offenses in its analyses, because information was not available at all ages for these offenses.
2 Do the findings uncovered in this chapter for males replicate for females?

# What Is the Role of Co-offenders, and How Does It Vary with Age?

One of the frequently documented observations about juvenile delinquency is that most offenses are committed with others rather than by persons acting alone (Breckinridge and Abbott, 1917; Reiss and Farrington, 1991) and that this is more characteristic of juveniles than of adults. From the perspective of the criminal career framework, three offending patterns characterize the issue of co-offending: (1) solo offending, where the individual engages in crimes only by himself; (2) a co-offending career, where the individual always offends with others; and (3) a mixed solo and co-offending career, where the individual evinces a mixture of solo and co-offending throughout his/her career, probably beginning with others and then moving into a solo pattern.

Extant criminological theory views the issue of co-offending as important. For example, differential association and social learning theories explicitly rely on the role of co-offending, either through attitudinal or skill transmission or actual offending with others, to explain the onset, persistence, and desistance of criminal activity. Moffitt's developmental taxonomy also implicates the role of co-offenders, but only for one group of offenders: the adolescence-limited. For Moffitt, life-course-persistent offenders do not require the aid and comfort of peers to engage in criminal activity. From her taxonomy, then, it would be expected that co-offending should be most prevalent in mid to late adolescence, just about when offending peaks in the aggregate age/crime curve, only to fall in early to middle adulthood because solo (including life-course-persistent) offenders are more persistent in offending.

**97**

The research that does exist tends to suggest that the incidence of co-offending is greatest for burglary and robbery and that juvenile offenders primarily commit their crimes with others, whereas adult offenders primarily commit their crimes alone (Reiss and Farrington, 1991). Although the decline in co-offending may, at first glance, be attributed to co-offenders dropping out, it seems to occur because males change from co-offending in their teenage years to lone offending in their 20s. Recent efforts continue to assess the extent of co-offending (Conway and McCord, 2002; Haynie, 2001; Sarnecki, 2001; Warr, 2002), but none have tracked co-offending patterns from childhood through adulthood.

While the role of co-offending is an important criminal career feature (Reiss, 1986), unfortunately there has been only a very limited amount of research on this topic, largely because of the lack of co-offending data in extant longitudinal studies. Many questions remain unanswered. For example, even if most criminal careers begin with co-offending, are solo offenders more likely to persist in offending? Is there selective desistance of persons who primarily co-offend or a shift from co-offending to solo offending, within a career, as offenders grow older? Does co-offending peak in mid to late adolescence in a fashion similar to the aggregate age/crime curve? Do those who have co-offended have shorter careers and/or a smaller number of offenses? Do they commit violent acts? Do these patterns change over age?

Clearly, longitudinal data on offending careers are required to establish whether there are changing patterns with age of offending alone or with others or whether the selective attrition of those who offend primarily with others accounts for the preponderance of solo offending at later ages (Reiss and Farrington, 1991:362–363). Fortunately, the CSDD contains measures that allow for an investigation of some of these aspects of co-offending.

In this chapter, we examine some of the aforementioned questions regarding co-offending and provide basic descriptive evidence regarding the patterning of co-offending with age in the CSDD. Additionally, we examine changes in solo offending with age, variation in co-offending by type of offense, changes in co-offending with experience in offending, co-offending in first offenses, and the general patterning (increase, decrease, stability) of co-offending with age.

## Methods

The criminal records of all 411 males specified whether each person committed his offense with, or was convicted with, others. In the majority of cases, the records also specified the name and date of birth of each co-offender.

## Measures

In this chapter, we focus on the longitudinal patterning of co-offending with age and how co-offending varies with other criminal career parameters, such as offending frequency and career length. For present purposes, co-offenders indicate the presence of an offender in addition to the study male.

## Data Analysis Approach

A mixture of graphical and correlational analyses are presented in this chapter, focusing on how co-offending relates to criminal activity between ages 10 and 40 in the CSDD.

## Results

First, we begin with a plot of the relationship between age and the total number of co-offenders at that age (Fig. 8.1). This graph represents a count of the total number of co-offenders aggregated from all crimes committed at that particular age. As can be seen from the figure, the age/co-offending curve is similar to the aggregate age/crime curve depicted in many data sets, both nationally and internationally, including the CSDD (see Chapter 4), largely because it reflects the number of offenses. The total number of co-offenders rises between ages 10 and 16, peaks at age 17, drops throughout the 20s, and approaches zero by the end of the follow-up period (age 40). The correlation between these two variables is $r = -.619$, significant at the $p < .05$ level.

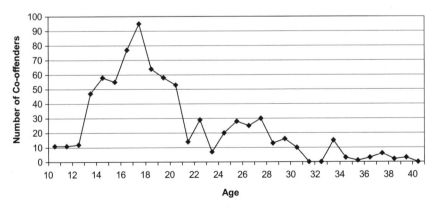

**Figure 8.1.** Relationship Between Age and the Total Number of Co-offenders

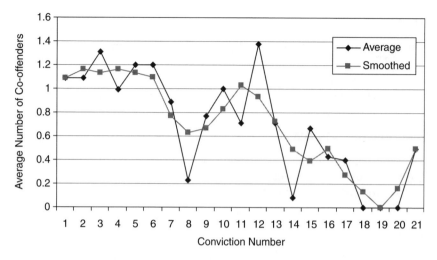

**Figure 8.2.** Relationship Between Average Number of Co-offenders Per Conviction and Conviction Number

Figure 8.2 presents the relationship between the average number of co-offenders per conviction number. Here, it can be seen that the two variables are negatively related to one another. At early conviction numbers, there is a higher average number of co-offenders; but as the conviction number increases, the average number of co-offenders decreases. (Because of small n's that cause some erratic spiking at higher conviction numbers, we also present a smoothed curve in Figure 8.2).

Next, we present a plot of the relationship between each of three variables and the age at conviction. The three variables of interest here are the total number of offenders at each age, the total number of offenses at each age, and the total number of co-offenders at each age. Figure 8.3 shows very clearly that all three variables rise between ages 10 and 16, peak at virtually the same ages 17/18, and then begin a drop toward zero by age 40. The similar peak and shape pattern observed signifies a very general process underlying co-offending, offending, and offenders in the CSDD.

Next, we turn to a series of different plots of co-offenders and three different criminal career parameters: career length in years (for those with two or more offenses), total convictions, and age at first conviction. First, regarding the relationship between the total number of co-offenders in a person's career and career length, Figure 8.4 shows that there is a fairly stable (and slightly positive) pattern to this relationship. Excluding

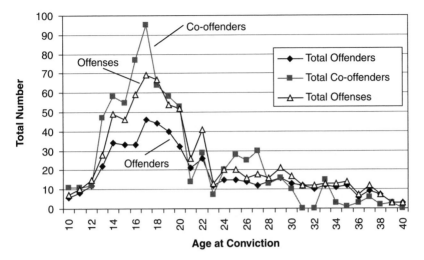

**Figure 8.3.** Relationship Between Age at Conviction and Total Number of Co-offenders at Each Age, Total Number of Offenses at Each Age, and Total Number of Offenders at Each Age

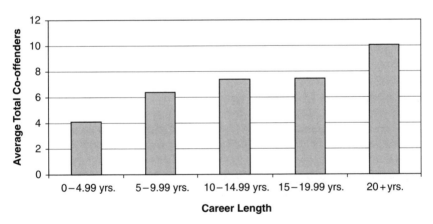

**Figure 8.4.** Relationship Between Total Number of Co-Offenders in Career and Career Length

one-time offenders, this figure shows that individuals with short career lengths (<5 years) tend to have a low number of co-offenders, while individuals with longer career lengths (upward of 10 years) have many more co-offenders. In fact, individuals with very lengthy careers (20 + years)

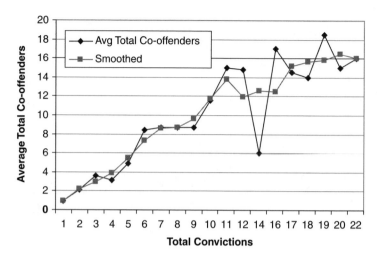

**Figure 8.5.** Relationship Between Average Total Number of Co-offenders and Total Number of Convictions

evince many co-offenders throughout their criminal careers (averaging more than 10 co-offenders), likely because this reflects a larger number of offenses.

Next, Figure 8.5 presents a graph of the relationship between the average (mean) total number of co-offenders and the total number of convictions between ages 10 and 40. As shown, individuals with very few convictions (<6) tend to have very few co-offenders throughout their careers, while individuals with many more convictions (16+) tend to have many more co-offenders over the course of their criminal career. In fact, these two variables are positively and very strongly related to one another ($r = .878$, $p < .05$). Hence, the total number of co-offenders really reflects the total number of offenses. (Because of a spiked data point, conviction 14, we also present the smoothed curve.)

We also examined the relationship between age at first conviction and the mean total number of co-offenders in a person's career. Given the results thus far, we suspect that these two variables will be inversely related. As Figure 8.6 shows, there is, in fact, a strong negative relationship between these two variables. Offenders with an early age at first conviction tend to have, on average, a higher average total number of co-offenders throughout their careers, while individuals with a later age at first conviction tend to have, on average, fewer co-offenders. As expected, the correlation between these two variables is negative and significant ($r = -.753$, $p < .05$).

Given the results on the relationship between the age at first conviction and co-offending, we thought it would be of interest to further probe the

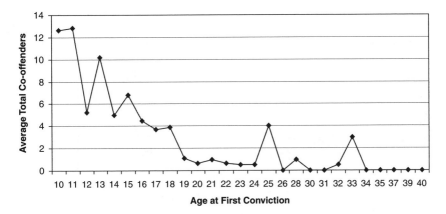

**Figure 8.6.** Relationship Between Age at First Conviction and Mean Total Number of Co-offenders in Person's Career

relationship between co-offending and onset age by splitting the sample of offenders into those who exhibit an early onset (<14) and those exhibiting a later onset (age 14+). There is also theoretical reason to believe that co-offending varies according to the "type" of offender (see Moffitt, 1993; Warr, 2002). To probe this potential relationship, we examined how co-offending varies according to whether the offender exhibited early or late onset. Figure 8.7 presents the relationship. As shown in this figure, the early-onset group averages a significantly higher number of co-offenders than does the late-onset group (t=4.593, p<.05).

Given this graphical evidence, we now turn toward a series of analyses designed to understand the changes in co- and solo offending with age. Table 8.1 shows how the incidence of co-offending varies with age in the CSDD. Several important findings emerge from this table. First, over the course of the career through age 40, over half (51.8 percent) of the offenses were committed alone. Very few offenses were committed by large numbers of offenders: three or more co-offenders were involved in 80 of the 760 (10.52 percent) of the total number of offenses. Further, the maximum number of verified co-offenders in one offense was nine.

The incidence of co-offending decreases with age.[1] The average number of co-offenders per offense decreased from 1.21 at ages 10–13 to 0.44 at ages 37–40, and the percentage of offenses committed alone

---

[1] The total age range was divided into periods according to English legal status: 10–13 (child); 14–16 (young person); and 17–20 (young adult). The remaining age bands (21+) were divided into approximately four-year periods.

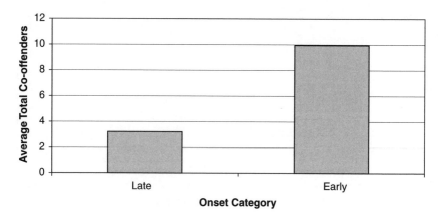

**Figure 8.7.** Relationship Between Early-/Late-Onset and Average Total Number of Co-offenders

Table 8.1. *Changes in Co-offending with Age in the CSDD*

| Age at Conviction | Number of Co-offenders | | | | Total Offenses | Percentage Alone | Avg. Number Co-offenders |
|---|---|---|---|---|---|---|---|
| | 0 | 1 | 2 | 3+ | | | |
| 10–13 | 15 | 25 | 12 | 8 | 60 | 25.0 | 1.21 |
| 14–16 | 60 | 39 | 31 | 24 | 154 | 38.9 | 1.12 |
| 17–20 | 109 | 74 | 31 | 28 | 242 | 45.0 | 0.90 |
| 21–24 | 57 | 27 | 11 | 5 | 100 | 57.0 | 0.64 |
| 25–28 | 44 | 13 | 4 | 9 | 70 | 62.8 | 0.68 |
| 29–32 | 53 | 5 | 1 | 3 | 62 | 85.4 | 0.25 |
| 33–36 | 38 | 4 | 3 | 2 | 47 | 80.8 | 0.34 |
| 37–40 | 18 | 4 | 2 | 1 | 25 | 72.0 | 0.44 |
| Total | 394 | 191 | 95 | 80 | 760 | 51.8 | 0.81 |

increased from 25 percent at ages 10–13 to 72 percent at ages 37–40.[2] Over all age groups (10–40), age was highly negatively correlated with the average number of co-offenders $(r = -.915)$ and positively with the percentage of offenses committed alone $(r = .916)$. At first glance, the finding that the percentage alone is increasing with age suggests that only the most determined offenders, those who do not need the aid and

---

[2] If we use the ages 33–36 bracket, the percentage alone is 80.8 percent and the average number of co-offenders is 0.34. The final age range (37–40) had a small number of individuals in the bracket.

encouragement of peers, remain offending into middle adulthood, as theorists like Moffitt (1993) and Warr (2002) would predict.

Next, we examine the variation in co-offending with offense type in the CSDD data. From the results presented in Table 8.2, which are ordered by the highest percentage alone, it seems clear that the extent of co-offending varies by the type of offense. In fact, Table 8.2 shows how co-offending varies with different types of crimes. Here, the most common crimes to involve co-offenders are burglary, robbery, and theft from motor vehicles. The average number of co-offenders was 1.25 in 127 burglary convictions; for robbery, it was 1.22 in 18 convictions; and for theft from motor vehicles, it was 1.10 in 38 convictions. Other crime types that were also likely to involve co-offenders included theft of motor vehicles, other thefts, and taking and driving away motor vehicles. Offenses classified as violent have somewhat below average numbers of co-offenders, including assault (0.47 in 51 offenses), threatening behavior (1.10 in 29 offenses), and possessing an offensive weapon (0.22 in 18 offenses). Many other offenses – such as fraud, sexual offenses versus a female, damage, and drug offenses – had low rates of co-offending. Also, across most offense types, when co-offending was present it was typically with only one other offender. Rarely, except for burglary, were there more than two offenders.[3]

Because some offenses are more likely to be committed at older ages (such as violence and fraud) and because co-offending decreases with age, it might be expected that offense types committed at older ages would tend to be solo offenses, Tables 8.3 (<18) and 8.4 (≥18) help to disentangle the relationship between co-offending and crime type according to age at offense.

Here, the average number of co-offenders decreased from 1.15 in the juvenile years (<18) to 0.61 in the adult years (≥18). This decrease occurs for most offense types, except for fraud, robbery, and insulting/threatening behavior. The decrease within all offense types suggests that the decrease in co-offending with age occurs independently of the changing pattern of offense types. Also, because the offense types with a high average number of co-offenders at juvenile ages also tend to have a high number at the adult ages and offense types with a low average number at juvenile ages tend to have a low number at adult ages, the relationship between co-offending and offense type, with a few exceptions (fraud and robbery), appears to be independent of age and reflects more of a change in offense type over age than a pattern based on age within offense type.

Next, we present an analysis depicting the relationship between the number of co-offenders and the serial conviction number. As shown in

---

[3] To be sure, some offense types have very small numbers (e.g., wounding), while others are inherently solo offenders (e.g., disqualified driving, weapons).

Table 8.2. *Co-offending in Different Types of Crime (Ordered by Highest % Alone)*

| Crime Type | No. Co-offenders | | | | No. Convic. | Percentage Alone | Mean No. Co-offenders |
|---|---|---|---|---|---|---|---|
| | 0 | 1 | 2 | 3+ | | | |
| Disqualified driving | 27 | 0 | 0 | 0 | 27 | 100.00 | 0.00 |
| Offensive weapon, possession of firearms | 16 | 1 | 0 | 1 | 18 | 88.88 | 0.22 |
| Sexual offenses versus female | 7 | 1 | 0 | 0 | 8 | 87.50 | 0.12 |
| Drug offenses | 16 | 3 | 0 | 1 | 20 | 80.00 | 0.30 |
| Assault | 40 | 4 | 1 | 6 | 51 | 78.43 | 0.47 |
| Fraud/forgery/deception | 37 | 4 | 7 | 2 | 50 | 74.00 | 0.48 |
| Theft as employee | 14 | 6 | 0 | 2 | 22 | 63.63 | 0.54 |
| Damage | 17 | 5 | 1 | 4 | 27 | 62.96 | 0.70 |
| Handling, receiving, unlawful possession | 21 | 11 | 1 | 2 | 35 | 60.00 | 0.54 |
| Theft from shops or market stalls | 32 | 12 | 9 | 2 | 55 | 58.18 | 0.65 |
| Theft of cycles or parts of cycles | 5 | 3 | 1 | 0 | 9 | 55.55 | 0.55 |
| Insulting or threatening behavior | 16 | 2 | 3 | 8 | 29 | 55.17 | 1.10 |
| Arson | 1 | 1 | 0 | 0 | 2 | 50.00 | 0.50 |
| Taking and driving away of motor vehicles | 40 | 33 | 10 | 7 | 90 | 44.44 | 0.82 |
| Other theft | 27 | 15 | 19 | 4 | 65 | 41.53 | 1.00 |
| Theft from machines | 7 | 6 | 1 | 3 | 17 | 41.17 | 1.00 |
| Theft of motor vehicles | 6 | 6 | 4 | 2 | 18 | 33.33 | 1.11 |
| Equipped to steal, suspected person, loitering | 10 | 13 | 3 | 4 | 30 | 33.33 | 1.03 |
| Robbery, conspiracy to rob | 6 | 6 | 2 | 4 | 18 | 33.33 | 1.22 |
| Sexual offenses versus male | 1 | 1 | 0 | 1 | 3 | 33.33 | 1.33 |
| Theft from motor vehicles | 12 | 15 | 6 | 5 | 38 | 31.57 | 1.10 |
| Burglary | 36 | 43 | 27 | 21 | 127 | 28.34 | 1.25 |
| Wounding | 0 | 0 | 0 | 1 | 1 | 0.00 | 3.00 |
| Total | 394 | 191 | 95 | 80 | 760 | | 0.81 |

Table 8.3. *Co-offending in Different Types of Crime (Under Age 18)*
*(Ordered by Highest % Alone)*

| Crime Type | No. Co-offenders | | | | No. of Convic. | Percentage Alone | Mean No. Co-offenders |
|---|---|---|---|---|---|---|---|
| | 0 | 1 | 2 | 3+ | | | |
| Fraud/forgery/deception | 4 | 0 | 0 | 0 | 4 | 100.00 | 0.00 |
| Offensive weapon, possession of firearms | 4 | 0 | 0 | 1 | 5 | 80.00 | 0.60 |
| Sexual offenses versus female | 4 | 1 | 0 | 0 | 5 | 80.00 | 0.20 |
| Assault | 5 | 0 | 0 | 2 | 7 | 71.42 | 0.85 |
| Theft of cycles or parts of cycles | 4 | 3 | 1 | 0 | 8 | 50.00 | 0.62 |
| Insulting or threatening behavior | 5 | 0 | 2 | 1 | 8 | 62.50 | 0.87 |
| Damage | 2 | 1 | 1 | 1 | 5 | 40.00 | 1.20 |
| Taking and driving away of motor vehicles | 17 | 16 | 7 | 5 | 45 | 37.77 | 1.00 |
| Theft from shops market stalls | 8 | 10 | 5 | 1 | 24 | 33.33 | 0.95 |
| Other theft | 9 | 8 | 8 | 2 | 27 | 33.33 | 1.11 |
| Handling, receiving, unlawful possession | 2 | 3 | 1 | 0 | 6 | 33.33 | 0.83 |
| Robbery, conspiracy to rob | 2 | 3 | 1 | 0 | 6 | 33.33 | 0.83 |
| Burglary | 18 | 16 | 15 | 19 | 68 | 26.47 | 1.51 |
| Theft from machines | 3 | 5 | 1 | 3 | 12 | 25.00 | 1.33 |
| Theft as employee | 1 | 3 | 0 | 0 | 4 | 25.00 | 0.75 |
| Equipped to steal, suspected person, loitering | 4 | 7 | 3 | 3 | 17 | 23.52 | 1.29 |
| Theft from motor vehicles | 4 | 9 | 4 | 5 | 22 | 18.18 | 1.45 |
| Theft of motor vehicles | 1 | 3 | 3 | 2 | 9 | 11.11 | 1.66 |
| Arson | 0 | 1 | 0 | 0 | 1 | 0.00 | 1.00 |
| Wounding | — | — | — | — | — | — | — |
| Sexual offenses versus male | — | — | — | — | — | — | — |
| Drug offenses | — | — | — | — | — | — | — |
| Disqualified driving | — | — | — | — | — | — | — |
| Total | 97 | 89 | 52 | 45 | 283 | | 1.15 |

Table 8.4. *Co-offending in Different Types of Crime (18 or Over)*
*(Ordered by Highest % Alone)*

| Crime Type | No. Co-offenders | | | | No. Convic. | Percentage Alone | Mean No. Co-offenders |
|---|---|---|---|---|---|---|---|
| | 0 | 1 | 2 | 3+ | | | |
| Theft of cycles or parts of cycles | 1 | 0 | 0 | 0 | 1 | 100.00 | 0.00 |
| Arson | 1 | 0 | 0 | 0 | 1 | 100.00 | 0.00 |
| Sexual offenses versus female | 3 | 0 | 0 | 0 | 3 | 100.00 | 0.00 |
| Disqualified driving | 27 | 0 | 0 | 0 | 27 | 100.00 | 0.00 |
| Offensive weapon, possession of firearms | 12 | 1 | 0 | 0 | 13 | 92.30 | 0.07 |
| Theft from machines | 4 | 1 | 0 | 0 | 5 | 80.00 | 0.20 |
| Drug offenses | 16 | 3 | 0 | 1 | 20 | 80.00 | 0.30 |
| Assault | 35 | 4 | 1 | 4 | 44 | 79.54 | 0.40 |
| Theft from shops or market stalls | 24 | 2 | 4 | 1 | 31 | 77.41 | 0.41 |
| Theft as employee | 13 | 3 | 0 | 2 | 18 | 72.22 | 0.50 |
| Fraud/forgery/deception | 33 | 4 | 7 | 2 | 46 | 71.73 | 0.52 |
| Damage | 15 | 4 | 0 | 3 | 22 | 68.18 | 0.59 |
| Handling, receiving, unlawful possession | 19 | 8 | 0 | 2 | 29 | 65.51 | 0.48 |
| Theft of motor vehicles | 5 | 3 | 1 | 0 | 9 | 55.55 | 0.55 |
| Taking and driving away of motor vehicles | 23 | 17 | 3 | 2 | 45 | 51.11 | 0.64 |
| Insulting or threatening behavior | 11 | 2 | 1 | 7 | 21 | 52.38 | 1.19 |
| Theft from motor vehicles | 8 | 6 | 2 | 0 | 16 | 50.00 | 0.62 |
| Other theft | 18 | 7 | 11 | 2 | 38 | 47.36 | 0.92 |
| Equipped to steal, suspected person, loitering | 6 | 6 | 0 | 1 | 13 | 46.15 | 0.69 |
| Robbery, conspiracy to rob | 4 | 3 | 1 | 4 | 12 | 33.33 | 1.41 |
| Sexual offenses versus male | 1 | 1 | 0 | 1 | 3 | 33.33 | 1.33 |
| Burglary | 18 | 27 | 12 | 2 | 59 | 30.50 | 0.96 |
| Wounding | 0 | 0 | 0 | 1 | 1 | 0.00 | 3.00 |
| Total | 297 | 102 | 43 | 35 | 477 | | 0.61 |

Table 8.5. *Co-offending Versus Serial Number of Convictions*

| Serial Conviction No. | Mean No. Co-offenders | N |
|---|---|---|
| 1 | 1.09 | 173 |
| 2 | 1.09 | 120 |
| 3 | 1.31 | 93 |
| 4 | 0.99 | 71 |
| 5 | 1.20 | 50 |
| 6 | 1.20 | 41 |
| 7 | 0.89 | 36 |
| 8 | 0.23 | 30 |
| 9 | 0.77 | 30 |
| 10 | 1.00 | 20 |
| 11 | 0.71 | 21 |
| 12 | 1.38 | 16 |
| 13 | 0.71 | 17 |
| 14 | 0.08 | 12 |
| 15 | 0.67 | 12 |
| 16 | 0.43 | 7 |
| 17 | 0.40 | 5 |
| 18 | 0.00 | 2 |
| 19 | 0.00 | 1 |
| 20 | 0.00 | 1 |
| 21 | 0.50 | 2 |
| Total | 1.01 | 760 |

| Serial Conviction Grouping | Mean No. Co-offenders | N |
|---|---|---|
| 1–5 | 1.13 | 507 |
| 6–10 | 0.83 | 157 |
| 11–15 | 0.74 | 78 |
| 16–21 | 0.33 | 18 |
| Total | 1.01 | 760 |

the top portion of Table 8.5, the average number of co-offenders varies with the serial number of the offense. The incidence of co-offending appears to be relatively constant through the 6th or 7th serial offense but then declines for later offenses, especially beginning at offense 13. We also present this information grouped in convictions of five because of low cell sizes, particularly at the high conviction numbers. As shown in the bottom panel of Table 8.5, the average number of co-offenders varies with the serial offenses. Specifically, the mean number of co-offenders significantly decreases as the number of convictions increases (F=3.061, p < .05).

The top portion of Table 8.6 shows how both the mean and total number of co-offenders vary with the total number of convictions. Here, it can be seen that the mean number of co-offenders appears relatively constant throughout much of the total number of convictions, only decreasing with very high numbers of total convictions. The bottom portion of Table 8.6 shows how the mean number of co-offenders varies with the total number of convictions, using four groupings of the total number of convictions. As shown, the average number of co-offenders does not appear to vary with the total number of convictions (F = 1.416, p > .05).

The top panel of Table 8.7 demonstrates how both the mean and total number of co-offenders vary according to age at first conviction. Here, it can be seen that individuals experiencing an earlier as opposed to later onset have both a higher mean and higher total number of co-offenders. To examine how early- and late-onset offenders vary across co-offending measures, a series of t-tests were performed according to the early-onset (<14) and late-onset (≥14) designations. Individuals who incur an early onset are significantly more likely than their late-onset counterparts to have a co-offender in their career (mean = .942 compared to mean = .658), have a higher mean number of co-offenders (mean = 1.278 compared to mean=.952), and have a higher total number of co-offenders (mean = 9.942 compared to 3.240) over their careers. The bottom panel of Table 8.7 demonstrates how the mean and total number of co-offenders vary according to age at first conviction, grouped in five-year age bands due to small cell sizes, especially at the top end of the onset continuum. As can be seen, individuals who experienced an onset between ages 10 and 14 incurred both a higher average and total number of co-offenders over the course of their career (F = 1.685, p > .05).

The relationship between career length and co-offending is presented in the top portion of Table 8.8. Here, it appears that while those with shorter career lengths had little experience with co-offending, both the mean and the total number of co-offenders stay relatively constant with career length. Due to small sample sizes, the relationship between co-offending and career length (partialed into six separate career length groupings because of small cell sizes) is again presented in the bottom panel of Table 8.8. With regard to the mean number of co-offenders, the career length groups do not significantly differ from one another (F = 0.356, p > .05); however, the career length groups and total number of co-offenders over the course of the career are significantly related

Table 8.6. *Co-offending Versus Total Number of Convictions*

| Total No. Convictions | Mean No. Co-Offenders | Total No. Co-offenders | N |
|---|---|---|---|
| 1 | .96 | .96 | 52 |
| 2 | 1.04 | 2.08 | 34 |
| 3 | 1.19 | 3.57 | 14 |
| 4 | .79 | 3.18 | 11 |
| 5 | .97 | 4.88 | 9 |
| 6 | 1.40 | 8.42 | 7 |
| 7 | 1.25 | 8.75 | 4 |
| 8 | 1.08 | 8.66 | 3 |
| 9 | .96 | 8.66 | 6 |
| 10 | 1.16 | 11.60 | 5 |
| 11 | 1.36 | 15.00 | 1 |
| 12 | 1.23 | 14.80 | 5 |
| 14 | .42 | 6.00 | 1 |
| 16 | 1.06 | 17.00 | 2 |
| 17 | .85 | 14.50 | 2 |
| 18 | .77 | 14.00 | 1 |
| 19 | .97 | 18.50 | 2 |
| 20 | .75 | 15.00 | 3 |
| 22 | .72 | 16.00 | 2 |
| Total | 1.02 | 4.67 | 760 |

| Total No. Convictions (Grouped) | Mean No. Co-offenders | N |
|---|---|---|
| 1–5 | 1.00 | 251 |
| 6–10 | 1.16 | 198 |
| 11–17 | 1.05 | 151 |
| 18–22 | 0.80 | 160 |
| Total | 1.01 | 760 |

($F = 9.986$, $p < .05$). Here, those individuals with lengthier criminal careers also have more co-offenders than their counterparts.[4]

In short, the decline in co-offending with the serial number of the offense suggests that experience in offending, both alone and with others,

[4] This is so because those with lengthy careers incur more offenses but not do not necessarily have more co-offenders per offense.

Table 8.7. *Co-offending Versus Age at First Conviction*

| Age at First Conviction | Mean No. Co-offenders | Total No. Co-offenders | N |
|---|---|---|---|
| 10 | 1.02 | 12.66 | 6 |
| 11 | 1.27 | 12.83 | 6 |
| 12 | 0.62 | 5.25 | 8 |
| 13 | 1.72 | 10.20 | 15 |
| 14 | 1.28 | 5.00 | 19 |
| 15 | 0.81 | 6.82 | 17 |
| 16 | 1.24 | 4.50 | 14 |
| 17 | 1.25 | 3.72 | 18 |
| 18 | 1.12 | 3.87 | 8 |
| 19 | 0.65 | 1.11 | 9 |
| 20 | 0.37 | 0.66 | 9 |
| 21 | 1.00 | 1.00 | 2 |
| 22 | 0.23 | 0.66 | 3 |
| 23 | 0.50 | 0.50 | 2 |
| 24 | 0.25 | 0.50 | 2 |
| 25 | 4.00 | 4.00 | 3 |
| 26 | 0.00 | 0.00 | 4 |
| 28 | 0.33 | 1.00 | 2 |
| 30 | 0.00 | 0.00 | 1 |
| 31 | 0.00 | 0.00 | 1 |
| 32 | 0.25 | 0.50 | 2 |
| 33 | 3.00 | 3.00 | 3 |
| 34 | 0.00 | 0.00 | 2 |
| 35 | 0.00 | 0.00 | 2 |
| 37 | 0.00 | 0.00 | 1 |
| 39 | 0.00 | 0.00 | 1 |
| 40 | 0.00 | 0.00 | 1 |
| Total | 1.02 | 4.67 | 164 |

| Onset Age (Grouped) | Mean Number of Co-offenders | N |
|---|---|---|
| 10–14 | 1.280 | 54 |
| 15–19 | 1.040 | 66 |
| 20–24 | 0.422 | 18 |
| 25–31 | 0.904 | 14 |
| 32–40 | 0.791 | 12 |
| Total | 1.021 | 164 |

Table 8.8. *Co-offending Versus Career Length*

| Career Length (Years) | Mean No. Co-offenders | Total No. Co-offenders | N |
|---|---|---|---|
| (1 time offenders) | 0.96 | 0.96 | 52 |
| <1 | 0.54 | 1.20 | 5 |
| 1 | 1.36 | 3.20 | 10 |
| 2 | 1.25 | 4.00 | 11 |
| 3 | 2.11 | 7.66 | 6 |
| 4 | 0.92 | 4.44 | 9 |
| 5 | 1.80 | 9.00 | 1 |
| 6 | 1.26 | 13.33 | 6 |
| 7 | 0.37 | 0.75 | 4 |
| 8 | 0.50 | 1.00 | 2 |
| 9 | 0.84 | 4.20 | 5 |
| 10 | 0.87 | 9.66 | 3 |
| 11 | 1.50 | 9.00 | 1 |
| 12 | 1.39 | 7.33 | 6 |
| 13 | 0.56 | 6.33 | 3 |
| 14 | 0.73 | 6.90 | 10 |
| 15 | 0.58 | 6.00 | 2 |
| 16 | 2.20 | 10.50 | 2 |
| 17 | 0.47 | 9.00 | 2 |
| 18 | 0.46 | 4.00 | 2 |
| 19 | 1.15 | 7.57 | 7 |
| 20 | 0.68 | 10.25 | 4 |
| 22 | 1.21 | 8.75 | 4 |
| 23 | 0.67 | 7.00 | 2 |
| 24 | 0.98 | 18.50 | 2 |
| 25 | 0.79 | 8.00 | 3 |
| Total | 1.02 | 4.67 | 164 |

| Career Length (Grouped) | Mean No. Co-offenders | Total No. Co-offenders | N |
|---|---|---|---|
| (1 time offenders) | 0.961 | 0.961 | 52 |
| 0.01–4.99 years | 1.246 | 4.097 | 41 |
| 5.00–9.99 years | 0.894 | 6.388 | 18 |
| 10.00–14.99 years | 0.936 | 7.391 | 23 |
| 15.00–19.99 years | 1.034 | 7.466 | 15 |
| 20.00–30.00 years | 0.887 | 10.066 | 15 |
| Total | 1.021 | 4.670 | 164 |

may explain some of the decline in co-offending with age. At the same time, that the rate of co-offending remains relatively constant for up to 10 or so offenses and then declines suggests that age may be more important than experience in explaining the decline in co-offending.

Next, we investigate how the number of co-offenders varies according to whether the first conviction was early or later. Out of 164 offenders, 35 experienced an onset prior to age 14. Of these 35, only 7 were solo offenders at their first conviction. Of the 35 individuals who started at or after age 21, 26 were solo offenders at their first conviction. Thus, with a later age at first conviction, the proportion of individuals not having a co-offender in their career increases.

Table 8.9 shows how the total number of offenses and the percentage of recidivists (i.e., those with two or three or more offenses throughout their career) vary with whether the individuals had a co-offender in their career, while controlling for age at first conviction. In the total sample, as shown earlier in Chapter 5, individuals with an early onset have both a higher mean number of convictions and a higher likelihood of recidivism. Some further interesting results are observed when the sample is disaggregated by whether they offended alone or with others on the first conviction (i.e., one, two, or three or more). At onset ages 10–13, it can be seen that those who committed their first offense alone also committed fewer offenses compared to those individuals in the same onset age bracket who had one, two, or three or more co-offenders at the first conviction. Interestingly, at ages 14–16, those who committed their first offense alone committed a higher total number of offenses compared to the one- and two-co-offenders groups, but not the three or more–co-offenders group.

Other interesting findings emerged from this table. For example, those individuals who had the most co-offenders at the first conviction (three or more) and who had the earliest onset ages (10–13) accumulated the highest number of offenses throughout their careers (mean=12.20). Additionally, solo offenders were generally less likely to accumulate many offenses and/or recidivate compared to their co-offending-group counterparts. In short, there appears to be no consistent tendency for solo offending in the first offense to be associated with few total offenses for all ages at first conviction.[5]

Next, we examine co-offending in the first offense versus recidivism[6] and co-offending in the second offense (and then second to third, and then third to fourth). This is examined for the total sample and then

---

[5] We would expect those with co-offenders to reoffend less because they may have been led into it, but we do not find this to be true. They could have been the recruiter, but the CSDD data do not allow an investigation of this possibility.
[6] 56.1 percent of the 164 offenders had a co-offender on their first conviction.

Table 8.9. *Number of Co-offenders in the First Conviction Versus Later Criminal Careers*

|  | Total | | | Number of Co-Offenders at First Conviction | | | | | | | | | | | |
|---|---|---|---|---|---|---|---|---|---|---|---|---|---|---|---|
|  | | | | 0 Co-offenders (Solo) | | | 1 Co-offender | | | 2 Co-offenders | | | 3 or more Co-offenders | | |
| Age at First Conviction | Mean No. Convic. | N | % Recid. | Mean No. Convic. | N | % Recid. | Mean No. Convic. | N | % Recid. | Mean No. Convic. | N | % Recid. | Mean No. Convic. | N | % Recid. |
| 10–13 | 8.77 | 35 | 91.00 | 7.57 | 7 | 85.71 | 8.56 | 16 | 100.00 | 8.00 | 7 | 71.43 | 12.20 | 5 | 100.00 |
| 14–16 | 5.62 | 50 | 84.00 | 6.23 | 17 | 82.35 | 5.64 | 14 | 85.71 | 4.64 | 17 | 82.35 | 8.50 | 5 | 100.00 |
| 17–20 | 2.63 | 44 | 61.36 | 2.63 | 22 | 68.18 | 2.35 | 14 | 42.86 | 7.00 | 1 | 100.00 | 2.571 | 7 | 71.43 |
| 21+ | 1.60 | 35 | 31.43 | 1.65 | 26 | 30.77 | 1.80 | 5 | 60.00 | 1.00 | 2 | 0.00 | 1.00 | 2 | 0.00 |
| Total | 4.63 | 164 | 68.29 | 3.61 | 72 | 59.72 | 5.26 | 49 | 75.51 | 5.33 | 27 | 74.07 | 6.125 | 16 | 75.00 |

disaggregated by age according to whether the first four (of all) offenses occurred prior to age 18 and then after age 18. The results may be found in Table 8.10.

Generally speaking, it seems clear that in the full sample the probability of a solo offense following another solo offense is always greater than the probability of a co-offender offense being followed by a solo offense or a co-offending offense. Therefore, there appears to be a tendency to co-offend or to offend alone. Also of interest is the finding that solo offenders on their first conviction were more likely than offenders who co-offended on their first conviction to exhibit fewer convictions over the course of the career (mean=3.6 compared to mean=5.4 convictions), and this is true among individuals who were solo offenders in the first through the fourth conviction. Interestingly, beginning with the fifth transition, those who were solo offenders compared to those who co-offended did not significantly vary on the total number of convictions throughout the career.

When the 23 individuals who had their first four (of all) offenses by age 18 are examined, the transition between the first and second and then the second and third convictions reveal a similar story – that is, solo offenders are more likely to continue being solo offenders than offending with co-offenders being followed by offending with co-offenders at the next conviction. The exception to this trend is for the transition between the third and fourth conviction. Here, co-offending at the third conviction is more likely to be followed by solo offending at the fourth conviction than solo offending at conviction three is to be followed by solo offending at conviction four.

Turning to the eight individuals who experienced their first four (of all) convictions at or after age 18, it can be seen that the transition between the first and second convictions seems to favor more of a tendency to stay within solo offending. Between convictions two and three, there appears to be a tendency to remain within solo offending (especially if one was a solo offender at conviction two). For the transition between convictions three and four, all eight offenders who experienced a third conviction became solo offenders on the fourth conviction, regardless if they were solo or co-offenders at the third conviction.

Co-offending may decrease with age because of changes in the population of offenders (e.g., if co-offenders tend to desist while solo offenders tend to persist – the Moffitt explanation) or because of behavioral changes within offenders (i.e., if any given offender becomes more likely to offend alone with age). Thus far, the analyses have shown that there appears to be no tendency for solo offenders in general to persist.

Another way of investigating this issue is to study changes within the criminal careers of persistent offenders (Reiss and Farrington, 1991:382).

Table 8.10. *Co-offending in One Offense Versus Recidivism and Co-offending in the Next Offense*

| | | Full Sample | | | | | | | | |
|---|---|---|---|---|---|---|---|---|---|---|
| Serial No. of Offense | C1 | Conviction 2 Alone | | | C2 | Conviction 3 Alone | | | C3 | Conviction 4 Alone | | |
| | N | Next Time | % | | N | Next Time | % | | N | Next Time | % |
| 1 alone | 43 | 26 | 60.4 | | | | | | | | |
| 1 with other | 69 | 26 | 37.6 | | | | | | | | |
| 2 alone | | | | | 34 | 18 | 52.9 | | | | |
| 2 with other | | | | | 44 | 11 | 25.0 | | | | |
| 3 alone | | | | | | | | | 23 | 14 | 60.8 |
| 3 with other | | | | | | | | | 41 | 22 | 53.6 |
| Total | 112 | | | | 78 | | | | 64 | | |

| | | First Four Offenses by Age 18 | | | | | | | | |
|---|---|---|---|---|---|---|---|---|---|---|
| Serial No. of Offense | C1 | Conviction 2 Alone | | | C2 | Conviction 3 Alone | | | C3 | Conviction 4 Alone | | |
| | N | Next Time | % | | N | Next Time | % | | N | Next Time | % |
| 1 alone | 7 | 5 | 71.4 | | | | | | | | |
| 1 with other | 16 | 3 | 18.7 | | | | | | | | |
| 2 alone | | | | | 8 | 5 | 62.5 | | | | |
| 2 with other | | | | | 15 | 4 | 26.6 | | | | |
| 3 alone | | | | | | | | | 9 | 4 | 44.4 |
| 3 with other | | | | | | | | | 14 | 8 | 57.1 |
| Total | 23 | | | | 23 | | | | 23 | | |

| | | First Four Offenses at Age 18+ | | | | | | | | |
|---|---|---|---|---|---|---|---|---|---|---|
| Serial No. of Offense | C1 | Conviction 2 Alone | | | C2 | Conviction 3 Alone | | | C3 | Conviction 4 Alone | | |
| | N | Next Time | % | | N | Next Time | % | | N | Next Time | % |
| 1 alone | 6 | 4 | 66.66 | | | | | | | | |
| 1 with other | 2 | 1 | 50.00 | | | | | | | | |
| 2 alone | | | | | 5 | 4 | 80.00 | | | | |
| 2 with other | | | | | 3 | 1 | 33.33 | | | | |
| 3 alone | | | | | | | | | 5 | 5 | 100.0 |
| 3 with other | | | | | | | | | 3 | 3 | 100.0 |
| Total | 8 | | | | 8 | | | | 8 | | |

To examine this, we classified 24 of the sample males as the most persistent offenders because each committed at least 10 offenses by age 40, thus constricting the sample even further than the Wolfgang et al. (1972) five-plus chronic-offender designation. In the aggregate, these 24 offenders (5.8 percent of the sample) committed 47.5 percent of all offenses – 361 of 760 offenses.

Table 8.11 shows some characteristics of the 24 most persistent offenders. Their criminal careers were largely characterized by equal numbers of solo and co-offending offenses. For example, 52.53 percent

Table 8.11. *Characteristics Associated with 24 Persistent Offenders (10+ Convictions) (Sorted by Highest Mean Number of Co-offenders)*

| Number | Total No. Convictions | Percentage Alone | Mean No. Co-offenders | Total Co-offenders in Career |
|---|---|---|---|---|
| 1 | 10 | 40.00 | 3.80 | 38 |
| 2 | 12 | 16.66 | 2.00 | 24 |
| 3 | 16 | 31.25 | 1.63 | 26 |
| 4 | 12 | 41.66 | 1.42 | 17 |
| 5 | 14 | 21.42 | 1.40 | 14 |
| 6 | 11 | 9.09 | 1.36 | 15 |
| 7 | 17 | 70.58 | 1.24 | 21 |
| 8 | 20 | 45.00 | 1.10 | 22 |
| 9 | 19 | 42.10 | 1.00 | 19 |
| 10 | 12 | 66.66 | 1.00 | 12 |
| 11 | 19 | 57.89 | .95 | 18 |
| 12 | 12 | 41.66 | .92 | 11 |
| 13 | 12 | 50.00 | .83 | 10 |
| 14 | 18 | 50.00 | .78 | 14 |
| 15 | 22 | 68.18 | .73 | 16 |
| 16 | 22 | 54.54 | .73 | 16 |
| 17 | 20 | 55.00 | .70 | 14 |
| 18 | 16 | 68.75 | .50 | 8 |
| 19 | 17 | 58.82 | .47 | 8 |
| 20 | 20 | 60.00 | .45 | 9 |
| 21 | 14 | 71.42 | .43 | 6 |
| 22 | 10 | 70.00 | .30 | 3 |
| 23 | 10 | 70.00 | .30 | 3 |
| 24 | 10 | 100.00 | .00 | 0 |
| Total | 365 | 52.53 | 1.00 | 344 |

Table 8.12. *Changes in Average Number of Co-offenders with Age for Persistent Offenders*

| | Mean No. Co-Offenders | | | | | |
|---|---|---|---|---|---|---|
| | 10+ Offenses[a] | | 6–9 Offenses[b] | | 1–5 Offenses[c] | |
| Age | Mean | N | Mean | N | Mean | N |
| 10–13 | 1.27 | 33 | 1.18 | 11 | 1.63 | 16 |
| 14–16 | 1.22 | 72 | 1.27 | 37 | 1.22 | 45 |
| 17–20 | 1.03 | 122 | 1.22 | 41 | 1.19 | 79 |
| 21–24 | 0.76 | 45 | 0.89 | 18 | 0.54 | 37 |
| 25–28 | 1.00 | 29 | 2.31 | 13 | 1.32 | 28 |
| 29–32 | 0.40 | 30 | 0.93 | 14 | 0.06 | 18 |
| 33–36 | 0.32 | 22 | 0.33 | 9 | 0.75 | 16 |
| 37–40 | 0.75 | 8 | 0.00 | 5 | 0.42 | 12 |
| Total | 0.95 | 361 | 1.16 | 148 | 1.00 | 251 |

*Notes:* [a] These are the persistent offenders (n = 24).
[b] These are individuals who committed between 6 and 9 offenses (n = 20).
[c] The are individuals who committed between 1 and 5 offenses (n = 120).

of the total crimes committed by persistent offenders were committed alone. One person (case 24) was exclusively a solo offender,[7] four cases were predominantly solo offenders (cases 7, 21, 22, 23), and one (case 6) was predominantly a co-offender.

Table 8.12 shows the average number of co-offenders of the 24 persistent offenders (who committed 10 or more offenses) in the first column. Here, it can be seen that the average number of co-offenders decreases with age, as did, during the third decade of life, the co-offending of the more occasional offenders (listed as those offenders who committed between six and nine offenses or between one and five offenses). Among the 24 persistent offenders, over all ages, the correlation between age at conviction and the average number of co-offenders was, as would be expected, negative and significant. It could be concluded, then, that the decrease in co-offending with age appears not to be caused by the persistence of solo offenders and/or the dropping out of co-offenders as Moffitt would suggest, but instead reflects changes within individual criminal careers.

In another investigation of the decrease of co-offending with age (not shown), the average number of co-offenders per offense during the

[7] This offender committed a total of 7 (out of 18) different crime types.

Table 8.13. *Age at Conviction and Co-offenders (24 Persistent Offenders, 361 Total Convictions)*

| | | No. Co-offenders | | | | |
|---|---|---|---|---|---|---|
| Age | 0 | Row % for 0 | Col % for 0 | 1 | 2 | 3+ |
| 10–13 | 10 | 5.2 | 30.3 | 12 | 5 | 6 |
| 14–16 | 33 | 17.1 | 45.8 | 16 | 10 | 13 |
| 17–20 | 60 | 31.1 | 49.2 | 36 | 15 | 11 |
| 21–24 | 25 | 13.0 | 55.6 | 13 | 4 | 3 |
| 25–28 | 18 | 9.3 | 62.1 | 7 | 2 | 2 |
| 29–32 | 26 | 13.5 | 86.7 | 3 | 0 | 1 |
| 33–36 | 17 | 8.8 | 77.3 | 3 | 2 | 0 |
| 37–40 | 4 | 2.1 | 50.0 | 3 | 0 | 1 |
| Total | 193 | | | 93 | 38 | 37 |

juvenile years (<18) is compared to the adult period (≥18) among the 24 persistent offenders. A number of findings emerged from this comparison. First, out of the 361 convictions among this select group, 193 had no co-offenders; and of those 193, 140 were committed during adulthood. Second, it was found that during the juvenile years the mean number of co-offenders was 1.19 as compared to 0.81 co-offenders, on average, during the adult years (t = 2.169, p<.05). For the 24 persistent offenders, the average decreased in 16 cases and increased in 6 cases.[8] Once again, the results indicate changes within individual criminal careers.

Finally, Table 8.13 displays a cross-tabulation of the age at conviction and the number of co-offenders (categorized as 0, 1, 2, and 3+). As can be seen here, the tendency to have co-offenders appears to be a feature of one's youth. The tendency is to decrease in co-offending, both in terms of proportion and number with increasing age at conviction.

## Comment: Is There Co-offending in the CSDD, and How Does Co-offending Vary with Age?

Despite much recognition, the role of co-offending generally, and within-individual criminal careers in particular, has been one of the most ill-studied of all criminal career dimensions. This omission is due more

---

[8] For two cases, one was exclusively a solo offender (case 24), and the other had no co-offenders nor offenses in adulthood because he died at age 17 (case 8).

likely to the lack of data than it is to the lack of criminologists' interest in the role of co-offending. Fortunately, the CSDD provides some information with regard to co-offending that allows for its study.

Throughout our analysis of the relationship between co-offending and various criminal career dimensions within the full sample, individual criminal careers, and a small group of persistent offenders, a number of important findings emerged. Descriptively speaking, the age/co-offending curve closely mimicked aggregate portrayals of the age/crime curve, with the mean co-offending peak at age 17 and then a decline through the 20s and 30s. Additionally, more co-offenders were related to a longer career length, the age at onset (early), and the total number of convictions.

When we examined the role of co-offending within criminal careers, several key findings emerged. First, the incidence of co-offending decreased with age primarily because individual offenders changed and became less likely to offend with others rather than because of selective attrition of co-offenders or persistence of those who offend primarily alone. As offenders age, it seems that they become more likely to offend alone, though most continue to commit *some* offenses with others. Second, exclusive solo offending was rare (only one person offended only alone) and exclusive co-offending (none) was uncommon at all ages, though there appears to be a tendency to remain in the category most common to the offender himself. Studies of the most persistent offenders showed that on average only 51.8 percent offended alone. Thus, their careers were filled with both solo and co-offending, though it was also the case that there were changes in the careers of persistent offenders with a movement from co- to more solo offending. Finally, there was also some evidence to suggest that co-offending varied by offense type, burglary and robbery being the most common involving co-offenders. Still, co-offending decreased with all offense types with age independently of changing patterns of offending types.

## Take-Home Messages

1 The age/co-offending relationship peaks in the late teenage years.
2 The incidence of co-offending decreases with age primarily because individual offenders change and become less likely to offend with others rather than because of selective attrition of co-offenders or persistence of those who offend primarily alone.
3 Co-offending appears more common for some crimes (burglary, robbery) than others.

**Unanswered Questions**

1 What is the process of co-offending generally and co-offender recruitment specifically?
2 Do some individual characteristics relate to co-offending patterns over the life-course?
3 Do females disproportionately co-offend with males or with one another?
4 What are the roles (leader versus follower) in co-offending groups, and how are they related to their respective criminal careers?

CHAPTER NINE

# Are Chronic Offenders Serious Offenders, and Does This Relationship Vary with Age?

Is there such a thing as a "chronic" offender – one whose frequent involvement in criminal activity is marked by serious offenses? The starting point for this question must be Wolfgang et al.'s (1972) finding that 6 percent of the 1945 Philadelphia Birth Cohort was responsible for over 50 percent of the criminal acts to age 17. Perhaps no finding in criminology is better known by students and scholars alike (Laub, 2004), while at the same time being hailed by policy makers and practitioners as central to crime reduction efforts (see Schumacher and Kurz, 1999). If only it were so easy to identify such individuals ahead of time (Blumstein et al., 1985; Gottfredson and Hirschi, 1990).

The concept of chronicity was first established by Wolfgang and colleagues and applied to offenders committing five or more offenses prior to age 18. The concept – and its operationalization – however, is ambiguous because of its arbitrary designation and truncation problems. We believe that chronicity is better discussed with regard to the various relevant constituent dimensions that can vary with age, like frequency and seriousness. The basic theme is that the number of offenses committed (and the opportunity for a larger number goes up with age) and the rate of offending may vary with age.

In this chapter, we examine how chronicity is related to seriousness of offending with age. We attempt to unpack the meaning of chronicity by linking frequency, seriousness, and duration of offending. In this regard, we attempt to demonstrate how an offender cannot be both chronic (i.e., committing many offenses) and serious because serious offenders tend to be locked up quickly (but only for short time periods), thus preventing their high involvement in crime.

**123**

Additionally, there is the question of whether the offenses committed by chronic offenders are more serious on average. Offenders designated as "chronic" should be expected to have both a high offending frequency and a high seriousness of offending over their careers, though the outward manifestations of their acts may change over the life-course. For example, among youngsters there should be little evidence of homicide, assault, and robbery, but many instances of kicking, pushing, and so forth (see Tremblay et al., 1999). As these youngsters enter into adolescence and then into adulthood, there should be fewer kicking and pushing episodes and more acts of assault and robbery.

## Methods

### Measures

Conviction records between ages 10 and 40 are used to examine the chronicity issue.

### Data Analysis

This chapter presents both descriptive and predictive analyses designed to understand chronicity.

## Results

First, we begin with a description of the pattern of chronic offending in the CSDD data. As noted in Chapter 4, the prevalence of offending in the CSDD is 39.9 percent, suggesting that 60 percent of the sample had no convictions by age 40. Table 9.1 presents the information necessary for identifying chronic offenders using the classic approach for the CSDD sample.

Applying Wolfgang et al.'s (1972) designation of chronic offending as those individuals with five or more offenses, it can be seen in the CSDD that chronic offenders represent 12.89 percent (53 of 411) of the full sample or 32.3 percent (53 of 164) of all offenders, but were responsible for about 72.89 percent (554 of 760) of all convictions. These results, like Wolfgang and colleagues', suggest that a small percentage of the cohort is responsible for a large share of the convictions. Figure 9.1a displays the relationship between conviction number and the percentage of the full and offender samples, while Figure 9.1b presents a graph of the cumulative area by conviction number (for offenders only).

Table 9.1. *Chronicity Analysis*

Full Sample (n = 411)

| k | Nk | Pnk | Ok | Pok | cPnk | cPok | area |
|---|----|-----|----|-----|------|------|------|
| 0 | 247 | 0.6009 | 0 | 0 | 1 | 1 | 0.6009 |
| 1 | 52 | 0.1265 | 52 | 0.0684 | 0.3990 | 1 | 0.1221 |
| 2 | 34 | 0.0827 | 68 | 0.0894 | 0.2725 | 0.9315 | 0.0733 |
| 3 | 14 | 0.0340 | 42 | 0.0552 | 0.1897 | 0.8421 | 0.0277 |
| 4 | 11 | 0.0267 | 44 | 0.0578 | 0.1557 | 0.7868 | 0.0202 |
| 5 | 9 | 0.0218 | 45 | 0.0592 | 0.1289 | 0.7289 | 0.0153 |
| 6 | 7 | 0.0170 | 42 | 0.0552 | 0.1070 | 0.6697 | 0.0109 |
| 7 | 4 | 0.0097 | 28 | 0.0368 | 0.0900 | 0.6144 | 0.0058 |
| 8 | 3 | 0.0072 | 24 | 0.0315 | 0.0802 | 0.5776 | 0.0041 |
| 9 | 6 | 0.0145 | 54 | 0.0710 | 0.0729 | 0.5460 | 0.0074 |
| 10 | 5 | 0.0121 | 50 | 0.0657 | 0.0583 | 0.4750 | 0.0053 |
| 11 | 1 | 0.0024 | 11 | 0.0144 | 0.0462 | 0.4092 | 0.0009 |
| 12 | 5 | 0.0121 | 60 | 0.0789 | 0.0437 | 0.3947 | 0.0043 |
| 14 | 1 | 0.0024 | 14 | 0.0184 | 0.0316 | 0.3157 | 0.0007 |
| 16 | 2 | 0.0048 | 32 | 0.0421 | 0.0291 | 0.2973 | 0.0013 |
| 17 | 2 | 0.0048 | 34 | 0.0447 | 0.0243 | 0.2552 | 0.0011 |
| 18 | 1 | 0.0024 | 18 | 0.0236 | 0.0194 | 0.2105 | 0.0004 |
| 19 | 2 | 0.0048 | 38 | 0.05 | 0.0170 | 0.1868 | 0.0007 |
| 20 | 3 | 0.0072 | 60 | 0.0789 | 0.0121 | 0.1368 | 0.0007 |
| 22 | 2 | 0.0048 | 44 | 0.0578 | 0.0048 | 0.0578 | 0.0001 |
| Total | 411 | 760 | | | | 1 | 0.9041 |

Delinquent Sample (n = 164), k ≥ 1

| k | nk | pnk | cpnk | area |
|---|----|-----|------|------|
| 1 | 52 | 0.3170 | 1 | 0.3062 |
| 2 | 34 | 0.2073 | 0.6829 | 0.1838 |
| 3 | 14 | 0.0853 | 0.4756 | 0.0695 |
| 4 | 11 | 0.0670 | 0.3902 | 0.0508 |
| 5 | 9 | 0.0548 | 0.3231 | 0.0383 |
| 6 | 7 | 0.0426 | 0.2682 | 0.0274 |
| 7 | 4 | 0.0243 | 0.2256 | 0.0145 |
| 8 | 3 | 0.0182 | 0.2012 | 0.0102 |
| 9 | 6 | 0.0365 | 0.1829 | 0.0186 |
| 10 | 5 | 0.0304 | 0.1463 | 0.0134 |
| 11 | 1 | 0.0060 | 0.1158 | 0.0024 |
| 12 | 5 | 0.0304 | 0.1097 | 0.0108 |
| 14 | 1 | 0.0060 | 0.0792 | 0.0018 |
| 16 | 2 | 0.0121 | 0.0731 | 0.0038 |
| 17 | 2 | 0.0121 | 0.0609 | 0.0028 |
| 18 | 1 | 0.0060 | 0.0487 | 0.0012 |
| 19 | 2 | 0.0121 | 0.0426 | 0.0019 |
| 20 | 3 | 0.0182 | 0.0304 | 0.0017 |
| 22 | 2 | 0.0121 | 0.0121 | 0.0003 |
| 164 | | | | 0.7598 |

k = Conviction number

Nk = Number of individuals convicted k times

Pnk = Fraction of the cohort with exactly k convictions

Ok = Number of offenses multiplied by the number of offenders, or K * Nk

Pok = Fraction of the offenses committed by member with exactly k offenses

cPnk = Fraction of sample members with k or more offenses

cPok = Fraction of the offenses committed by cohort members with at least k+1 offenses

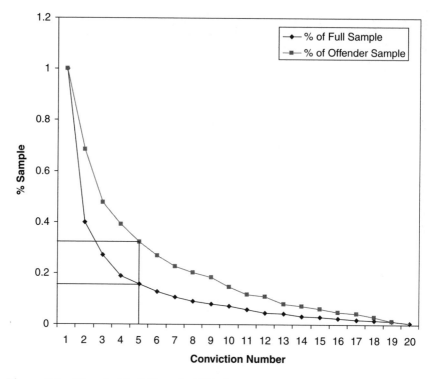

**Figure 9.1a.** Threshold of Chronic Offender

## Comparing Offense Skewness

Fox and Tracy (1988) outlined a measure of offense skewness, termed "alpha ($\alpha$)," which makes full use of the offense distribution in order to allow researchers to make comparisons about chronicity both within and between different sets of data. This coefficient of offense skewness is the area between the curve and the diagonal line of the even distribution (i.e., one in which all cohort members commit the same number of offenses). Alpha measures the extent of departure of the cumulative offense curve from the diagonal. The curve is piecewise linear (Fox and Tracy, 1988:263), so one must first calculate the area by

$$\text{Area} = \sum \text{Pn}_k(\text{Po}_k/2 + \text{cPo}_{(k+1)}) - 0.5,$$

where $\text{Pn}_k$ is the fraction of the cohort with exactly $k$ offenses, $\text{Po}_k$ is the fraction of the offenses committed by members with exactly $k$ offenses, and $\text{cPo}_{(k+1)}$ is the fraction of the offenses committed by cohort members

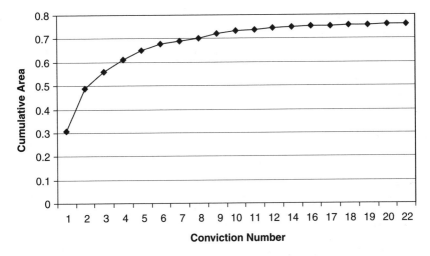

**Figure 9.1.b.** Cumulative Area by Conviction Number (Offenders Only)

with at least $k+1$ offenses. Fox and Tracy (1988:264) note that the area achieves a value of 0 if every cohort member had the same number of offenses, and the area approaches a limit of one-half if all offenses were committed by the same person. To obtain the measure of skewness, alpha ($\alpha$), the area between the observed curve and the diagonal is doubled:

$$\alpha = 2 \sum Pn_k(Po_k/2 + cPo_{(k+1)}) - 1.$$

Alpha ranges from 0 for complete equality in offense share to 1 for complete unevenness in offense share. Although there is no standard criterion for deciding when skewness is or is not substantial, this coefficient has the desirable property that allows it to be compared against other measures of alpha calculated for other cohort studies. In referring to the two Philadelphia birth cohorts, Fox and Tracy (1988:265) make this point explicit:

> The primary question still remains concerning which cohort has the more pronounced chronic offender effect, and this question is best answered by the kind of coefficient we discussed above and apply below [alpha]. Thus, does the 1958 birth cohort, with 7% of the cohort committing 61% of the offenses, represent a situation of more, less, or equal skewness in chronic offensivity than the 1945 cohort, in which 6% of the members committed 52% of the offenses?

Although alpha is influenced by both the distribution of offenses among offenders and the prevalence of offending itself, by calculating

Table 9.2. *Comparison of Alpha Across Studies*

| Study | Full Sample Alpha | Offender Sample Alpha |
|---|---|---|
| Philadelphia Birth Cohort I (1945) | 0.81 | 0.47 |
| Philadelphia Birth Cohort II (1958) | 0.83 | 0.50 |
| Philadelphia Perinatal Project | 0.88 | 0.47 |
| Providence Perinatal Project | 0.93 | 0.44 |
| Seattle Social Development Project | 0.82 (court records) 0.75 (self-reports) | 0.49 (court records) 0.72 (self-reports) |
| Stockholm | 0.94 | 0.71 |
| CSDD | 0.80 | 0.51 |

alpha for both the offenders only and the full cohort, one can obtain a measure of the skewness in offense share distribution without the effect of prevalence.[1]

Before proceeding, two cautions should be noted. First, one should always inspect cumulative offense plots when interpreting alpha. Second, one must be careful about truncation points in the offense data. Because alpha assumes that the offenses held by a group are evenly distributed among its members, it assumes that there is no remaining skewness beyond the truncation point (Fox and Tracy, 1988:271–272).[2]

Data for assessing offense skewness can be found in Table 9.1. As stated earlier, alpha is calculated by subtracting 1 from twice the sum of the area. Among the full sample, alpha was equal to .80. Among the offenders, alpha is equal to .51. We thought it would be particularly useful and interesting to see how these estimates compare to those obtained in other longitudinal studies (Table 9.2).

With one exception, the results for the CSDD are quite similar to those obtained from the three Philadelphia studies (the 1945 birth cohort, the 1958 birth cohort, and both the Philadelphia and Providence Perinatal Projects; see Fox and Tracy, 1988; Piquero, 2000b; Piquero and Buka,

[1] A larger prevalence implies that offensivity is more widely spread; thus, the distribution is less skewed (Fox and Tracy, 1988:269).
[2] The data in the present research are truncated at age 40, when most members would likely have terminated their offending, a point we will return to later. The true offense distributions are retained as they were found in the data.

2002) and from court records obtained from the Seattle Social Development Project (SSDP; see Farrington et al., 2003). The exception in the CSDD concerns the alpha coefficient among offenders. In the CSDD, it is higher than some of the other coefficients shown in Table 9.2, indicating that the effect of chronic offenders on the aggregate offense rate is more substantial in the CSDD than in the other cohorts.[3] Nevertheless, it is important to note the striking similarity of $\alpha$'s across cohort studies.

Because research has shown that chronic offenders exhibit an early onset and tend to be involved in violent offending, we next investigate these issues with the CSDD data. We begin this analysis by considering those individuals with five or more convictions as chronic offenders, a definition of chronicity that identifies 53 individuals with five or more convictions through age 40. We compare these individuals to two other groups of offenders: one-timers and below-chronics (those with two, three, or four convictions). Of the 164 offenders, 52 were one-timers; 59 had two, three, or four convictions; and 53 had five or more convictions through age 40.

Table 9.3 presents a series of comparisons where means are presented for career length, age at first conviction, age at last conviction, early onset (first conviction prior to age 14), the fraction of the group that had at least one violent offense, and the mean number of violent convictions per member of the group. As can be seen, individuals meeting the chronic-offender designation of five or more convictions exhibited the most extreme offending across all the measures. For example, chronic offenders had longer criminal careers (averaging over 15 years), were more likely to exhibit an early onset of offending (before age 14), were more likely to have a later age at last conviction, were more likely to be early-onset offenders, were more likely to commit a violent offense, and accumulated many more violent convictions than the other offender groups. Tukey's B post hoc comparison tests indicated that the chronic offenders were always significantly different from the other two offender groups on all of the comparisons.

Additionally, chronic offenders were significantly more likely to be involved in a number of different crime types (an average of 5.73 different crime types) compared to below-chronics (2.3 different crime types) and one-timers (1 crime type). Chronic offenders were also more likely to be involved in theft offenses, shoplifting, theft of motor vehicles, burglary, receiving stolen property, weapons violations, and robbery than the other two offender groups (see Table 9.3).

---

[3] The SSDP alpha coefficients using self-report records are lower for the full sample (as expected, reflecting differences in prevalence) and much higher for the offender sample. In the Stockholm official records, alpha is higher than it is for the CSDD.

Table 9.3. *Chronic Offender Mean-Level Comparisons*

| Group | N | Mean Career Length | Mean Age at First Conviction | Mean Age at Last Conviction | % Early Onset | % Violent Offender | Mean No. Violent Convictions |
|---|---|---|---|---|---|---|---|
| (1) One-timers | 52 | 0.00 | 22.52 | 22.52 | 5% | 13% | 0.13 |
| (2) Below-chronics | 59 | 6.28 | 17.76 | 24.20 | 16% | 30% | 0.33 |
| (3) Chronics | 53 | 15.04 | 14.19 | 29.3 | 41% | 50% | 1.01 |
| F-value | | 112.97* | 28.73* | 12.46* | 11.84* | 9.36* | 13.63* |
| Tukey's B test[a] | | 1/2/3 | 1/2/3 | 3/1,2 | 3/1,2 | 3/1,2 | 3/1,2 |

| Offense type[b] | One-timer | Below-chronics | Chronics | F-value |
|---|---|---|---|---|
| Shoplifting | 7.69% | 15.25% | 43.40% | 12.43* |
| Burglary | 13.46% | 22.03% | 79.25% | 44.11* |
| Robbery | 0.00% | 1.69% | 15.09% | 7.56* |
| Violence | 13.46% | 30.51% | 50.94% | 9.36* |
| Variety Index[c] | 1 | 2.32 | 5.73 | 193.25* |

*p < .05
[a]Tukey's B post hoc tests of significance should be interpreted in the following manner: 1/2/3 indicates that the three groups are significantly different from one another; 3/1,2 indicates that group 3 is significantly different from both groups 1 and 2, but groups 1 and 2 are not significantly different from one another.
[b]For the four crime types listed (shoplifting, burglary, robbery, and violence), the percentage listed indicates the percentage of individuals in each of the offender groups who have committed this crime type at least once over their career.
[c]The Variety Index is a count of the number of different crime types (out of 18 different types) engaged in by the offender. Higher values indicate a higher number of different crime types committed.

Table 9.4. *Logistic Regression Predicting Violent Offender (No/Yes)*

| Variable | B | SE | Exp(B) |
|---|---|---|---|
| Early onset | 0.164 | 0.433 | 1.178 |
| Chronic offender | 1.225 | 0.378* | 3.405 |
| Constant | −1.250 | 0.234* | |
| Chi-square (df) | 13.146 (2) | | |
| Nagelkerke R-square | 0.108 | | |

*$p < .05$. B = unstandardized regression coefficient. SE = standard error. EXP(B) = Exponentiated B coefficients.

We also estimated a logistic regression model predicting whether the individual was convicted of a violent offense at least once by age 40 (see Table 9.4). The predictors in this model included chronic-offender status (where those with five or more offenses were coded 1 and all others were coded 0) and early onset.[4] As would be expected, chronic-offender status was the only variable to emerge as significant in this analysis, and its effect was positive, strong, and significant.

Is the offending of the chronics spread out over time, or is it condensed in a select few years? Using the chronicity definition of five-plus convictions (n=53), we examined the number of years that elapsed between the first and fifth convictions (regardless of whether the subject had more than five convictions). For those subjects with five or more convictions, we found that the average number of years between the first and fifth convictions was 6.35 years (the median was somewhat lower – 5 years), with minimum and maximum values of 1 and 23 years, respectively.[5] Within this range, 60.4 percent of the chronic offenders accumulated their first five convictions in the five years between their first and fifth conviction. Over the course of their careers, these 53 chronic offenders accumulated many offenses, the majority of which were thefts and burglaries.

To further examine this issue, we selected the 5 males out of the pool of 53 chronic offenders who accumulated their first five convictions in one year or less. These five males accounted for a total (regardless of the first 5 convictions) of 58 of the 760 convictions (only one of these men had

---

[4] The bivariate correlation between chronicity and early onset was r = .346, p < .05.
[5] Of course, some chronic offenders offend well past a fifth offense. The average time between the first and last conviction among those with five or more convictions was a little over 15 years (median = 15 years).

only 5 convictions). When we inspected the type of crimes committed by each of these men in their first five convictions, the majority (n=14) of the 25 crime types were for some sort of theft: one robbery, two burglaries, one assault, and several other nonviolent crimes. This inspection reveals that among those chronics who accumulated their five crimes in the span of one year, their offending careers were marked by nonviolent crimes, which typically do not lead to incarceration, especially not to lengthy incarceration.[6] In short, chronic offenders are likely to simply be frequent but not very violent offenders. It is hard to be a violent offender and be able to commit many acts of crime because violent acts are more likely to be detected and followed by lengthy incarceration stints, which are still pretty rare themselves, especially in the United Kingdom at that time.

## A Different Approach to Identifying Chronic Offenders

Several authors have noted that the use of a five-plus category to designate chronic offenders is arbitrary (Blumstein, Farrington, and Moitra, 1985). In particular, Blumstein et al. argue that the calculation used by Wolfgang et al. that identifies chronic offenders as 6 percent of the Philadelphia 1945 Birth Cohort, overdramatizes the chronic-offender effect because many cohort members (about two-thirds of the 1945 Philadelphia Birth Cohort) will never be arrested. Instead, they urge that the ever-arrested subjects should be the base used to calculate the chronic-offender effect. These researchers also argued, based on evidence presented in Blumstein and Moitra (1980), that the proportion of chronic offenders observed by Wolfgang et al. (1972) could have resulted from a homogeneous population of persisters. Blumstein and Moitra (1980) tested the hypothesis that all persisters (those with three or more arrests) could be viewed as having the same re-arrest probability. Such an assumption could not be rejected. Although those with five or more arrests accounted for the majority of arrests among the persisters, such a result could have occurred even if all subjects with three or more arrests had identical recidivism probabilities (Blumstein et al., 1985:189). Thus, the chronic offenders who were identified retrospectively as those with five or more arrests could not have been distinguished prospectively from below-chronics, with three or four arrests, and never were distinguished in any analyses of the cohort.

Given this concern, we set out to examine recidivism probabilities in the CSDD through age 40 in order to determine if those with five or more

---

[6] Recall that incarceration spells were exceedingly rare in the CSDD.

Table 9.5. *Recidivism Probabilities CSDD Through the First 10 Convictions*

| Offense Number | Recidivism Probability | |
|---|---|---|
| 1 | 0.399 (164/411) | |
| 2 | 0.682 (112/164) | |
| 3 | 0.696 (78/112) | |
| 4 | 0.820 (64/78) | |
| 5 | 0.828 (53/64) | |
| 6 | 0.830 (44/53) | 84.5%[a] |
| 7 | 0.840 (37/44) | |
| 8 | 0.891 (33/37) | |
| 9 | 0.909 (30/33) | |
| 10 | 0.800 (24/30) | |

[a]Average between 4 and 10.

convictions (based on the five-plus chronic-offender designation) were a relatively more homogeneous group of chronic offenders or whether the numeric designation of 5 is problematic in the CSDD data.

Recidivism probabilities through the first 10 convictions are found in Table 9.5. As can be seen, the recidivism probabilities begin at .399 (the prevalence of offending in the CSDD) and jump quickly (because of the large proportion of one-time offenders who do not recidivate) to .682 for offense two, as expected. Between offense two and three, the recidivism probability stays in the 60 percent range, at which point it evinces a large increase at offense four, where the recidivism probability is .82. After offense four, the recidivism probabilities increase very slowly and are quite stable, only to decrease slightly at offense 10 (.80). Because the recidivism probabilities are very close and based on a small number of individuals, we conclude that beginning at offense four, the recidivism probabilities are quite stable and can be seen to reflect a homogeneous group of persisters (with an average recidivism probability of 84.5 percent). Figure 9.2 graphically presents this information. The recidivism probabilities, especially the flattening and stability of recidivism beginning at offense four, are quite clear here and confirm the benefit from partitioning the persister population.

The observed difference between a recidivism probability of .69 (at conviction three) and .82 (at conviction four) may appear small, but it can make an appreciable difference to the amount of subsequent offending.

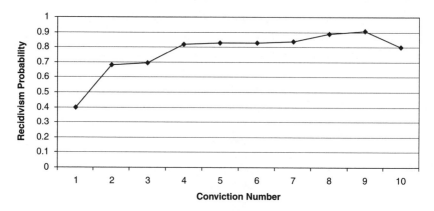

**Figure 9.2.** Recidivism Probabilities – CSDD


This effect is highlighted by a focus on the probability of *non*-recidivism, which is reduced from .31 to .18. For the geometric distribution, the expected number of future convictions after any given conviction from the third conviction onward is $q/(1-q)$, so that if q=.696, then each persister can expect to experience an additional 2.289 convictions; if the recidivism probability is .82, however, the expected number of future convictions is 4.55, which is 98 percent ((4.55–2.289)/2.289) larger.

In short, this brief analysis of the recidivism probabilities in the CSDD indicates that (1) there is a rapidly increasing probability of recidivism through the first few (three or four) involvements with the law; and (2) a higher but stable recidivism rate for subsequent involvement – at least 80 percent (averaging 84.5 percent) – at and after the fourth conviction. This estimate is comparable to those obtained by Blumstein et al. (1985:192) for the Philadelphia 1945 Birth Cohort Study, where they found that the recidivism rate increased to about 80 percent between the sixth and seventh arrest, and to the 1942 Racine, WI, Birth Cohort, where Blumstein and colleagues (1985:194) found that the recidivism rate increased to about 88 percent between the fifth and sixth arrest. The rise in the observed aggregate recidivism probability, then, reflects the changing composition of the offenders at each stage of involvement; the desisters stop relatively early and so leave a residue composed increasingly of the high-recidivism persisters (see also Blumstein et al., 1985:216). From a policy perspective, these results suggest the possibility of early discrimination between the more serious and less serious offenders, and also "[endorse] the appropriateness of representing the typical observation of growth in recidivism probability with successive involvements with

Table 9.6. *Chronic-Offender Mean-Level Comparisons Using Recidivism Probability Detected Chronic-Offender Status as Four-Plus*

| Group | Mean Career Length | Mean Age at First Conviction | % Early Onset | % Violent Offender | Mean No. Violent Convictions |
|---|---|---|---|---|---|
| (1) One-timers | 0.00 | 22.52 | 5% | 13% | 0.13 |
| (2) Below-chronics | 6.02 | 17.60 | 14% | 27% | 0.29 |
| (3) Chronics (4+) | 13.73 | 14.92 | 39% | 50% | 0.93 |
| F-value | 92.28* | 25.44* | 11.84* | 9.36* | 13.63* |
| Tukey's B test | 1/2/3 | 1/2/3 | 3/1,2 | 3/1,2 | 3/1,2 |

*p > .05

the criminal justice system as a process involving a changing mix of a high- and low-recidivism group that is increasingly composed of the high-recidivism group" (Blumstein et al., 1985:217).

With this in hand, we decided to revisit our earlier analysis based on Wolfgang et al.'s arbitrary designation of the chronic offender as being an individual with five or more offenses. We alter this designation, based on the objective recidivism probabilities shown above, to four or more offenses and repeat the analysis comparing key criminal career outcomes. The offender groups are represented as one-timers (n = 52), below-chronics (two or three offenses, n = 48), and chronics (four or more offenses, n = 64).

Table 9.6 presents a series of mean-level comparisons across the offender groups for a series of crime outcomes. As can be seen from this table, chronic offenders (using the four-plus designation) once again are significantly different from the other two offender groups. Chronics are more likely to have lengthier criminal careers (almost 14 years, on average), evince an earlier age at first conviction, be designated as "early onset," be a violent offender, and accumulate more violent offenses by age 40. Clearly, the probability of being a violent offender increases with the number of offenses. When we contrast the mean-level comparisons for chronics using the four-plus (Table 9.6) and the five-plus (Table 9.3) designations, the two groups appear very similar, as expected, with a slight tendency for the five-plus chronics to exhibit a slightly higher value on the outcomes. This suggests that the cut point between four and five convictions is not particularly sensitive.

As a further illustration of the longitudinal patterning of criminal activity among chronic offenders, we plotted the relationship between age and crime for those 64 offenders meeting the chronic-offender designation

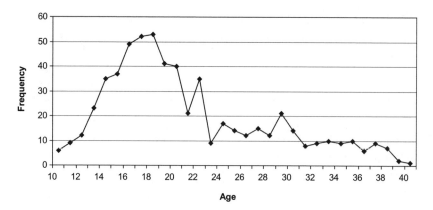

**Figure 9.3.** Relationship Between Age and Crime for Chronic Offenders (Defined as Four-Plus Convictions)

of four or more convictions. Figure 9.3 displays the common aggregate age/crime curve: As can be seen, it reproduces the classic depiction of the age/crime curve. Here, the peak number of convictions (53) among the 64 chronics is at age 18, followed by age 17 (52 convictions). Beginning at age 18, the number of convictions declines sharply, leveling off at about age 23 to a stable rate of about 10 per year.

Finally, we calculated $\lambda$ (using the number of offenses divided by the number of offenders at that age) for the 64 chronic offenders and plotted the age/lambda curve, the results of which may be found in Figure 9.4. Because of the erratic nature of some of the estimates, we also present the smoothed estimates in this figure. Here, it can be seen that $\lambda$ rises to a peak in the mid to late teens. It then begins to decrease in the early 20s and becomes fairly stable throughout much of the decade, hovering around 1.3–1.4 between ages 23 and 29. Beginning at about age 30, $\lambda$ steadily declines through age 40.

## Comment: Chronicity, Violence, Recidivism, and Age

Criminologists interested in the longitudinal patterning of criminal activity have consistently recognized that a small subset of individuals in any cohort (sample) is responsible for a large proportion of the group's criminal activity. In the past, researchers have designated those individuals with five or more offenses as "chronic." This definition of chronicity, however, is arbitrary, and it is unknown whether other definitions of chronicity, based on more-objective criteria, would identify the same

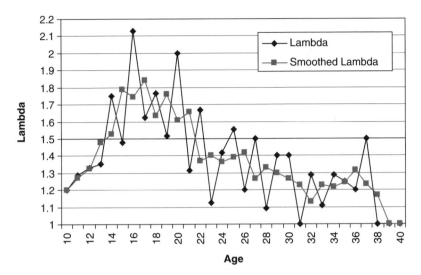

**Figure 9.4.** Lambda Estimates Among Chronics (Four-Plus Convictions)

individuals and/or lead to similar substantive conclusions. Fortunately, the CSDD provides a window through which to study the chronicity question and its dimensions.

Using the Wolfgang et al. conceptualization of chronicity (five or more offenses), we found that 12.89 percent of the full sample, or 32.3 percent of the offender sample, was responsible for 72.89 percent of the 760 convictions by age 40. When we examined and compared the degree of offense skewness in the CSDD data to other prominent longitudinal studies of crime over the life-course, we found that the effect of chronic offenders on the aggregate offense rate was more substantial in the CSDD compared to the other cohorts. Further, and as would be expected, the chronic offenders had longer criminal careers, were more likely to have an early onset, were more likely to have a later age at last conviction, were more likely to have committed a violent crime, and were more likely to have engaged in a wide variety of crimes. Finally, over half of the chronics accumulated their first five convictions in less than five years.

As an alternative to this more subjective approach to conceptualizing chronicity, we calculated the recidivism probabilities for the CSDD conviction data. Specifically, we found that the recidivism probabilities increased sharply through the first three convictions and then, beginning at conviction number four, the recidivism probability was stable at about 84.5 percent. Thus, we believe that those 64 individuals at offense number four and above could be considered a more appropriate and more homogeneous group of chronic offenders. Finally, among these 64 chronic offenders, λ was stable through age 20 and dropped somewhat until age 24, at which point it once again remained stable through the mid 30s and then began to decrease by age 40.

## Take-Home Messages

1 A small group of individuals is responsible for a large proportion of the offending activity.
2 The five-plus designation appears more arbitrary than a true reflection of the persister population in the CSDD. An inspection of recidivism probabilities indicates that four-plus is a better depiction of chronicity because at four-plus convictions the recidivism probability is reaching a fairly stable level, averaging 84.5 percent.
3 Chronics differ from all other offender groups (one-timers, below-chronics who incur two or three convictions) on most meaningful criminal career dimensions, including onset age and violence.

## Unanswered Questions

1 What are the factors that prospectively distinguish chronics from others?
2 Are the chronic offenders identified as those individuals with five or more convictions also identified as the highest-rate offenders using other methodologies, such as the trajectory methodology?
3 How should time be considered in a definition of chronicity?

# Trajectories of Offending

Are there distinct patterns of offending over time such that some individuals follow one course (e.g., peaking in adolescence and desisting as adulthood approaches) over another (e.g., peaking early in life, remaining active throughout life, and hardly desisting later in life)? Or is it the case that most offenders follow a similar path to offending such that it is unnecessary to postulate distinct patterns of offending and the theoretical and methodological complexity associated with them? Such questions strike at the heart of classic and contemporary criminological debates as well as policy discussions, options, and decisions.

One set of theorists claims that there are two different groups of offenders, each exhibiting a distinctive shape, peak, and pattern of offending over the life-course (e.g., Moffitt, 1993; Patterson, 1993). The first group is believed to be characterized by a very small number of individuals who evince an early onset of offending and a fairly flat trajectory of criminal activity throughout much of the life-course. These individuals offend early, offend more often while active, and are relatively unlikely to desist. A second group of offenders is believed to be characterized by a relatively large number of individuals who first engage in delinquent and criminal activity in their teenage years; however, at some point in their early adulthood these individuals curtail their offending activity and move on to more conventional adult patterns. The peak, shape, and patterning of these two groups of offenders, as well as the causal factors associated with membership in each group, are believed to be quite different from one another: One group mimics the age/crime curve, while the other deviates from it significantly. In short, the typological/developmental-friendly approach claims that the aggregate depiction of the age/crime curve does not hold at the individual level and instead indicates that there are heterogeneous and important subpopulations of offenders that are "masked" when aggregating the offending population and thinking of them as homogeneous.

A second set of theorists claims that aggregate depictions of the age/crime curve hold well for all offenders and that meaningful subpopulations of offenders are rare (Gottfredson and Hirschi, 1990). Thus, distinctions made within offender populations, especially those based on some sort of early/late-onset designation, are viewed as complicated and unnecessary because early and late starters all eventually desist and the causes of offending for both groups are viewed as more similar than different. In short, theorists critical of typological perspectives claim that the complexity necessitated by group-based models is unwarranted.

In an effort to sort out the validity of these claims, scholars have studied offending trajectories. A trajectory defines the developmental course of a behavior over age (or time). In criminology, trajectories of crime are longitudinal patterns of criminal activity, typically from birth to (ideally) death. Recently, there has been much interest in documenting these offending patterns as one way to assess the validity of the typological/general approaches to criminal activity over the life-course (see review in Piquero, 2005).

For example, early research on offending trajectories indicated that while the two-group pattern anticipated by some theories was found, other distinct offender groups emerged from offending data, thus challenging both the a priori two-group model and a strict one-group model (Nagin and Land, 1993). Other studies examined whether the same number of groups emerged across multiple data sets, and they again concluded that there were multiple trajectories of criminal activity (D'Unger et al., 1998). Sampson and Laub (2003) examined this issue using the world's longest longitudinal study, tracing the offending careers of five hundred Boston-area males between the ages of 7 and 70 who had been in a reformatory as juveniles. Their analysis indicated that although there could have been multiple types or groups of offenders, the common theme of the various groups was desistance. That is, there was little evidence of a flat trajectory when examining all offenses (though some evidence of a flat trajectory with regard to alcohol/drugs); and by age 60 or so, all offense trajectories approached 0. Ezell and Cohen (2005) used groups of three different serious youthful offender parolees from the California Youth Authority followed into the second and third decades of life to examine patterns of persistence/desistance. These authors found distinct offender trajectories, with different shapes and levels of offending after parole, but with the commonality that toward the end of the respective follow-up periods, most offending had either declined to 0 or was declining. On the other hand, Blokland et al. (2005), using Dutch offender data, found that a group termed "high-rate persisters" engaged in crime at a very substantial rate even after age 50.

In this chapter, we examine the offending trajectories of the 411 South London males between ages 10 and 40. Additionally, we also examine (1) how the emerging offender classes vary across a number of different criminal career dimensions, (2) whether the males identified as chronic in Chapter 10 are similarly identified as among the high-rate offenders in this chapter, and (3) whether individual and environmental risk factors distinguish between trajectories.

## Methods

To examine trajectories of offending in the CSDD data, we examined total convictions between ages 10 and 40.

## Data Analysis

Mixture, or group-based, models are useful for modeling unobserved heterogeneity in a population, especially in the case of criminal activity where it is believed that there are unobserved subpopulations differing in their parameter values over the life-course (Nagin, 2005). Although there are several software packages that allow for the estimation of trajectories, here we employ the group-based procedure developed by Nagin and Land (1993) and programmed into the SAS computer package by Jones and colleagues (2001). This procedure, referred to as PROC TRAJ, is available from the website of the National Consortium on Violence Research (www.ncovr.org).

Because we are dealing with count data, the Poisson model is potentially appropriate here; however, more zeros are present in the CSDD conviction data than would be expected in the purely Poisson model, so we use the zero-inflated poisson, or ZIP model (Jones et al., 2001:382). To evaluate model fit, we follow extant research and use the Bayesian Information Criterion (BIC). BIC – or the log-likelihood evaluated at the maximum likelihood estimate less one-half the number of parameters in the model times the log of the sample size (Schwarz, 1978) – tends to favor more-parsimonious models than likelihood ratio tests when used for model selection. For a given model, BIC is calculated as

$$\mathrm{BIC} = \log(L) - 0.5k\log(\mathrm{N}),$$

where $L$ is the value of the model's maximized likelihood, $N$ is the sample size, and $k$ is the number of parameters in the model, which is determined by the order of the polynomial used to model each trajectory and the number of groups (Nagin, 2005). Following previous research (D'Unger et al., 1998), we use an iterative procedure to identify meaningful groups. The approach we take is to begin with a one-group model and continue along the modeling space to two, three, four, five, and six groups, until we maximize the BIC.[1] We also examine trajectories using different types of polynomials (constant-only, linear, quadratic, and cubic) in order to determine which approach best characterizes the offending activity of the CSDD sample through age 40.[2] Our approach in this chapter is best viewed as descriptive: Are there meaningful subgroups in the CSDD, what do their offending trajectories look like, and how do they vary across criminal career dimensions?

## Results

We conducted a search of all possible models within the class for $k \leq 6$, and for four different polynomial orders (constant, linear, quadratic, cubic), thereby representing 24 different model procedures. The quadratic provided the best fit to the data. Table 10.1 gives the BIC values for the best-fitting models in the CSDD data using a number of different numbers of trajectory groups with quadratic fit. The BIC values indicate a substantial improvement in the model specification and fit to the data as the number of trajectories is increased from one to two. There are further improvements in the model fit as the number of latent classes is increased from two to three and so forth. The application of the BIC rule implies that the model with five latent classes should be chosen and further that there is strong evidence that the five-group quadratic model is the best five-group model considered.[3] It is important to note: "[B]ecause the

---

[1] According to D'Unger et al. (1998:1627), "This statistical criterion favors model parsimony by extracting a penalty for complicating a model (by adding parameters) that increases with the log of the sample size. Furthermore, this BIC (or Schwarz) criterion for model selection embodies the intuitive notion that, when the analyst complicates a model by adding parameters, the payoff in terms of a decrease in the log maximized-likelihood function of the model should be larger than this penalty."

[2] It is the case that various trajectory estimations can provide similarly reasonable fits to the data, be they cubic, quadratic, or mixed models. It is through the use of descriptive plots, the fit between actual and predicted values, as well as more formal criteria (e.g., BIC), that we arrive at our decision regarding the final set of trajectory estimations presented in the text.

[3] It is important to note here that previous trajectory analyses using the CSDD data through age 32 indicated that a four-group model provides the best fit to the data (Roeder et al., 1999). The addition of eight more years of conviction data, through age 40, indicates that this additional information provides more information for the model to better describe

Table 10.1. *BIC Values for Quadratic Trajectory Estimates*

| Number of Groups | Quadratic |
|---|---|
| 1 | − 2674.02 |
| 2 | − 2327.26 |
| 3 | − 2296.80 |
| 4 | − 2275.70 |
| 5 | − 2260.48* |
| 6 | −2268.39 |

*Best fit by BIC criterion

groups are intended as an approximation of a more complex underlying reality, the objective is not to identify the 'true' number of groups. Instead, the aim is to identify as simple a model as possible that displays the distinctive features of the population distribution of trajectories" (Nagin and Tremblay, 2005). In this regard, it is useful to think of the trajectories as clusters of similar individual trajectories, like cluster analysis, but in trajectory space.

## Offense Trajectories

To aid in the substantive interpretation of the nature of the trajectories of criminal careers identified and estimated in the CSDD data through age 40, the predicted conviction trajectories (i.e., predicted on the basis of estimated model parameters) for each of the five categories implied by the model are plotted in Figure 10.1a. Figure 10.1b contains the observed conviction trajectories for the five groups. Because it is easier to see the differences in the predicted conviction trajectories (due to smoothing), we focus our attention there in Figure 10.1a. We also present, in Figures 10.1c through 10.1g, the observed and predicted conviction trajectories for each of the five groups. Note the difference in scale on the y-axis (number of convictions) across the five groups; they vary widely according to the nature of offending evinced by the distinct groups.

distinct classes. The substance of this finding, according to Eggleston et al. (2004), is that with more data the groups become more finely converged (see also Nagin and Tremblay, 2005). We return to this point in more detail later in this chapter.

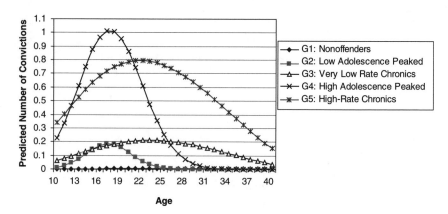

**Figure 10.1a.** Five-Group Predicted Conviction Trajectories

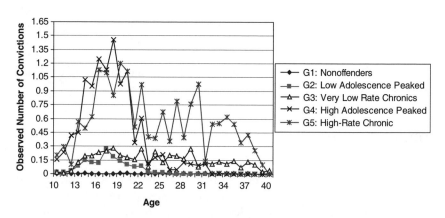

**Figure 10.1b.** Five-Group Observed Conviction Trajectories

There are five trajectories in this figure; and for ease of presentation, we provide labels for their description.[4] The first group, whom we label *nonoffenders*, represents 62.3 percent of the sample. These individuals exhibit virtually zero convictions across all ages.[5] The second group, *low adolescence peaked*, includes 18.6 percent of the sample and shows an

---

[4] These labels are not meant to reify the existence of these groups. We find it easier, however, to talk about these trajectory systems with descriptive names as opposed to abstract labels (i.e., group 1, group 2, etc.).

[5] Of course, there may be some individuals in this group who do have one or more convictions throughout the observation period; nevertheless, they more clearly resemble other individuals in this group as opposed to individuals in other offending groups.

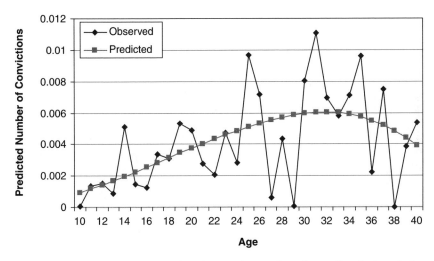

**Figure 10.1c.** Group 1 (Nonoffenders) Observed and Predicted Conviction Trajectories

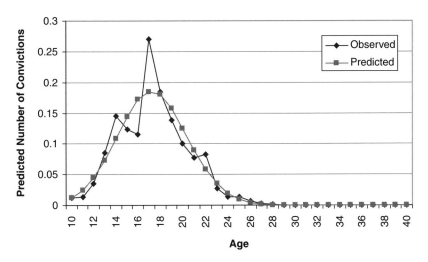

**Figure 10.1d.** Group 2 (Low Adolescence Peaked) Observed and Predicted Conviction Trajectories

increase of conviction rates during the early to mid adolescence period, only to be followed in late adolescence/early adulthood by a rapid decline toward zero convictions. In fact, by the early 20s these individuals exhibit virtually zero convictions through age 40. The third group, very low rate chronics, is represented by 11.3 percent of the sample and

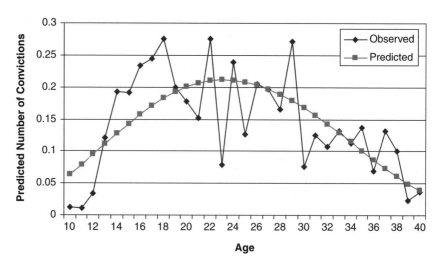

**Figure 10.1e.** Group 3 (Very Low Rate Chronics) Observed and Predicted Conviction Trajectories

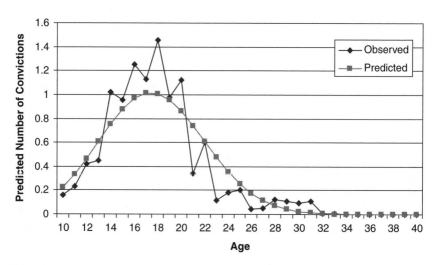

**Figure 10.1f.** Group 4 (High Adolescence Peaked) Observed and Predicted Conviction Trajectories

follows the same beginning and peak of conviction activity as the low adolescence peaked group; but while the latter group's conviction activity drops toward zero in the early 20s, the conviction activity of the very low rate chronics remains low but stable throughout the remainder of

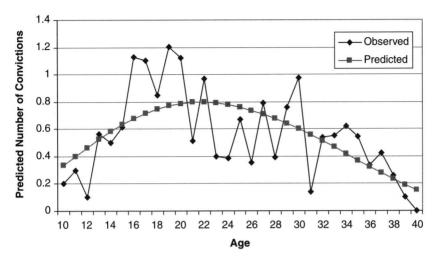

**Figure 10.1g.** Group 5 (High-Rate Chronics) Observed and Predicted Conviction Trajectories

the observation period until the very late 30s. The fourth group, high adolescence peaked, includes only 5.4 percent of the sample, but it exhibits the highest conviction rates throughout approximately the first half of the observation period (the first two decades of life). For this group of individuals, observed conviction rates, which are over 1.0 for several years, peak in the mid to late teenage years and then begin the classic rapid decline throughout the late 20s and early 30s. For these individuals, it is not until about the mid 30s that conviction rates approach zero. The fifth and final group, high-rate chronics, comprises about 2.5 percent of the sample. The conviction rate for this group, however, is quite different from the other four groups. For members of this trajectory group, the overall shape and level is similar to the high adolescence peaked; however, for the high-rate chronics, conviction rates remain quite high in the 20s and throughout most of the 30s. Thus, their offending activity is relatively high and stable throughout much of the observation period.[6]

For ease of presentation, Figure 10.2 also presents the total number of convictions at each age for the eight males in the high-rate chronic group. As can be seen, these eight males accumulated 152 of the 760 total convictions in the data set. At age 19, all eight men offended, accumulating

[6] Across all trajectory systems, by about age 40 offending is minimal.

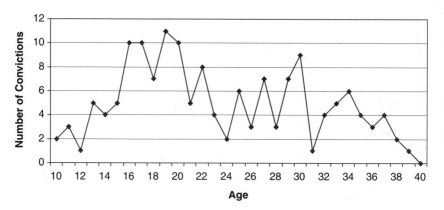

**Figure 10.2.** Total Number of Convictions for High-Rate Chronics

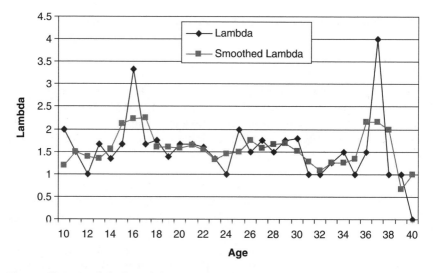

**Figure 10.3.** Lambda for High-Rate Chronics.
*Note:* The λ at age 40 is equal to 0 because there were no offenders nor offenses at this age among the high-rate chronics.

11 convictions at that age. It is only around the mid 30s that the conviction frequency declines. Figure 10.3 also displays the average λ (and a smoothed λ) for the eight males, and not surprisingly, λ is quite high among this small, select group of males and especially stable throughout much of the observation period.

In short, these findings support some of the common developmental taxonomies indicating an adolescence-peaked group whose offending declines with adulthood and a second group whose offending is chronic and stable throughout much of the observation period. At the same time, other distinctive developmental trajectories are identified that suggest that more than two groups are needed to characterize the offending careers of this sample, thereby calling into question a strict two-group offender typology.

## Model Estimates and Posterior Probability Assignments

In Table 10.2, we present the parameter estimates for the selected model. Additionally, for each individual we computed the maximum posterior membership probabilities. The results for the group average are found in Table 10.3. Specifically, we follow the model's ability to sort individuals into the trajectory group to which they have the highest probability of belonging (the "maximum probability" procedure). Based on the model coefficient estimates, the probability of observing each individual's longitudinal pattern of offending is computed, conditional on his being, respectively, in each of the latent classes. The individual is assigned to the group to which he has the highest probability of belonging. For example, an individual with a cluster of offenses in adolescence will more than likely be assigned to one of the adolescence-peaked classes. This procedure, of course, does not guarantee perfect assignments (i.e., posterior probability assignments equal to 1.0 for each individual).

The mean assignment probability for each group is quite high, suggesting that the large majority of individual trajectories can be classified to a particular group trajectory with high probability. For example, for group 1 (nonoffenders), the mean posterior probability was .91; for group 2, the mean posterior probability was .80; for group 3 (very low rate chronics), it was .84 (median = .89); for group 4 (high adolescence peaked), it was .91 (median = .98); and for group 5 (high-rate chronics), it was .98 (median = .99). In general, it is clear that the model has little ambiguity when making these assignments, but the greatest ambiguity is associated with the low adolescence peaked class (group 2), where the mean probability is .80.[7] Other studies in the trajectory research tradition

---

[7] The median assignment probabilities in this study are somewhat higher when compared to an investigation by Roeder et al. (1999) using the CSDD data through age 32. At least two of their median posterior probabilities were under .80, and some probabilities were under .70

Table 10.2. *Parameter Estimates and Group Assignment Probabilities*

| Group | Parameter | Estimate | SE | T |
|---|---|---|---|---|
| 1 | Intercept | −4.791 | 0.369 | −12.950 |
|   | Linear | 0.39 | 0.508 | 0.769 |
|   | Quadratic | −0.085 | 0.607 | −0.140 |
| 2 | Intercept | −8.227 | 2.824 | −2.913 |
|   | Linear | −11.463 | 4.757 | −2.410 |
|   | Quadratic | −4.678 | 1.949 | −2.400 |
| 3 | Intercept | −1.372 | 0.248 | −5.532 |
|   | Linear | −0.412 | 0.350 | −1.176 |
|   | Quadratic | −0.284 | 0.339 | −0.839 |
| 4 | Intercept | −2.829 | 0.607 | −4.661 |
|   | Linear | −5.282 | 0.895 | −5.902 |
|   | Quadratic | −2.095 | 0.439 | −4.762 |
| 5 | Intercept | −0.097 | 0.234 | −0.416 |
|   | Linear | −0.426 | 0.287 | −1.484 |
|   | Quadratic | −0.185 | 0.314 | −0.59 |
|   | Alpha0 | −0.873 | 0.679 | −1.286 |
|   | Alpha1 | 0.576 | 0.575 | 1.002 |
|   | Alpha2 | 0.748 | 0.676 | 1.106 |
| BIC |  | −2260.485 (n = 411) | | |
| **Group Membership** | | | | |
| 1 | (%) | 62.297 | 5.019 | 12.412 |
| 2 | (%) | 18.574 | 4.505 | 4.123 |
| 3 | (%) | 11.282 | 2.489 | 4.532 |
| 4 | (%) | 5.388 | 1.300 | 4.143 |
| 5 | (%) | 2.457 | 0.937 | 2.622 |

have also yielded, at times, somewhat low group probabilities for certain offender classes (see Roeder et al., 1999).

## Summary Statistics

Table 10.4 reports summary statistics on the offending trajectories displayed in Figure 10.1, including the predicted mean offending rate; the predicted rates at ages 10, 18, 25, and 40; the minimum and maximum rates; and the age at the maximum rate. Overall, the predicted mean

for the first (25th) quartile. It may be that, among other reasons, the addition of eight more years of conviction data led to these differences.

Table 10.3. *Posterior Probabilities for Group Assignments: Mean (Median)*

| Group | Prob. (G1) | Prob. (G2) | Prob. (G3) | Prob. (G4) | Prob. (G5) | 25th Percentile | 75th Percentile |
|---|---|---|---|---|---|---|---|
| 1 Nonoffenders (n = 271) | .91 (.91) | .07 (.07) | .01 (.00) | .00 (.00) | .00 (.00) | .91 | .91 |
| 2 Low adolescence peaked (n = 67) | .10 (.04) | .80 (.79) | .07 (.03) | .01 (.00) | .00 (.00) | .70 | .94 |
| 3 Very low rate chronics (n = 44) | .04 (.00) | .04 (.00) | .84 (.89) | .03 (.00) | .03 (.00) | .72 | .98 |
| 4 High adolescence peaked (n = 21) | .00 (.00) | .01 (.00) | .03 (.00) | .91 (.98) | .03 (.00) | .85 | .99 |
| 5 High-rate chronics (n = 8) | .00 (.00) | .00 (.00) | .00 (.00) | .00 (.00) | .98 (.99) | .99 | 1.00 |

*Note:* Minimum and maximum values presented for the group/prob(group) combination

offending rate is lowest for group 1 (nonoffenders), and increases for each of the succeeding groups to a maximum mean predicted offending rate of 0.562 for the high-rate chronics (group 5).

Even at age 10, the groups already appear distinguishable on offending, with the high adolescence peaked and high-rate chronic groups exhibiting predicted offending rates >.2. At ages 10, 18, 25, and 40, the results indicate that with one exception (group 1, nonoffenders), the predicted offending rate increases between ages 10 and 18, as would be expected. Between ages 18 and 25, however, the predicted rate of offending is not homogeneous across the groups. For the low adolescence peaked group (group 2, comprising 18.6 percent of the sample), the predicted offending rate decreases from .179 to .009, or almost 95 percent; and for the high adolescence peaked group, the group that had the highest peak in mid/late adolescence, the predicted rate of offending decreases from 1.009 to .254, or about 75 percent. For the very low rate chronic and the high-rate chronic groups, however, the predicted rates of offending between ages 18 and 25 are increasing. Between ages 25 and 40, all four offending groups (excluding group 1, nonoffenders) saw their predicted rate of offending decrease, especially the very low rate chronic (which decreased from .207 to .038, or about 81 percent) and the high adolescence peaked (which decreased from .254 to .000) groups. Finally, while the offending rate of the high-rate chronic group decreased from .760 to .153 between ages 25 and 40, it still had a nonzero offending rate at age 40.

A few other observations from Table 10.4 are worthy of attention. First, the minimum predicted rate of offending of the high-rate chronic group is .153, while all other offender groups started at .000 at age 10 or, in the case

Table 10.4. *Summary Characteristics of Offending Groups*

| Group | Predicted Mean Offending Rate | Predicted Offending Rate – Age 10 | Predicted Offending Rate – Age 18 | Predicted Offending Rate – Age 25 | Predicted Offending Rate – Age 40 | Min. Offending Rate | Max. Offending Rate | Age at Maximum Offending Rate |
|---|---|---|---|---|---|---|---|---|
| 1 Nonoffenders | .004 | .009 | .003 | .005 | .003 | .000 | .006 | 32 |
| 2 Low adolescence peaked | .046 | .011 | .179 | .009 | .000 | .000 | .185 | 17 |
| 3 Very low rate chronics | .143 | .064 | .182 | .207 | .038 | .038 | .211 | 23 |
| 4 High adolescence peaked | .353 | .227 | 1.009 | .254 | .000 | .000 | 1.013 | 17 |
| 5 High-rate chronics | .562 | .338 | .748 | .760 | .153 | .153 | .796 | 22 |

of the very low rate chronic group, the still low .038. Second, with regard to the maximum predicted rates of offending, the high adolescence peaked and high-rate chronic groups evince maximum rates over .50, with the high adolescence peaked group exhibiting the largest maximum rate of 1.013. While the maximum rate of the high adolescence peaked group is the highest, their offending is concentrated (and peaking) in the late teenage years. The shape of offending for this group closely resembles aggregate depictions of the age/crime curve. Third, the age at the maximum rate varies across the groups as well. Although they certainly differ in their degree of offending, the low adolescence peaked and high adolescence peaked groups peak at age 17. The very low rate chronic group, whose offending rate is low but quite stable over much of the observation period, peaks at age 23 (.211), while the high-rate chronic group peaks at age 22 (.796). Fourth, the predicted offending rates of the high adolescence peaked and high-rate chronic groups are quite similar at age 10; at age 18, the high adolescence peaked group has a higher rate (1.009), but by age 25 the predicted rate of offending for this group has decreased to .254, while for the high-rate chronics it has remained relatively flat between ages 18 and 25 (.748 and .760, respectively). Further, the predicted rate of offending for the high-rate chronic group remains above .5 from age 13 to 32, and this group (along with the very low rate chronic group) does not reach its minimum predicted offending rate until age 40, the last age of observation in the CSDD.

In short, the predicted rates of offending among the groups vary over the observation period. The groups evince different minimum and maximum rates, as well as ages at the maximum rate. Further, while the maximum rate of one group of offenders may be higher than another, it does not necessarily follow that their pattern of offending is long-lived. In fact, the offending of the high adolescence peaked group, with the highest predicted offending rate, was not long-lived. These individuals resemble closely the aggregate age/crime curve, with a sharp rise in adolescence, a high peak in late adolescence, and then a decline to very low rates of offending in early adulthood.[8] Other offender groups do not peak during adolescence and instead evince fairly stable offending rates throughout much of the observation period.

## Offending Classes and Criminal Career Dimensions

Table 10.5 compares the mean values of 12 important criminal career dimensions of the members of each of the five groups: (1) the percentage

---

[8] Some readers will observe that the offending rate of this group closely matches Moffitt's (1993) adolescence-limited offender typology.

of all cohort members in each group, (2) the total number of convictions, (3) the average number of convictions per group member, (4) the percentage of all the cohort's offenses committed by individuals in the group, (5) the average career length measured as the time between first and last conviction, (6) the mean age at first conviction, (7) the mean age at last conviction, (8) the proportion of individuals in the group who were violent offenders, (9) the total number of violent convictions, (10) the percentage of all the cohort's violent offenses committed by individuals in the group, (11) the mean number of total co-offenders throughout the careers of individuals in the group, and (12) the percentage of individuals in the group who were ever incarcerated.

As can be seen from this table, the groups vary across most variables in important (and expected) ways. Across most comparisons, the non-offender group has, as expected, the fewest number of offenses, has the shortest career length, has the latest age at first conviction, and is the least likely to be incarcerated. The low adolescence peaked group is more similar to the nonoffender group than to the other three offender classes, and in general it evinces more offending and more risk than the non-offenders on the other offending measures displayed in Table 10.5. The very low rate chronic, high adolescence peaked, and high-rate chronic groups deserve more commentary.

Recall that the very low rate chronic group (11.3 percent of the sample) evinces a low but fairly stable rate of offending throughout much of the observation period. Individuals in this group were responsible for over 28 percent of the sample's offenses, for a total of 215 convictions by age 40 and with an average of 4.88 convictions per group member. Additionally, individuals in this group had an average career length of 14 years and were 32 years old, on average, at their last conviction.

As shown earlier, the high adolescence peaked group – 21 members and 5.4 percent of the CSDD cohort – closely resembles the classic depiction of the age/crime curve. Individuals in this small group were responsible for 31.84 percent of all cohort offenses, accumulated 242 total convictions by age 40, and had an average number of 11.52 convictions by age 40. On average, individuals in this class had career lengths of about 10.84 years, exhibited their first conviction at age 13, and were, on average, 24 years old at their last conviction.[9]

Finally, the eight individuals in the high-rate chronic group, who represented about 2.5 percent of all cohort members, accumulated 152

---

[9] Some readers may observe that the percentages found in the figure do not perfectly coincide with the number of individuals in each group. This is normal. With sample sizes of at least one hundred individuals, they should be close, but they will almost never be exactly the same.

Table 10.5. *Offending Groups and Criminal Career Dimensions*

| Variable | Group 1 Nonoffenders (n = 271) | Group 2 Low Adolescence Peaked (n = 67) | Group 3 Very Low Rate Chronics (n = 44) | Group 4 High Adolescence Peaked (n = 21) | Group 5 High-Rate Chronics (n = 8) |
|---|---|---|---|---|---|
| Cohort members (%) | 62.3 | 18.6 | 11.3 | 5.4 | 2.5 |
| Total No. of convictions | 27.0 | 124.0 | 215.0 | 242.0 | 152.0 |
| Average No. of convictions | 0.099 | 1.850 | 4.886 | 11.523 | 19.000 |
| Cohort offenses (%) | 3.55 | 16.31 | 28.28 | 31.84 | 20.0 |
| Mean career length (yrs) | 0.328 | 1.714 | 14.524 | 10.849 | 22.325 |
| Mean age at first conviction | 30.79 | 16.40 | 17.18 | 13.00 | 13.00 |
| Mean age at last conviction | 31.468 | 18.600 | 32.329 | 24.401 | 35.753 |
| Violent offender (%) | 0.022 | 0.134 | 0.477 | 0.428 | 0.875 |
| Total No. of violent convictions | 6.0 | 9.0 | 30.0 | 16.0 | 20.0 |
| Cohort violent offenses (%) | 7.40 | 11.11 | 37.03 | 19.75 | 24.69 |
| Total No. of co-offenders (mean) | 0.958 | 2.283 | 4.204 | 13.809 | 14.375 |
| Incarcerated at any time (%) | 0.007 | 0.029 | 0.090 | 0.619 | 0.875 |

Table 10.6. *Cross-Tabulation of Trajectory Class Membership and Chronic Offender Designation Using Recidivism Based Probability (4 +, n = 64) and Wolfgang et al. 5 + Designation for Chronic Offender (n = 53)*

|  | Group 1 Nonoffenders | Group 2 Low Adolescence Peaked | Group 3 Very Low Rate Chronics | Group 4 High Adolescence Peaked | Group 5 High-Rate Chronics |
|---|---|---|---|---|---|
| Chronics (5 +) | 0 | 3 | 21 | 21 | 8 |
| Chronics (4 +) | 0 | 5 | 30 | 21 | 8 |

convictions by age 40 and had, on average, 19 convictions each. These eight men accumulated about 20 percent of all cohort offenses. Additionally, individuals in this group had career lengths of about 22 years, were 13 years old at their first conviction, and were about 35 years old at their last conviction. Further, almost every individual in this group was a violent offender, the eight men accumulating almost one-quarter of all violent convictions in the cohort. Further, 87.5 percent of them were incarcerated at least once during the study period. Lastly, members of this group averaged the highest number of co-offenders.

It may be of interest to examine where the chronic offenders, discussed in Chapter 9, show up with regard to trajectory membership. Using the five-plus designation for chronic offenders, Table 10.6 tabulates the chronic offenders with respect to membership in each of the groups from the five-group trajectory model. Here, the 53 offenders are distributed across the four offender groups (there were no chronic offenders in the nonoffender group) in the following way: 3 were in group 2 (low adolescence peaked), 21 were in group 3 (very low rate chronic), 21 were in group 4 (high adolescence peaked), and 8 were in group 5 (high-rate chronic).

When we used the below-chronic-based chronic-offender designation of four-plus (Table 10.6), the 64 offenders were distributed across the trajectory classes in the following manner: 5 were in group 2 (low adolescence peaked), 30 were in group 3 (very low rate chronic), 21 were in group 4 (high adolescence peaked), and 8 were in group 5 (high-rate chronic).

From the trajectory-based analysis, the two groups that offended at the highest rates and for the longest periods of time were groups 3 and 5 (the very low rate and the high-rate chronics). The five-plus designation places 29/53 (54.71 percent) of the males in those two groups, while the four-plus designation places 38/64 (59.37 percent) of the males in those two groups. However, this also indicates that some of the chronic offenders did not offend for long periods of time and instead kept their high-offending activity contained to very short periods of time. The difference in the two models concerns groups 2 (low adolescence peaked) and 3 (very low rate chronics). Because there are more individuals in the four-plus chronic designation than there are in the five-plus chronic designation, it is likely that one by-product of this is that more individuals using the four-plus designation were placed in the very low rate chronic group than in the low adolescence peaked group. Thus, the four-plus designation is likely correctly placing the males with more offenses in the group that has more (and more stable) offending over the observation period.

In any event, while the four-plus designation places more individuals in the highest peak and stable offending groups, many chronics were identified to be in the high adolescence peak group, whose offending is short-lived and who peak in adolescence. This reinforces the point of considering both frequency and duration when studying chronicity. In our view, the trajectory method seems to be a better mechanism for identifying chronics than the arbitrary five-plus designation or even the recidivism-based four-plus designation. The trajectory method allows us to examine the shape, level, and patterning of chronic offenders over time, whereas the five-plus designation does not allow us to examine these issues at all. The "static" definition(s) of chronicity treat heterogeneous offenders as being more homogeneous than they really are (i.e., they are truly spread across four distinct offender trajectories). The comparisons in this section highlight the importance of describing patterns of behavior, in this case chronicity, over time as opposed to conceptualizing the phenomenon in an arbitrary manner.

## Age 33 to Age 40: A Comment

In prior CSDD analyses, Nagin and colleagues (D'Unger et al., 1998; Nagin et al., 1995; Roeder et al., 1999) identified four groups of latent classes through age 32 in the CSDD data. In the current study, with eight additional years of observation, through age 40, one additional latent class (for a total of five classes) emerged. Why is this the case?

One potential answer, among others, is that, because the number of groups and the shape of each group's trajectory are not fixed realities, both of these features of the trajectory model may be altered by the variety of information in the data set, including both the number of cases/individuals and the number of periods of observation (Nagin and Tremblay, 2005). And while the limited research undertaken on this issue seems to suggest that the number of trajectory groups in the preferred model does not change beyond a minimal threshold involving three hundred to five hundred cases, the length of the follow-up period does appear to matter. This occurs because a trajectory group is a cluster of individuals following a similar trajectory, and as more periods of data are added the cluster may split into subgroups following divergent trajectories (Nagin and Tremblay, 2005). This is especially the case for changes (desistance) in offending that occur in the 30s and beyond, when many criminal careers are winding down.

Between ages 33 and 40, there were a total of 72 convictions. Thus, out of the 760 total convictions, 10.78 percent of them occurred after age 32. These 72 convictions were distributed across the offending classes in the following manner: the nonoffender group had 12 convictions; the low adolescence peaked group had 0 convictions; the very low rate chronic group had 35 convictions; the high adolescence peaked group had 0 convictions, and the high-rate chronic group had 25 convictions. Clearly, the very low rate chronic and the high-rate chronic groups contributed much of the new conviction information after age 32 (60 of 72 new convictions). This is no surprise for by age 32 the predicted offending rates are small, except for the very low rate chronic group, whose predicted rate is still >.10, and the high-rate chronic group, whose predicted rate is still >.50, and both groups do not reach their minimums until the last observation age (40).

This discussion of the age-32 and (the current study's) age-40 analyses offers two important points. First, as stated earlier, the groups are not "immutable entities. They are instead statistical devices for summarizing key features of the data used in the analysis" (Nagin and Tremblay, 2005). Second, our analysis of the conviction records through age 40 shows that more data "allows for more refined statistical inferences" (Ibid.). The age-40 analysis, then, becomes an elaboration of previous analyses with the CSDD data that becomes possible with eight additional years of conviction data. The estimates from the current study, then, should not be used to suggest that all previous analyses with the CSDD data through age 32 are incorrect; to the contrary, the results of the current study are merely an extension of those previous results with additional years of information.

In short, these analyses show the importance of having as much and as long a set of data as possible for identifying and charting the natural history of offending, especially because "the phenomenon under study has yet to unfold entirely" (Nagin and Tremblay, 2005). That said, given the very low base rate of offending at ages 38–40 in the CSDD data, we anticipate that the substantive conclusions drawn in this study regarding the offending classes will likely hold with additional data collection efforts.

## Comment: What Are the Trajectories of Offending to Emerge from the CSDD?

Researchers have long been interested in charting the course of criminal activity over time. From early descriptive data on this issue, theorists developed theories that contain either a single or multiple pathways to offending. Recently, methodological and statistical techniques have caught up with extant theory and have developed approaches that allow researchers to better assess the strength of theorists' hypotheses. In this chapter, we examined the offending trajectories of the 411 South London males using conviction records from ages 10 to 40. Several important findings have emerged from our analyses.

First, recall that the best-fitting model was a five-group quadratic model. These five groups include: (1) nonoffenders (62.3 percent), who had very low and/or zero rates of offending over the observation period; (2) low adolescence peak (18.6 percent), who had very low rates of offending and a peak in adolescence; (3) very low rate chronics (11.3 percent), who had very low but stable rates of offending over the observation period; (4) high adolescence peak (5.4 percent), who had many offenses during the adolescent years and a peak at age 17 followed by a quick decline to (close to) zero rates of offending in early adulthood; and (5) high-rate chronics (2.5 percent), who offended at a fairly high and stable rate throughout the entire observation period.

Second, average posterior membership probability assignments were high, with all exceeding .80 and several exceeding .90. Probabilities were also quite high between the 25th (.70) and 75th (.91) percentiles. These findings indicate that individuals appear to be placed into the groups with a high degree of certainty.

Third, at age 10, the groups were already distinguishable on their offending rates. By age 21, several had already peaked, and by age 25 most were on the decline, except for the high-rate chronic group, whose offending was stable throughout much of this period. In fact, the high-rate chronic group attained its minimum predicted rate of offending at age 40, the last age of observation, and even then the predicted rate of offending was >.10.

Fourth, the five groups differed significantly from one another on a number of criminal career dimensions, including the number of convictions and the proportion of the cohort's total convictions, violent offending, and career length. In particular, the eight males who comprised the high-rate chronic group accumulated 152 convictions by age 40, a full 20 percent of the cohort's total offenses. Their career lengths were, on average, about 20 years, with an average age at first conviction of 13 and at last conviction of 35.

Fifth, when the trajectory-based group assignments were compared to the chronicity definitions utilized in Chapter 9, we found some similarities and some differences. Across both the four- and five-plus chronicity designations, most chronic offenders were placed into the most offense prone of the groups emerging from the trajectory-based analysis. At the same time, many offenders identified as chronic using the static definition constrained their offending activity to a very short time interval. This finding suggests that the richness of the trajectory methodology may be better suited to studying the chronicity issue because it does a better job of describing the shape, peak, and patterning of criminal activity over time. As such, the trajectory approach can assess both frequency and time when studying the chronicity issue.

Finally, we compared the results obtained from this study of the conviction records to age 40 to those to age 32 obtained in previous research using the CSDD conviction data. The eight additional years of conviction records were important to have because of an extra 72 convictions and also because this new information allows the groups to be better defined. Because longitudinal data are best for studying how a phenomenon develops, changes, and ceases over time, more information helps to provide a sharper portrait of the natural history of offending over age.

In short, the trajectories emerging from the CSDD data indicate the heterogeneity that exists in these individual trajectories. The results indicate that there appear to be distinct groups of offenders, whose shape, peak, and patterning of criminal activity vary over the life-course, and that the groups vary across a number of important criminal career dimensions.

## How Do the Groups Vary According to Risk Factors Measured at Ages 8–10?

In this section, we examine how the groups vary across a series of individual and environmental (e.g., parent, family, school) risk factors measured prior to involvement in criminal activity (ages 8–10). A major aim of the CSDD was to measure as many factors as possible that could be causes or correlates of offending. Psychologists (both male and female) interviewed and tested males in their schools when they were aged 8–9, 10–11, and 14–15. The school tests measured such individual characteristics as intelligence, attainment, personality, and psychomotor impulsivity. In addition to interviews and tests with the boys, interviews with their parents were carried out by female psychiatric social workers who visited their homes. These took place about once a year, from when the boy was about 8 until he was 14–15 and in his last year of compulsory education. The primary informant was the mother, although many fathers were also seen. The parents provided details about such matters as the boy's daring or nervousness, family income, family size, their employment histories, their history of psychiatric treatment, their child-rearing practices (including attitudes, discipline, and parental disharmony), their closeness of supervision of the boy, and his temporary or permanent separation from them. The teachers completed questionnaires when the boys were about 8, 10, 12, and 14, furnishing data about their troublesome and aggressive school behavior, their restlessness and poor concentration, their school achievement, and their truancy. Delinquency rates of secondary schools were obtained from the local education authority. Because the first conviction could not occur before age 10, we used only risk factors collected between ages 8 and 10 in order to preserve temporal ordering. The CSDD is fortunate to have collected a wide array of important variables related to particular patterns of criminal activity, especially those advanced by developmental criminologists.

Specifically, of the 27 different risk factors, 15 are environmental and 12 are individual. The environmental risk factors include: (1) harsh attitude/discipline of parents (age 10), (2) teen mother at birth of first child, (3) behavior problems of siblings (age 8), (4) criminal record of parent(s) (age 10), (5) delinquent older sibling(s) (age 10), (6) large family size (age 8), (7) poor housing (age 10), (8) low family income (age 8), (9) parental disharmony (age 8), (10) neurotic/depressed father (age 10), (11) neurotic/depressed mother (age 10), (12) low SES (age 10), (13) separated parents (age 10), (14) poor supervision (age 10), and (15) high delinquency rate of school (age 11). The individual risk factors included (1) junior school attainment (age 10), (2) daring disposition (age 10), (3) short height (age 10), (4) low nonverbal IQ (age 8), (5) nervous/withdrawn boy (age 10), (6) high extraversion (age 10), (7) high neuroticism (age 10), (8) psychomotor impulsivity (age 10), (9) dishonest (age 10), (10) unpopular (age 10), (11) troublesome (age 10), and (12) lacks concentration/restless (age 8). Coding for all risk factors was dichotomous: 1 = "ok," 2 = "bad," so that higher scores indicate presence of the particular risk factor.

We present several comparisons of the groups across these risk factors. First, we begin with an analysis of variance, where we compare the means of the risk factors identified above across the five groups to emerge from the trajectory analysis. Second, we estimate a series of logistic and multinomial logistic regression models, where we attempt to discriminate between group membership using the 27 risk factors. Third, we combine the environmental ($\alpha = .77$) and individual ($\alpha = .57$) risk factors into two separate constructs and examine how they discriminate between the groups. Finally, we sum up all the risk factors into an overall scale ($\alpha = .76$) to examine how the overall set of risk factors discriminates across groups.

Table 10.7. *Analysis of Variance Results for Risk Factors Across Group Membership: Percentages (%) Presented*

| Risk Factor | Group 1 Nonoffender | Group 2 Low Adol. Peaked | Group 3 Very LR Chron. | Group 4 High Adol. Peaked | Group 5 High-Rate Chronics | F-Test |
|---|---|---|---|---|---|---|
| *Environmental* | | | | | | |
| Harsh attitude/ discipline of parents | 25 | 23 | 39 | 65 | 75 | 6.53* |
| Teen mother | 18 | 22 | 34 | 42 | 50 | 3.82* |
| Behavior problems of siblings | 32 | 42 | 53 | 69 | 50 | 3.68* |
| Criminal record of parents | 18 | 37 | 43 | 42 | 87 | 10.43* |
| Delinquent older sibling | 07 | 12 | 14 | 48 | 25 | 9.10* |
| Large family size | 18 | 28 | 36 | 57 | 50 | 6.80* |
| Poor housing | 30 | 55 | 36 | 62 | 38 | 5.32* |
| Low family income | 18 | 22 | 27 | 67 | 50 | 8.27* |
| Parental disharmony | 19 | 34 | 33 | 37 | 38 | 2.86* |
| Neurotic father | 20 | 22 | 26 | 31 | 12 | 0.50 |
| Neurotic mother | 29 | 40 | 39 | 30 | 37 | 0.97 |

| | | | | | |
|---|---|---|---|---|---|
| Low SES | 18 | 16 | 18 | 38 | 50 | 2.65* |
| Separated parents | 15 | 30 | 41 | 24 | 63 | 6.86* |
| Poor supervision | 14 | 25 | 27 | 37 | 50 | 3.95* |
| High delinquency rate school | 15 | 24 | 32 | 50 | 33 | 5.14* |
| *Individual* | | | | | | |
| Junior school attainment | 16 | 28 | 35 | 79 | 25 | 12.33* |
| Daring disposition | 21 | 39 | 45 | 62 | 75 | 9.79* |
| Short height | 15 | 21 | 15 | 38 | 37 | 2.50* |
| Low nonverbal IQ | 19 | 30 | 36 | 57 | 50 | 6.18* |
| Nervous/withdrawn | 27 | 13 | 29 | 25 | 00 | 2.32* |
| High extraversion | 27 | 31 | 31 | 33 | 50 | 0.67 |
| High neuroticism | 27 | 31 | 34 | 38 | 25 | 0.48 |
| Psychomotor impulsivity | 21 | 30 | 27 | 52 | 63 | 4.62* |
| Dishonest | 19 | 28 | 43 | 47 | 63 | 5.64* |
| Unpopular | 29 | 34 | 38 | 47 | 63 | 1.88 |
| Troublesome | 14 | 28 | 34 | 71 | 75 | 16.86* |
| Lacks concentration/restless | 15 | 16 | 30 | 57 | 37 | 6.82* |

*p < .05

The analysis of variance results, partialed by environmental/individual risk factors and group membership, are presented in Table 10.7. For ease of presentation, we show the percentage of each group possessing the risk factor. As can be seen, for all but two of the environmental risk factors and all but three of the individual risk factors, there are significant differences across the five groups. Overall, two main findings emerge from this analysis. First, groups 4 (high adolescence peaked) and 5 (high-rate chronics) evidence more of the risk factor across both the environmental and individual domains when compared to the other three groups. In other words, a higher percentage of individuals in groups 4 and 5 possess the risk factors displayed in Table 10.7. Second, there is no clear pattern as to whether one of these two groups (especially the high-rate chronic group) evinces more of a risk factor than the other group; however, the trend was in that direction, especially for the individual risk factors that would be expected to differentiate among offenders (such as impulsivity, daring disposition, troublesome, etc.).

Next, we present a series of logistic regression models, where we compare the ability of the 27 risk factors to differentiate among the offender groups.[10] Before we examine the differences among the offender groups, we present a baseline comparison between the nonoffenders (group 1) and the other offender groups combined (groups 2–5). Because inserting all 27 risk factors into a single model will greatly affect the regression estimates due to multicollinearity, we present the results of a forward stepwise logistic regression model, using the Forward: Wald procedure. These results may be found in Table 10.8.

As would be expected, a number of variables appear to discriminate between offenders and nonoffenders. For example, in step 1, one environmental risk factor, criminal record of parents, significantly discriminated between offenders and nonoffenders. Specifically, nonoffenders were less likely to have parents who had a criminal record. In step 2, criminal record of parents retained significance, but the individual risk factor, daring disposition, also emerged as significant, indicating that it was predictive of being an offender. Results from step 3 carried forward the significant effects of the criminal record of parents and the boy's daring disposition, and a third variable, the individual risk factor of junior school attainment, emerged as a significant predictor, indicating that boys who did not attain junior school were more likely to be

---

[10] Originally, we estimated a multinomial logistic regression model, where we estimated the effect of the 27 risk factors on the various comparisons of group memberships. Unfortunately, given the low sample size in some of the groups and the large number of risk factors examined, the results were not stable. Therefore, we decided to only present the single logistic regression results where we differentiate among two groups at a time.

Table 10.8. *Logistic Regression Analysis Discriminating Between Nonoffenders vs. Offenders (Forward Stepwise: Wald). Significant Effects Only*

| Variable | Step 1 B(SE) | Exp(B) | Step 2 B(SE) | Exp(B) | Step 3 B(SE) | Exp(B) | Step 4 B(SE) | Exp(B) | Step 5 B(SE) | Exp(B) |
|---|---|---|---|---|---|---|---|---|---|---|
| *Environmental* | | | | | | | | | | |
| Criminal record of parents | 1.21 (.29)* | 3.36 | 1.13 (.30)* | 3.12 | 1.05 (.30)* | 2.86 | 0.94 (.31)* | 2.56 | 0.87 (.31)* | 2.40 |
| Poor housing | | | | | | | | | .65 (.29)* | 1.91 |
| *Individual* | | | | | | | | | | |
| Junior school attainment | | | | | 1.06 (.33)* | 2.91 | 1.08 (.33)* | 2.95 | 1.07 (.34)* | 2.92 |
| Daring disposition | | | 1.05 (.28)* | 2.87 | 1.05 (.29)* | 2.87 | 0.92 (.30)* | 2.52 | 0.85 (.30)* | 2.35 |
| Dishonest | | | | | | | 0.77 (0.32)* | 2.15 | 0.74 (.32)* | 2.10 |
| −2LL | 344.02 | | 330.5 | | 319.95 | | 314.20 | | 309.19 | |
| Nagelkerke $R^2$ | 0.086 | | 0.148 | | 0.194 | | 0.218 | | 0.239 | |

All models include constant. *p < .05.

offenders. In step 4, aside from the three previous risk factors, the individual risk factor of dishonesty emerged as a positive, a significant risk factor for offenders compared to nonoffenders. Finally, in step 5, an additional environmental risk factor, poor housing, was predictive of being an offender. In short, the forward stepwise logistic regression analysis indicated that two environmental risk factors – criminal record of parents and poor housing – and three individual risk factors – daring disposition, dishonesty, and junior school attainment – successfully discriminated between offenders and nonoffenders.[11]

When we attempted to estimate logistic regression models discriminating between each of the offender groups using the 27 risk factors, we were unsuccessful because of the very low sample sizes in the offender groups and the high number of correlated risk factors to be considered, a problem that has plagued similar lines of research (see Laub and Sampson, 2003). To circumvent this problem, we decided to collapse the 15 environmental factors into a scale, the 12 individual factors into a scale, and all 27 risk factor items into one overall scale and then used these three scales to discriminate among the offender groups. For all three scales, we counted the occurrences of each risk factor; this, then, provided us with a count of the number of each respective risk factor, within the more general domain of risk, for which to make between-group comparisons. An analysis of variance for each of the three risk composites was significant. With regard to the environmental risk factor composite (range 0–13), the respective mean scores were as follows: (1) nonoffenders, mean = 2.87, (2) low adolescence peaked, mean = 4.19, (3) very low rate chronics, mean = 4.61, (4) high adolescence peaked, mean = 6.66, and (5) high-rate chronics, mean = 7.00. As expected, with increasing offending rates and levels there is a corresponding higher average number of risk factors for the environmental risk factor composite, and this result was significant (F=17.16, p < .05). Turning to the individual risk factor composite (range 0–10), which was significantly different across the five groups (F = 21.59, p < .05), the corresponding group averages were (1) nonoffenders, mean = 2.42, (2) low adolescence peaked, mean = 3.22, (3) very low rate chronics, mean = 3.79, (4) high adolescence peaked, mean = 5.66, and (5) high-rate chronics, mean = 5.62. Finally, with regard to the overall (environmental and individual risk) composite (range 0–22), once again the analysis of variance was significant (F = 27.63, p < .05). The specific group averages were

[11] A full logistic regression model containing all 27 risk factors was also estimated, and these results showed the same five variables cited above to be significant discriminators between offenders and nonoffenders.

Table 10.9. *Logistic Regression Discriminating Between Groups 2–5*
*(Offenders) and Group 1 (Nonoffenders)*

| Variable | B | SE(B) | Exp(B) |
|---|---|---|---|
| Risk factor composite | −0.21 | 0.03* | 0.80 |
| Constant | 7.97 | 0.03 | |
| Model chi-square/df | 42.20/1 | | |
| Nagelkerke R-square | 0.20 | | |

*p < .05

(1) nonoffenders, mean = 5.30, (2) low adolescence peaked, mean = 7.41, (3) very low rate chronics, mean = 8.40, (4) high adolescence peaked, mean = 12.33, and (5) high-rate chronics, mean = 12.62.

Taking this one step further, we take our risk composite score and assess whether it can discriminate between nonoffenders and offenders, as well as among the offender trajectories. In Table 10.9, we estimate a logistic regression model to sort between offenders and nonoffenders and find that, as expected, individuals scoring high on the risk factor composite are significantly less likely to be in the nonoffender group. Next, we estimate a multinomial logistic regression model where we examine the effect of the risk factor composite across the five trajectory groups (see Table 10.10). In this model estimation, the reference group is group 5 (high-rate chronics). We expect that membership in groups 1 through 4 (not including group 5, high-rate chronics) will have lower risk factor composite scores, and the results provide support for this hypothesis (excluding group 4, high adolescence peaked). High scores on the risk factor composite are associated with a lower likelihood of membership in each of the four groups compared to the high-rate chronic group. In other words, individuals in the high-rate chronic group score higher on the risk factor composite compared to three of the other four groups. In this multinomial logistic regression model, the risk factor composite does not appear able to distinguish between individuals in groups 4 (high adolescence peaked) and 5 (high-rate chronics).[12]

Next, we estimate a series of logistic regression models where we use the risk factor composite to discriminate between two of the offender

---

[12] We also estimate this same model in a different fashion, using nonoffenders as the reference category. As would be expected, the risk factor composite score was positively and significantly correlated with membership in each of the four offender groups compared to membership in the nonoffender group.

Table 10.10. *Multinomial Logistic Regression Discriminating Among Five Offender Trajectories (Reference Group is Group 5, High-Rate Chronics)*

| Variable | Group 1 Nonoffenders B/SE(B) EXP(B) | Group 2 Low Peaked Adol. B/SE(B) EXP(B) | Group 3 Very Low Rate Chronics B/SE(B) EXP(B) | Group 4 High Adol. Peaked B/SE(B) EXP(B) |
|---|---|---|---|---|
| Risk factor Composite | −0.56/0.12* (0.56) | −0.40/0.12* (0.66) | −0.37/0.12*(0.68) | −0.16/0.12 (0.84) |
| Constant | 24.27/5.13* | 17.57/5.11* | 15.61/5.24* | 7.31/5.26 |
| Model Chi-square/df | 64.56/4 | | | |
| Nagelkerke R-square | 0.24 | | | |

*$p < .05$

groups, repeating this analysis for all potential comparisons. These results are found in Table 10.11.

In the top portion of the table, group 2 (low adolescence peaked) is compared to groups 3 (very low rate chronics), 4 (high adolescence peaked), and 5 (high-rate chronics). The risk factor composite is unable to discriminate between groups 2 and 3 but is able to do so between groups 2 and 4 and groups 2 and 5. This is to be expected because groups 4 and 5 have very different patterns of offending than group 2, both in terms of overall shape and level differences through age 40. In short, higher scores on the risk factor composite are associated with membership in groups 4 and 5 relative to group 2.

The bottom portion of the table presents comparisons of groups 3 (very low rate chronics) and 4 (high adolescence peaked), 3 and 5 (high-rate chronics), and 4 and 5. When comparing groups 3 and 4 and groups 3 and 5, the risk factor composite score exhibits a positive and significant effect, indicating that higher scores on the risk factor composite are associated with membership in groups 4 and 5, respectively, compared to group 3. In the final comparison, between groups 4 and 5, the risk factor composite score is not able to discriminate between the two offender groups.

In sum, the results from Table 10.11 indicate that groups 4 (high adolescence peaked) and 5 (high-rate chronics) are not distinguishable on the risk factor composite, but that groups 2 (low adolescence peaked) and 3 (very low rate chronics) are distinguishable on the risk factor composite from groups 4 and 5. Additionally, groups 2 and 3 do not differ on the risk factor composite.

Next, we examined the mean values of the individual and environmental risk factor scores across the five groups. As would be expected, the risk level was highest among those offenders who evinced the most offending. When we calculated the mean value for the environmental risk factor score, we found that the high-rate chronic group had the highest mean value (mean = 23.50), followed by the high adolescence peaked (mean = 21.93), very low rate chronic (mean = 20.19), low adolescence peaked (mean = 19.41), and nonoffender (mean = 17.98) groups. Finally, when we examined the mean value for the individual risk factor score, we found that the high-rate chronic (group 5) and high adolescence peaked (group 4) groups had the highest mean scores (mean = 17.62 and mean = 17.66, respectively), followed by the very low rate chronic (mean = 15.58), low adolescence peaked (mean = 15.05), and nonoffender (mean = 14.25) groups.

Because we may want to separate the environmental and individual risk portions of the risk factor composite, we estimated an additional

Table 10.11. *Logistic Regression Estimates Comparing Offender Groups to Each Other*

| Variable | Group 2 (Low Adol. Peaked) Group 3 (Very Low Rate Chronics) | | | Group 2 (Low Adol. Peaked) Group 4 (High Adol. Peaked) | | | Group 2 (Low Adol. Peaked) Group 5 (High-Rate Chronics) | | |
|---|---|---|---|---|---|---|---|---|---|
| | B | SE(B) | Exp(B) | B | SE(B) | Exp(B) | B | SE(B) | Exp(B) |
| Risk factor composite | 0.03 | 0.06 | 1.03 | 0.22 | 0.08* | 1.25 | 0.47 | 0.17* | 1.60 |
| Constant | −1.93 | 2.10 | | −9.61 | 3.08 | | −20.23 | 6.93 | |
| Model chi-square/df | 0.30/1 | | | 9.23/1 | | | 15.95/1 | | |
| Nagelkerke R-square | 0.01 | | | 0.23 | | | 0.51 | | |

| Variable | Group 3 (Very Low Rate Chronics) Group 4 (High Adol. Peaked) | | | Group 3 (Very Low Rate Chronics) Group 5 (High-Rate Chronics) | | | Group 4 (High Adol. Peaked) Group 5 (High-Rate Chronics) | | |
|---|---|---|---|---|---|---|---|---|---|
| Risk factor composite | 0.18 | 0.08* | 1.19 | 0.42 | 0.17* | 1.52 | 0.15 | 0.12 | 1.16 |
| Constant | −7.31 | 3.25 | | −17.68 | 7.11 | | −6.78 | 5.11 | |
| Model chi-square/df | 5.24/1 | | | 11.29/1 | | | 1.74/1 | | |
| Nagelkerke R-square | 0.2 | | | 0.51 | | | 0.13 | | |

$*p < .05$

multinomial logistic regression model where we include two independent composite variables: environmental risk and individual risk.[13] These results are found in Table 10.12. Throughout this table, the high-rate chronics serve as the reference group. When comparing nonoffenders to the high-rate chronics, it can be seen that high scores on both the environmental and individual risk composites are associated with a lower likelihood of membership in the nonoffender group compared to the high-rate chronic group. With regard to the low adolescence peaked group, the results indicate that high scores on both the environmental and individual risk composites are associated with a lower likelihood of membership in the low adolescence peaked group compared to the high-rate chronic group, though the coefficient for the environmental risk composite is significant only at $p < .10$. With regard to the very low rate chronic group, only individual risk is a significant discriminator. High scores on the individual risk composite are associated with a lower likelihood of membership in the very low rate chronic group compared to the high-rate chronic group. Finally, when the comparison is between the high adolescence peaked group and the high-rate chronic group, neither the environmental nor the individual risk composite scale is a significant discriminator. In short, groups 4 (high adolescence peaked) and 5 (high-rate chronics) appear indistinguishable on the environmental and individual risk composites, while the individual risk composite appears able to distinguish the high-rate chronic group (group 5) from groups 1 (nonoffenders), 2 (low adolescence peaked), and 3 (very low rate chronics), but not from group 4 (high adolescence peaked).

We also estimated a series of logistic regressions where we used the environmental and individual risk composites to discriminate among the offender groups. In these analyses, we found that in no case did the environmental risk composite discriminate between the offender groups (2–5). However, the individual risk composite did discriminate in four of the six comparisons: between groups 2 and 4 ($p < .05$), groups 2 and 5 ($p < .05$), groups 3 and 4 ($p < .10$), and groups 3 and 5 ($p < .10$). In the first two comparisons, higher scores on the individual risk composite were associated with membership in groups 4 and 5, respectively, compared to group 2, while in the second two comparisons higher scores on the individual risk composite were associated with membership in groups 4 and 5, respectively, compared to group 3. As has been the case, neither the environmental nor the individual risk composite was able to

---

[13] The individual and environmental composite risk factor scales are positive and significantly correlated ($r = .451$, $p < .05$).

Table 10.12. *Multinomial Logistic Regression Discriminating Between Five Offender Trajectories Using Environmental and Individual Risk Composite*

| | Group 1 Nonoffenders B/SE(B) EXP(B) | Group 2 Low Adol. Peaked B/SE(B) EXP(B) | Group 3 Very Low Rate Chronics B/SE(B) EXP(B) | Group 4 High Adol. Peaked B/SE(B) EXP(B) |
|---|---|---|---|---|
| Environmental risk | − 0.42/0.17 (0.65)* | − 0.31/0.17 (0.73)+ | − 0.28/0.18 (0.75) | − 0.19/0.18 (0.82) |
| Individual risk | − 0.86/0.28 (0.42)* | − 0.62/0.28 (0.53)* | − 0.58/0.29 (0.55)* | − 0.12/0.29 (0.88) |
| Constant | 26.15/5.53 | 19.20/5.51 | 17.22/5.63 | 7.11/5.49 |
| Model chi-square/df | 69.56/8 | | | |
| Nagelkerke R-square | 0.26 | | | |

+p < .10; *p < .05 Reference group is Group 5, High-Rate Chronics.

Table 10.13. *Logistic Regression Estimates Comparing Offender Groups to Each Other*

| Variable | Group 2 (Low Adol. Peaked) Group 3 (Very Low Rate Chronics) | | | Group 2 (Low Adol. Peaked) Group 4 (High Adol. Peaked) | | | Group 2 (Low Adol. Peaked) Group 5 (High-Rate Chronics) | | |
|---|---|---|---|---|---|---|---|---|---|
| | B | SE(B) | Exp(B) | B | SE(B) | Exp(B) | B | SE(B) | Exp(B) |
| Environmental risk | 0.02 | 0.08 | 1.02 | 0.08 | 0.12 | 1.08 | 0.31 | 0.20 | 1.37 |
| Individual risk | 0.04 | 0.15 | 1.04 | 0.51 | 0.22* | 1.67 | 1.03 | 0.46* | 2.82 |
| Constant | −2.00 | 2.28 | | −11.55 | 3.66 | | −26.57 | 9.87 | |
| Model chi-square/df | 0.31/2 | | | 11.59/2 | | | 18.55/2 | | |
| Nagelkerke R-square | 0.01 | | | 0.29 | | | 0.58 | | |

| Variable | Group 3 (Very Low Rate Chronics) Group 4 (High Adol. Peaked) | | | Group 3 (Very Low Rate Chronics) Group 5 (High-Rate Chronics) | | | Group 4 (High Adol. Peaked) Group 5 (High-Rate Chronics) | | |
|---|---|---|---|---|---|---|---|---|---|
| | B | SE(B) | Exp(B) | B | SE(B) | Exp(B) | B | SE(B) | Exp(B) |
| Environmental risk | 0.07 | 0.13 | 1.07 | 0.32 | 0.20 | 1.37 | 0.22 | 0.21 | 1.25 |
| Individual risk | 0.37 | 0.21[+] | 1.45 | 0.93 | 0.51[+] | 2.54 | 0.04 | 0.27 | 1.05 |
| Constant | −8.38 | 3.66 | | −24.31 | 11.11 | | −6.55 | 5.18 | |
| Model chi-square/df | 6.34/2 | | | 13.00/2 | | | 1.91/2 | | |
| Nagelkerke R-square | 0.24 | | | 0.57 | | | 0.14 | | |

[+]p < .10; *p < .05

discriminate between groups 4 and 5. A summary of these appears in Table 10.13.

**Take-Home Messages**

1 Five distinct trajectories were identified in the CSDD data through age 40.
2 These five groups evinced distinct offending patterns, both in terms of onset, persistence, and desistance between ages 10 and 40.
3 The groups varied, as expected, on several criminal career dimensions. For example, the high-rate chronic group (group 5, comprised of eight boys) had an average of 19 convictions by age 40, had an average career length of 22 years, and had a higher likelihood of being convicted for a violent offense.
4 More information post age 32 allowed for a clearer depiction of the natural history of offending into middle adulthood.
5 Important environmental and individual risk factors not only distinguished between nonoffenders and offender, but between membership in different offender trajectories.

**Unanswered Questions**

1 What predictors early in life distinguish these offending trajectories?
2 What life events alter these offending trajectories upward or downward?

# Developing Estimates of Duration and Residual Career Length

How long do criminal careers last? Is their duration short (a few years), medium (several years), or long (many years)? Do some identifiable offenders have longer careers than other offenders? Are careers in one crime type longer than those in another crime type? Can estimates of career length be obtained given the truncation observed in many longitudinal data sets? What about residual career length, or the expected time remaining in an offender's career at the time of a particular intervention (such as incarceration)? Can we develop estimates of an offender's expected time left in a career?

Career length questions are central to both theory and policy, but the policy questions are particularly salient. For example, if offenders have short careers, then criminal justice policies such as three-strikes laws, with their lengthy incarceration terms, may waste scarce resources. This will be the case because offenders' careers are likely to be over well before the end of their lengthy incarceration. Thus, knowledge of career lengths, particularly residual career lengths, can provide important information for policy guidance. Additionally, information on the correlates associated with both short and long careers will be of use in attempts to modify criminal careers. For example, a strong relationship between legitimate employment and termination of criminal careers may suggest greater attention to employment facilitation as a useful policy intervention (Blumstein et al., 1986:85).

Research has examined the career length issue in one of three ways. First, some studies have examined juvenile careers or adult careers, but fewer have *combined* juvenile and adult careers. Second, other studies have

examined the sequence of events in individual careers, providing estimates of termination probabilities after each arrest. These studies have
examined how termination probabilities change with the accumulation of
further arrests, what the expected number of future arrests is at any point
in a career, and whether there are any bases for prospectively identifying
"persisters," those who go on to have long records with large numbers of
crimes or arrests.[1] The third approach to career length has been to focus
on the actual duration of criminal careers, by estimating the time that
elapses between the first and last crimes committed.

The literature on duration has been growing, but it is still sparse. Early
work by Greene (1977), Greenberg (1975), and Shinnar and Shinnar
(1975) arrived at estimates ranging from 5 to 12 years. Blumstein et al.'s
(1982) work on residual career length arrived at the finding that most
careers last about five years. Spelman's (1994) analysis of the Rand
Inmate Survey data indicated that most careers lasted between six and
seven years. The two exceptions to these relatively small career length
estimates are the ones obtained by Piquero et al. (2004) and Laub and
Sampson (2003). Using a longitudinal sample of California Youth
Authority wards, Piquero et al. (2004) found that the average career
length of these highly selected offenders was 17 years. Laub and Sampson's (2003) follow-up of the Glueck Boston delinquent sample to age 70
generated an average career length estimate of 25 years between the first
and the last arrest.[2]

The research on residual career length, or the expected time still
remaining in a career, has been scant. Blumstein et al. (1982) presented
one of the few studies conducted on residual career length. A key finding
from this study is the authors' articulation of a three-phase depiction of
the criminal career. In the first phase, the "break-in" period in the early
years of the career, dropout rates decrease as those with short careers
terminate, and so the mean residual career length of those remaining
increases. This result – residual career length of the offender group that
stays active increasing – is a consequence of the changing composition of
the offender population. Through their 20s, the more committed
offenders persist and the less committed drop out, so the residual average
career length of the remaining group increases as a result. This initial
phase lasts for the first 10 to 12 years of a career. In the second, "stable,"
period, beginning around age 30 for 18-year-old starters, there are likely
to be stable residual career lengths. During this second phase, the

---

[1] Termination probabilities are, of course, the inverse of recidivism probabilities, an issue
dealt with in Chapter 10.
[2] Of course, all of these estimates depend on the length of the observation period.

dropout rate is at its minimum and the expected time remaining in the career is longest (i.e., about 10 additional years regardless of the prior duration of careers). Thus, during this phase, regardless of the number of years a person has been active in a career, the expected time remaining is similar. Then, in the final, "burnout," period, around age 41 character-ized by increasing dropout rates, the expected time remaining in a career gets shorter.

Residual career length (RCL) and residual number of offenses (RNO) provide information on the time remaining in criminal careers and future rates of offending. Knowledge about RCL and RNO can potentially have important theoretical and policy implications. From a theoretical view-point, RCL and RNO reflect the age/crime curves of active offenders. In a follow-up to age 70, Laub and Sampson (2003) found that participation and incidence rates declined with age, even among serious and violent offenders. As Blumstein et al. (1982:11) pointed out: "The observation of declining population arrest rates with age ... has led to the conventional wisdom that imprisonment after age 30 is not efficient because these older offenders are likely to be soon terminating their criminal careers." Although the proportion of individuals who are active in offending after age 30 is relatively small, Blumstein et al. (1982:11) argued: "It is not clear ... whether the expected future career length of those few who are still criminally active at age 30 is also small." An assessment of RCL and RNO at each age could identify ages where active offenders are most likely to cease offending and ages where they are most likely to persist. Piquero et al. (2003:479) outlined the policy implications associated with estimates of residual career length:

> Knowledge on career length and residual career length is perhaps one of the most critical areas of research that could best inform criminal justice policies because it deals directly with sentencing and incapacitation deci-sions, which are now so strongly driven by ideology rather than empirical knowledge. For example, if research shows that residual criminal-career lengths average around five years, then criminal justice policies advocating multi-decade sentences will waste scarce policy resources. Similarly, as offenders continue to be incarcerated in late adulthood when their residual career lengths have diminished, then not only will incarceration space be wasted, but the costs of health care for such offenders will tend to increase, thereby exerting further strain on the scarce resources of an already taxed criminal justice system.

In this chapter, we develop estimates of duration and residual career length using the official conviction records from the CSDD. Though we recognize that the data used in this book are truncated at age 40, there is very little offending past age 40 in most offending careers, with the exception of a very small number of serious offenders (see Sampson and Laub, 2003). So we suspect that our estimates, though on the conservative side, will largely capture career length. The specific focus on residual career length serves three main purposes: By examining distributions of RCL and RNO for the CSDD males, (1) it seeks to explore issues relating to termination of criminal careers; (2) it aims to examine the distribution of RCL and RNO according to various criminal career indicators that are available in official records (serial number of convictions, time since the last conviction, age of onset, co-offending, and offense type); and (3) it assesses the ability to predict RCL and RNO based on these variables (i.e., information available to decision makers in the criminal justice system).

## Methods

### Measures

We use the conviction information available in the CSDD to examine issues related to duration, career length, and residual career length. For the first portion of the analysis on duration, we employ the information on ages at conviction for the convicted males in the CSDD. Our principal measure of career length is the number of years between the age at first and last conviction. We take this measure of career length and compare it to other criminal career parameters in the CSDD data. We focus our attention here on the 112 males who were convicted two or more times.

Then, we turn our attention to the issue of residual career length. RCL refers to the number of years remaining in the criminal career up to the last recorded conviction, whereas RNO is defined as the number of offenses remaining in the criminal career. For instance, if a respondent is convicted for one offense in each year at ages 16, 24, 30, and 38, his respective residual career lengths would be 22, 14, 8, and 0 years, and his residual number of offenses would be 3, 2, 1, and 0. From the initial sample of 411 boys, 164 had at least one conviction; of these, 6 died before age 35. Of the remaining 158 offenders, 49 were convicted only once and were excluded from the analyses. Thus, estimates of RCL and RNO could be derived for 109 males,[3] who committed a total of 676 convicted offenses up to age 40. Results were only presented up to age 35 (see explanation below), resulting in a total of 647 convictions.

---

[3] There were a total of 112 individuals who were convicted two or more times. However, three of these individuals offended multiple times in the same year and thus were excluded.

Because studies of crime rates in relation to age have traditionally relied on official arrest data in order to have demographic information, these distributions have been left-hand censored: First arrests and convictions rarely occur in childhood and rather tend to occur in adolescence. In contrast, the distributions of RCL and RNO are right-hand censored: Observations stop at a given age, even though offenders may not have ceased offending at this point in the life-course (see Piquero et al., 2003). Although criminal career research has generally found that a relatively small proportion of offenders remain criminally active after age 40 (Blumstein and Cohen, 1987; Le Blanc and Fréchette, 1989), estimates of residual criminal career lengths are affected by "false desistance" imposed by the right-hand censoring (see Blumstein et al., 1986). It has been suggested that certain desistance can occur only when offenders have died (Blumstein et al., 1982). In the present study, the records of convictions were available up to age 40, which may have underestimated the number of years and offenses remaining in the criminal careers of individuals who persisted in crime after this period. Thus, males with a conviction at age 39 could not have a residual criminal career length greater than one year, even if they may persist in offending for many subsequent years. Although we do not wish to minimize the problem of false desistance, following up individuals over a 30-year span is still a considerably long observation period: Past studies have based their analysis of termination on much shorter observation periods (Ayers et al., 1999: three-year follow-up during adolescence; Elliott, Huizinga and Menard, 1989: seven-year follow-up during adolescence).

One step was undertaken to address this issue: The results were only presented for offenses committed up to age 35 in order to minimize the biases associated with false desistance. Thus, in this study the maximum possible residual career length at age 35 is five years; this cutoff point was used on the basis that a five-year crime-free period is better evidence of career termination than a one-year crime-free period (Kurlychek, Brame, and Bushway, 2006).

## Data Analysis Approach

We provide both descriptive and correlational evidence in this chapter as we attempt to understand the patterning of career length in the CSDD.

## Results: Career Length Duration

Because the large proportion of one-time offenders skewed the average career length downward (because their career length is equal to zero),

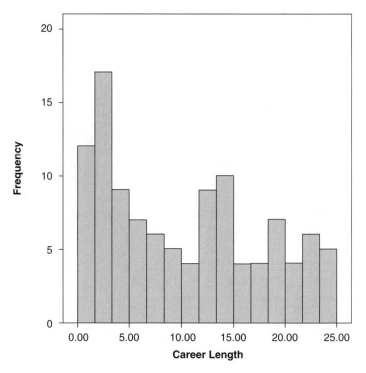

**Figure 11.1.** Histogram of Career Length

we excluded one-time offenders from these calculations. This left us with a total of 112 individuals with two or more convictions. Their average career length, or the duration interval from the first to last conviction, was 10.431 years. When we removed the three individuals whose ages at first and last conviction were in the same year, the average career length was 10.183 (n = 109). In the analyses that follow, we use the 109 males who were convicted two or more times in at least two different years.

We begin with a plot of the histogram of career length using the sample of 109 individuals. As shown in Figure 11.1, many careers are relatively short (38 percent are under 6 years in duration), but a handful of careers (12.5 percent) are over 20 years long. Table 11.1 presents the information on career length as a function of age at first conviction. Here, it can be seen that the average career lengths of the six men first convicted at age 10 are almost the longest, over 13 years. Through the middle teens, in fact, the average career length is quite long – over 10

Table 11.1. *Relationship Between Age at First Conviction and Average Career Length (Two-Plus Offenders)*

| Age at First Conviction | N | Average Career Length |
|---|---|---|
| 10 | 6 | 13.382 |
| 11 | 5 | 11.94 |
| 12 | 7 | 12.17 |
| 13 | 14 | 12.874 |
| 14 | 14 | 12.448 |
| 15 | 15 | 13.533 |
| 16 | 12 | 11.016 |
| 17 | 11 | 6.727 |
| 18 | 5 | 7.915 |
| 19 | 4 | 6.064 |
| 20 | 5 | 9.096 |
| 22 | 2 | 3.108 |
| 24 | 2 | 10.069 |
| 26 | 2 | 7.519 |
| 28 | 1 | 2.855 |
| 32 | 1 | 4.698 |
| 33 | 2 | 3.006 |
| 34 | 1 | 1.462 |
| Total | 109 | 10.183 |

years. From age 17 forward, with the exception of the two men first convicted at age 24, the average career length is much shorter.

Figure 11.2 presents the relationship between age at last conviction and career length. Here, there is a trend toward longer criminal careers with an older age at last conviction. In fact, individuals who were older than 35 at their last conviction had career lengths of over 10 years, on average. As would be expected, this relationship is positive and significant ($r = .788$, $p < .05$).

Next, we plotted the relationship between age at first conviction and career length (Figure 11.3). Here, lengthy career lengths are confined to the earliest ages of first conviction (13–18). In fact, for those experiencing their first conviction between ages 10 and 16, the average career length was over 10 years. As the age at first conviction increased (i.e., the offender was older at the time of first conviction), career length decreased. As expected, this relationship is negative and significant ($r = -.336$, $p < .05$).

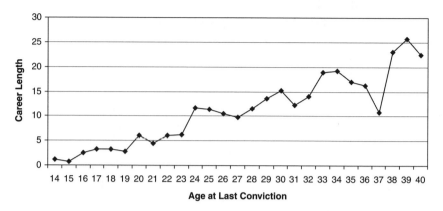

**Figure 11.2.** Relationship Between Age at Last Conviction and Career Length

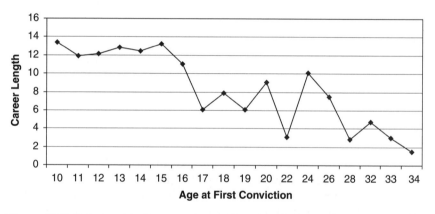

**Figure 11.3.** Relationship Between Age at First Conviction and Career Length

Next, we plotted the relationship between career length and the total number of convictions between ages 10 and 40. Given the hypotheses that high-frequency offenders tend to have longer careers (Moffitt, 1994) and that a longer career provides more time to accumulate convictions, we would expect that individuals with longer careers will accumulate many more convictions than those with shorter careers. As shown in Figure 11.4, there is a positive relationship between the total number of convictions and the average career length. Specifically, individuals with few convictions had relatively short careers, while those with many convictions had

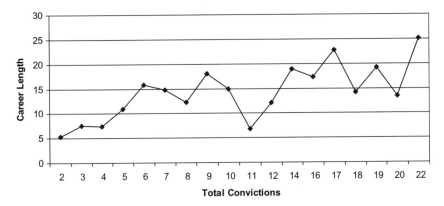

**Figure 11.4.** Relationship Between Total Number of Convictions and Career Length

relatively long careers. Total convictions and career length exhibited a positive and significant correlation ($r = .542$, $p < .05$).

Next, we examined the relationship between the difference in years between the age at last conviction and age at follow-up (age 40) and career length. As seen in Figure 11.5, the peak of career length is much higher and earlier in the chart (when the difference between the two ages is much smaller) and it slowly decreases as the age gap increases. As would be expected, as the difference in years between the final age at follow-up and the age at last conviction increases, the average career length is rather small. This is confirmed by the negative and significant correlation between the two variables ($r = -.788$, $p < .05$).

An interesting set of questions emerges with regard to the role of incapacitation. One point of view asserts that incapacitation slows or stalls criminal careers, while another view suggests that individuals with longer careers will have more incarceration experiences because they are most likely to come to the attention of authorities. To provide some evidence on this question, we examined the mean career length by whether the subject experienced an incarceration event at any point between ages 10 and 40. We note here that only 26 men experienced some incarceration experience, and the majority did not spend much time in facilities. The analysis showed that those individuals who were incarcerated at some point throughout the observation period had lengthier careers than their counterparts (mean $= 13.923$ compared to mean $= 9.012$). The two groups, stratified on incarceration experience, exhibited significantly different career lengths ($t = 3.040$, $p < .05$).

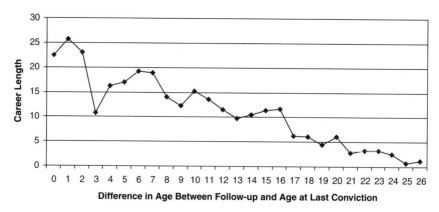

**Figure 11.5.** Relationship Between Difference in Years Between Age at Last Conviction and Age at Follow-up (Age 40) and Career Length

But simply using an indicator of whether a subject was incarcerated may hide the fact that some individuals might have been incarcerated multiple times and that the career lengths could differ according to the number of incarceration stints. To examine this issue, we assessed the relationship between career length and the number of incarcerations experienced by the 109 offenders. Here, we uncovered a step-function increase between the second and third incarceration stint, such that career lengths exceeded 20 years for those subjects with three or more incarceration stints. As would be expected, individuals with zero incarcerations had the lowest average career length, while the lone individuals who had four or five incarcerations, respectively, had career lengths of 20 years each.[4]

It is also of interest to examine the relationship between career length and violence. Some theorists believe that individuals with longer careers also tend to engage in violent activity. For example, Blumstein et al. (1982) found longer criminal careers for violent offenders compared to property offenders. To examine this question, we calculated the average career length for individuals who had accumulated at least one violent conviction by age 40 (n = 45) compared to individuals who had not (n = 64)[5] among the two-plus offenders. We found that violent offenders did, indeed, have longer criminal careers (average of 13.288 years) compared to nonviolent

[4] There were too few individuals who had incarceration stints (n = 26) generally; and when parceled into the distinct number of incarceration stints, the sample sizes were too small to conduct tests of statistical significance.

[5] This was actually 67 males, but recall that 3 males experienced their two or more convictions during the same year and thus were excluded.

offenders (average of 8.0 years). As expected, violent offenders had significantly longer career lengths ($t = 3.875$, $p < .05$).

We also investigated the relationship between the number of violent convictions and career length. We would anticipate that with an increase in the number of violent convictions, there should be a corresponding increase in career length, or, conversely, individuals with longer careers are more likely to accumulate one or more violent convictions. This relationship was confirmed. Although violence is a rare event in the CSDD data – with very few multiple violent offenders, thus precluding us from a useful graphical portrayal – there is a positive and significant relationship between career length and the number of violent convictions ($r = .377$, $p < .05$).

## Time Intervals Between Offenses

Table 11.2 shows the average time intervals between offenses during the criminal careers of the South London males; n offenses generate n−1 time intervals. This table is based only on offenders with at least two offenses (at least one time interval), and therefore it excludes the 52 one-time offenders. This has the effect of leading to a small number of cases as offenses increase in number. For the 112 individuals with at least one time interval, the difference in years between the first and second conviction was, on average, 3.276 years. There was however, a wide range around this mean (SD = 4.00), likely because the second conviction for some offenders did not occur until their 20s or 30s. In fact, the maximum value for the first time interval is 26 years.

For those individuals with at least two time intervals, we calculated the difference in years between the ages at their second and third convictions. For these 78 individuals, the average time interval decreased to 2.05 years, and the variance around that mean decreased. As one proceeds along Table 11.2, it can be seen that the mean (as well as the variance and maximum values) begins to decrease with increasing numbers of convictions. This should not be a surprise because individuals with many more convictions tend not to have their offenses spread out over time; instead, such offenses appear to cluster together. For example, among those 53 individuals with five or more convictions, the average time interval between convictions was less than one year.

## Comment: What is the Average Career Length, and How Does It Relate to Other Criminal Career Parameters?

The duration of time between the beginning and end point of a criminal career (i.e., career length) has been of interest to both criminologists and

Table 11.2. *Average Time Intervals Between Offenses (in Years)*

| Age Difference | N | Mean |
|---|---|---|
| Age 2–Age 1 | 112 | 3.276 |
| Age 3–Age 2 | 78 | 2.051 |
| Age 4–Age 3 | 64 | 2.156 |
| Age 5–Age 4 | 53 | 0.962 |
| Age 6–Age 5 | 44 | 2.909 |
| Age 7–Age 6 | 37 | 1.351 |
| Age 8–Age 7 | 33 | 1.151 |
| Age 9–Age 8 | 30 | 2.300 |
| Age 10–Age 9 | 24 | 1.125 |
| Age 11–Age 10 | 19 | 1.631 |
| Age 12–Age 11 | 18 | 0.833 |
| Age 13–Age 12 | 13 | 2.000 |
| Age 14–Age 13 | 13 | 1.307 |
| Age 15–Age 14 | 12 | 0.583 |
| Age 16–Age 15 | 12 | 0.666 |
| Age 17–Age 16 | 10 | 2.000 |
| Age 18–Age 17 | 8 | 1.250 |
| Age 19–Age 18 | 7 | 0.714 |
| Age 20–Age 19 | 5 | 1.600 |
| Age 21–Age 20 | 2 | 1.500 |
| Age 22–Age 21 | 2 | 1.000 |

This table excludes one-time offenders.

policy makers alike. For theorists, knowledge about the length of criminal careers provides important descriptive information and is likely linked to other criminal career dimensions, such as onset age, persistence, and violence. For policy makers, knowledge about the length of criminal careers provides information that is useful for purposes of intelligent sentencing policy. To the extent that criminal careers are, on average, shorter rather than longer, this would suggest a policy of shorter as opposed to lengthier incarceration lengths.

Unfortunately, there has been limited research on criminal career length generally and residual career length in particular. This is so because many longitudinal data sets have been truncated (right-hand censoring) in the early or late 20s and thus do not provide follow-up information on criminal activity into adulthood. In fact, only two longitudinal studies contain detailed information on criminal activity up to and past age 40: the

Sampson and Laub (2003) follow-up of the Glueck Boston delinquent sample and the CSDD.

The purpose of this chapter was to provide descriptive and correlational evidence regarding the duration of criminal careers in the CSDD. Though we recognize that the data are truncated at age 40, there is very little (high-rate) offending past age 40 in most offending careers. Moreover, a comparison of the career length estimates obtained in this study (using the through-age-40 data) compared to a previous investigation with the through-age-33 CSDD conviction data (Farrington and Maughan, 1999; Farrington, Lambert, and West, 1998) indicate very little difference in terms of average career length.[6] In short, while our estimates should be viewed as conservative, they will largely capture most career lengths. With this caveat in hand, several key findings emerged from this effort.

First, most careers are of short duration. In fact, 40 percent of all careers were under 2 years in length, and only 9 percent were greater than 20 years. Generally speaking, among the full sample of 164 offenders the average career length was 7 years. Excluding one-time offenders, the average career length increased to over 10 years.

Second, higher career lengths were associated with an older age at last conviction, an earlier age at first conviction, and a higher number of convictions. That is, individuals with lengthier criminal careers were more likely to be of an older age at their last conviction, to have an earlier age at their first conviction, and to have accumulated a higher number of convictions by age 40.

Third, individuals incarcerated at some point in their lives were more likely to have lengthier criminal careers. This should not be surprising because individuals with lengthier careers are more likely to accumulate many more offenses, and with many more offenses comes a higher likelihood (i.e., opportunity) of coming to the attention of formal legal authorities.

Fourth, violent offenders had lengthier criminal careers than nonviolent offenders. On average, the career lengths of individuals who were convicted of at least one violent offense were about five years longer than the careers of individuals who were not convicted of a violent offense by age 40.

Fifth, the average time interval between offenses, for those individuals with at least two offenses, was 3.27 years. This time interval decreased with increasing numbers of convictions, suggesting that offenses were not very spread out over time among those individuals accumulating many more offenses.

---

[6] In Farrington and Maughan (1999), overall career length among all offenders, on average, was just under six years, whereas in our study it was just over seven years, a difference of one year with eight additional years of data.

In short, the fact that the majority of careers among the South London males were, on average, 10 years long suggests that lengthy incarceration stints (20+ years) are likely to waste scarce correctional resources. In fact, through age 40 only 15 males had career lengths of more than 20 years. As they should be, these 15 males were distributed into groups 3 (very low rate chronic) and 5 (high-rate chronic) from the trajectory-based analysis in the preceding chapter, the two groups who had the most stable and lengthiest predicted offending rates to age 40.

## Take-Home Messages

1 Among the 112 offenders in the CSDD sample with two or more convictions by age 40, the average career length was over 10 years.
2 Onset age is strongly related to career length. Individuals who experience an early onset have longer criminal careers.
3 Individuals with a later age at last conviction were more likely to have lengthier criminal careers.
4 Career length is predictive of an individual's total number of convictions. Those with longer careers had, on average, many more offenses throughout their careers.
5 Career length was also associated with the presence of at least one incarceration stint. That is, individuals who were incarcerated at least once by age 40 had lengthier criminal careers than those who were not incarcerated at all.
6 On average, the time interval between the first and second conviction was about 3.27 years. With increasing conviction frequency, the average time between intervals decreased.

## Unanswered question

1 What factors relate to career length?

## Results: Residual Career Length

The next portion of this chapter[7] addresses the time and number of offenses remaining in the career according to other criminal career

---

[7] This portion of Chapter 11 borrows extensively from Lila Kazemian and David P. Farrington (2006), "Exploring Residual Career Length and Residual Number of Offenses

indicators and the ability to predict RCL and RNO based on information available in official records.

The distributions of RCL and RNO according to six variables will be presented: Most of these variables have been used in previous studies (listed in parentheses below), estimating the length of criminal careers or recidivism. These variables are (1) age on offense, not on conviction (respondent's age at the time of the offense; Blumstein et al., 1982; Carney, 1967; Silver et al., 2000), (2) conviction number (nth convicted offense; Ashford and LeCroy, 1988; Blumstein et al., 1982; Carney, 1967; Horwitz and Wasserman, 1980; Scarpitti and Stephenson, 1971; Silver et al., 2000), (3) the time since the last convicted offense (in years; Barnett, Blumstein, and Farrington, 1989; Blumstein et al., 1982), (4) age of onset (juvenile onset: first conviction occurred before age 17; adult onset: first conviction occurred at age 17 or later; Ashford and LeCroy, 1988; Blumstein et al., 1982; Blumstein et al., 1986; Carney, 1967; Farrington et al., 1998; Piquero et al., 2004; Scarpitti and Stephenson, 1971; Silver et al., 2000), (5) the number of co-offenders (Le Blanc and Fréchette, 1989; Reiss and Farrington, 1991), and (6) offense type (Blumstein et al., 1982; Carney, 1967; Horwitz and Wasserman, 1980).

Offense type is a dichotomous variable that contrasts violent offenses (robbery, physical assault, wounding, insulting or threatening behavior, possession of an offensive weapon, and sex offenses) with nonviolent offenses (shoplifting, theft of vehicles, theft from vehicles, joyriding, theft of cycles, theft from machines, theft from work, other theft, burglary, fraud, receiving, suspicious behavior, drug offenses, arson, damage, and disqualified driving). It would have been interesting to study the impact of incarceration on patterns of residual career length (possible deterrent or criminogenic effects); however, the number of incarcerated individuals was small, and it was not possible to include this variable in the analyses.

*Distributions of Residual Career Length and Residual Number of Offenses*

*Age on Offense.* Figure 11.6 shows the distribution of RCL and RNO. Two striking observations emerge from this figure. First, there is a steady drop in RCL and RNO with age. The impressive degree of linearity of these distributions is noteworthy (RCL: $r = -0.96$, $p < .0001$; RNO: $r = -0.89$, $p < .0001$). Second, the fluctuations occurring in both RCL and RNO distributions are very similar. In fact, residual career length and residual number of offenses are significantly correlated ($r = 0.69$, $p < .0001$).

for Two Generations of Repeat Offenders," *Journal of Research in Crime and Delinquency* 43:89–113. Permission for reprint granted from Sage Publications.

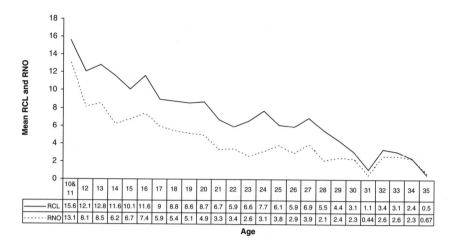

| | 10&11 | 12 | 13 | 14 | 15 | 16 | 17 | 18 | 19 | 20 | 21 | 22 | 23 | 24 | 25 | 26 | 27 | 28 | 29 | 30 | 31 | 32 | 33 | 34 | 35 |
|---|---|---|---|---|---|---|---|---|---|---|---|---|---|---|---|---|---|---|---|---|---|---|---|---|---|
| RCL | 15.6 | 12.1 | 12.8 | 11.6 | 10.1 | 11.6 | 9 | 8.8 | 8.6 | 8.7 | 6.7 | 5.9 | 6.6 | 7.7 | 6.1 | 5.9 | 6.9 | 5.5 | 4.4 | 3.1 | 1.1 | 3.4 | 3.1 | 2.4 | 0.5 |
| RNO | 13.1 | 8.1 | 8.5 | 6.2 | 6.7 | 7.4 | 5.9 | 5.4 | 5.1 | 4.9 | 3.3 | 3.4 | 2.6 | 3.1 | 3.8 | 2.9 | 3.9 | 2.1 | 2.4 | 2.3 | 0.44 | 2.6 | 2.6 | 2.3 | 0.67 |

Age

**Figure 11.6.** Relationship Between Average Official Residual Career Length (in Years) and Residual Number of Offenses at Each Age, 10–35 Years Old (n = 647 Convicted Offenses). Correlation between age and residual career length: r = −0.96, p < .0001 (n = 25). Correlation between age and RNO: r = −0.89, p < .0001 (n = 25). Mean residual length: 8.1 years. Mean residual residual number of offenses: 5 offenses.

*Serial Number of Conviction.* Figure 11.7 shows that both residual career length and residual number of offenses tend to decline after each successive conviction, and both distributions display a considerable degree of linearity (RCL: r = −0.91, p < .0001; RNO: r = −0.77, p < .0001). Declines with successive convictions are less steep than declines with age. Despite the high degree of linearity, the residual number of offenses remains relatively stable up to the 11th conviction. Why does RNO not decrease as steadily as RCL with each successive conviction? It may be that the sample convicted at each serial conviction number includes an increasing proportion of persisters as opposed to desisters (see Blumstein, Farrington, and Moitra, 1985). In other words, there may be an increasing proportion of individuals who continue committing offenses at high rates.

*Time Since the Last Conviction.* The distributions of RCL and RNO according to the time between the last and current conviction are presented in Figure 11.8. These distributions are characterized by increased fluctuations in comparison with previous figures, but they still remain linear (RCL: r = −0.73, p < .05; RNO: r = −0.77, p < .05). Once again, the similarity of patterns between the RCL and RNO distributions is striking. Both distributions show a considerable increase between three

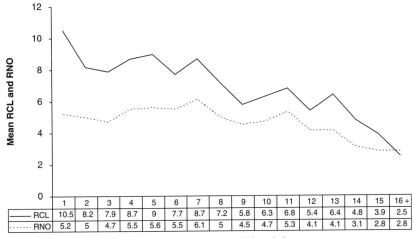

| | 1 | 2 | 3 | 4 | 5 | 6 | 7 | 8 | 9 | 10 | 11 | 12 | 13 | 14 | 15 | 16 + |
|---|---|---|---|---|---|---|---|---|---|---|---|---|---|---|---|---|
| ——— RCL | 10.5 | 8.2 | 7.9 | 8.7 | 9 | 7.7 | 8.7 | 7.2 | 5.8 | 6.3 | 6.8 | 5.4 | 6.4 | 4.8 | 3.9 | 2.5 |
| ······· RNO | 5.2 | 5 | 4.7 | 5.5 | 5.6 | 5.5 | 6.1 | 5 | 4.5 | 4.7 | 5.3 | 4.1 | 4.1 | 3.1 | 2.8 | 2.8 |

**Serial Number of Convictions**

**Figure 11.7.** Relationship Between Average Official Residual Career Length (in Years) and Residual Number of Offenses after Each Conviction (n = 647 Convicted Offenses). Correlation between serial conviction number and residual career length: $r = -0.91$, $p < .0001$ (n = 16). Correlation between serial conviction number and RNO: $r = -0.77$, $p < .0001$ (n = 16).

and five years since the last conviction, followed by a substantial decrease. Despite these fluctuations, RCL and RNO tend to decline as the time lag between the last and current convicted offense increases, which suggests that individuals who are convicted at relatively short time intervals tend to have longer RCL and RNO; these are likely to be high-rate offenders.

*Age of Onset.* Past research has repeatedly shown that an early onset predicts many offenses and a long duration of criminal activity (Blumstein et al., 1982; Farrington et al., 1990; Le Blanc and Fréchette, 1989; Moffitt, 1993; Piquero et al., 2004). The analyses carried out in this section explore whether the relationship between RCL/RNO and age varies according to age of onset. Table 11.3 shows the average residual career length and residual number of offenses according to age on offense and juvenile onset versus adult onset. In both age groups (17–24 and 25–35), RCL and RNO were higher for individuals who had first been convicted between 10 and 16 years old (overall RCL for juvenile onsetters: 7.5; overall RCL for adult onsetters: 4.8; overall RNO for juvenile onsetters: 4.7; overall RNO for adult onsetters: 1.9). Thus, for different ages on offenses, age of onset is negatively related to RCL/RNO. Discrepancies between the RCL and RNO

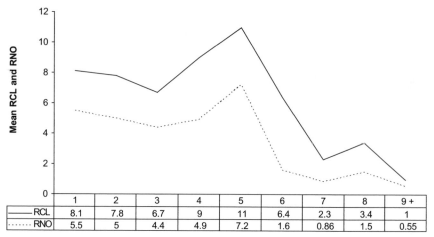

| | 1 | 2 | 3 | 4 | 5 | 6 | 7 | 8 | 9 + |
|---|---|---|---|---|---|---|---|---|---|
| —— RCL | 8.1 | 7.8 | 6.7 | 9 | 11 | 6.4 | 2.3 | 3.4 | 1 |
| ······ RNO | 5.5 | 5 | 4.4 | 4.9 | 7.2 | 1.6 | 0.86 | 1.5 | 0.55 |

**Time Since Last Conviction (in Years)**

**Figure 11.8.** Relationship Between Average Official Residual Career Length (in Years) and Residual Number of Offenses According to the Time Since Last Conviction ($n = 519$ Convicted Offenses). Correlation between the time since the last conviction and residual career length: $r = -0.73$, $p < .05$ ($n = 9$). Correlation between the time since the last conviction and RNO: $r = -0.77$, $p < .05$ ($n = 9$). Average time since the last conviction: 2.7 years.
*Note:* First offenses were excluded from this distribution (time since last offense $= 0$).

of juvenile and adult onsetters are greater for offenses committed between ages 17 and 24, which suggests a greater effect of age of onset on RCL and RNO during this period (in contrast to the 25–35 period); this interaction between the age on offense and age of onset is statistically significant for both RCL and RNO. Thus, age of onset predicts RCL and RNO.

*Co-offending.* Average RCL and RNO in relation to the number of co-offenders are presented in Table 11.4. The average number of co-offenders was 0.8, with 53 per cent of offenses involving no co-offenders at all. Residual career length and residual number of offenses did not vary significantly according to the number of co-offenders; both one-way analyses of variance were insignificant. These findings suggest that the number of co-offenders does not predict RCL and RNO.

*Offense Type.* Table 11.5 shows the distribution of residual career length and residual number of offenses according to the age on offense

Table 11.3. *Average Residual Career Length and Residual*
*Number of Offenses According to Age on Offense and*
*Age of Onset*

| Age on offense (n = 470) | 17–24 | 25–35 | 36+ | Total |
|---|---|---|---|---|
| *RCL* | | | | |
| Juvenile onset | 9.1 (n = 232) | 4.2 (n = 118) | — | 7.5 (n = 350) |
| Adult onset | 5.2 (n = 82) | 4 (n = 38) | — | 4.8 (n = 120) |
| Total | 8.1 (n = 314) | 4.2 (n = 156) | — | 6.8 (n = 470) |
| *RNO* | | | | |
| Juvenile onset | 5.6 (n = 232) | 2.8 (n = 118) | — | 4.7 (n = 350) |
| Adult onset | 2.1 (n = 82) | 1.5 (n = 38) | — | 1.9 (n = 120) |
| Total | 4.7 (n = 314) | 2.5 (n = 156) | — | 4 (n = 470) |

Table Key:
RCL according to
1. Age on offense            $F = 22.7$, $df = 1$, $p < .0001$
2. Age of onset             $F = 10.5$, $df = 1$, $p < .01$
3. Age on offense × age of onset $F = 8.0$, $df = 1$, $p < .01$

RNO according to
1. Age on offense            $F = 16.5$, $df = 1$, $p < .0001$
2. Age of onset             $F = 33.7$, $df = 1$, $p < .0001$
3. Age on offense × age of onset $F = 7.4$, $df = 1$, $p < .01$

and offense type (violent versus nonviolent). Although the overall average RCL and RNO were similar for both offense types, these figures are generally higher for violent offenses committed at the youngest ages (10–16). This suggests that the effect of offense type on RCL and RNO is attenuated with age. Two-way analyses of variance show that offense type and the interaction between age and offense type did not have a significant effect on RCL and RNO. However, significance tests may have been affected by the small number of convictions for violent offenses in comparison to nonviolent offenses.

## Can Risk Scores Predict RCL and RNO?

In order to investigate the predictability of RCL and RNO based on variables available in criminal records, risk scores were computed based

Table 11.4. *Average Residual Career Length and Residual Number of Offenses per Number of Co-offenders (n = 631 Convicted Offenses)*

| Number of Co-offenders | RCL | RNO |
|---|---|---|
| 0 (n = 333) | 7.59 | 4.55 |
| 1 (n = 166) | 8.85 | 5.42 |
| 2 (n = 81) | 9.38 | 5.41 |
| 3 (n = 31) | 9.16 | 6.45 |
| 4 or more (n = 20) | 8.4 | 5.7 |

RCL according to the number of co-offenders: $F = 1.83$, $df = 4$, ns
RNO according to the number of co-offenders: $F = 2$, $df = 4$, ns
Average number of co-offenders: 0.8

on the four most influential variables: age on offense, conviction number, time since the last conviction, and age of onset. The variables that were not dichotomous were dichotomized (using the median as the cutoff point), and a cumulative score ranging from 0 to 4 was created by summing the four scores. The predictive validity of the risk scores was investigated according to their ability to predict RCL and RNO (see Tables 11.6 and 11.7); RCL and RNO were dichotomized in low and high categories.

Results show that individuals with higher-risk scores tend to have more years remaining in their criminal careers and to commit more offenses. All four chi-square tests were significant, but chi-square measures only deviations from chance expectation, not the linearity of relationships.

ROC curves assess the predictive efficacy of classification schemes, when the outcome variable has two categories. In other words, the ROC curve "plots the probability of a 'hit' versus the probability of a 'false positive'" and is a measure that is "unaffected by changes in sample size and row and column totals ..." (Farrington et al., 1996:515). The area under the ROC curve is a better measure of predictive efficiency in $4 \times 2$ tables than chi-squared because it measures the linearity of the relationship. Farrington et al. (1996) developed a measure ("AROC") that varies from 0 to 1 (i.e., from chance to perfect prediction): $AROC = 2 \times (A - 0.5)$, where $A$ = area under the ROC curve. AROC obtained for RCL and RNO were both significant (RCL: $A = .631$, $sd = .025$, $AROC = .262$, $p < .05$; RNO: $A = .681$, $sd = .024$, $AROC = .362$, $p < .05$). Although these predictions are significantly better than chance, neither is greater than

Table 11.5. *Average Residual Career Length and Residual Number of Offenses According to Age on Offense and Offense Type, 10–35 Years Old (n = 645 Convicted Offenses)*

| Age on offense | 10–16 | 17–24 | 25–35 | Total |
|---|---|---|---|---|
| *RCL* | | | | |
| Nonviolent offenses | 11.5 (n = 161) | 8 (n = 261) | 4.1 (n = 121) | 8.1 (n = 543) |
| Violent offenses | 14.6 (n = 16) | 8.7 (n = 53) | 4.3 (n = 35) | 8.1 (n = 104) |
| Total | 11.8 (n = 177) | 8.1 (n = 314) | 4.2 (n = 156) | 8.1 (n = 647) |
| *RNO* | | | | |
| Nonviolent offenses | 7.5 (n = 161) | 4.7 (n = 261) | 2.6 (n = 121) | 5 (n = 543) |
| Violent offenses | 9.2 (n = 16) | 4.9 (n = 53) | 2.3 (n = 35) | 4.7 (n = 104) |
| Total | 7.6 (n = 177) | 4.7 (n = 314) | 2.5 (n = 156) | 5 (n = 647) |

Table Key:
RCL according to
   1. Age on offense:            $F = 39.8$, $df = 2$, $p < .0001$
   2. Offense type:              $F = 3.4$, $df = 1$, $p < .10$
   3. Age on offense × offense type: $F = 1.2$, $df = 2$, ns

RNO according to
   1. Age on offense:            $F = 33.7$, $df = 2$, $p < .0001$
   2. Offense type:             $F = 1.2$, $df = 1$, ns
   3. Age on offense × offense type: $F = 0.93$, $df = 2$, ns

AROC $= 0.5$, which suggests that they are nearer to chance than to prefect prediction on the 0–1 scale.

In short, these results suggest that these risk scores are significant, but not highly predictive of RCL and RNO. This finding highlights the difficulties associated with predictions based on information included in official records, that is, information that is most often available to decision makers in the criminal justice system.

### Comment: What Do We Learn from Residual Career Lengths?

One of the striking findings of this study is the remarkable linearity of the distributions of RCL and RNO, particularly according to the age on offense. As offenders got older, their number of remaining years of active offending declined; similar results were observed for the residual number of offenses. This general decline is consistent with the age/crime

Table 11.6. *Distribution of Residual Career Length According to Risk Scores (n = 519 Convicted Offenses)*

| RCL Risk Score | Low (0–7 Years) | High (8 Years or More) | Total |
|---|---|---|---|
| 1 | 70% (n = 67) | 30% (n = 29) | 100% (n = 96) |
| 2 | 56% (n = 108) | 44% (n = 85) | 100% (n = 193) |
| 3 | 50% (n = 66) | 50% (n = 66) | 100% (n = 132) |
| 4 | 35% (n = 34) | 65% (n = 64) | 100% (n = 98) |
| Total | 53% (n = 275) | 47% (n = 244) | 100% (n = 519) |

$x^2 = 25.2$, df = 3, p < .0001 AROC = .262, p < .05

Table 11.7. *Distribution of Residual Number of Offenses According to Risk Scores (n = 519 Convicted Offenses)*

| RNO Risk Score | Low (0–3 Offenses) | High (4 Offenses or More) | Total |
|---|---|---|---|
| 1 | 74% (n = 71) | 26% (n = 25) | 100% (n = 96) |
| 2 | 58% (n = 112) | 42% (n = 81) | 100% (n = 193) |
| 3 | 35% (n = 46) | 65% (n = 86) | 100% (n = 132) |
| 4 | 33% (n = 32) | 67% (n = 66) | 100% (n = 98) |
| Total | 50% (n = 261) | 50% (n = 258) | 100% (n = 519) |

$x^2 = 50.9$, df = 3, p < .0001 AROC = .362, p < .05

curve: Both suggest increasing dropout rates with increasing age. Sampson and Laub (2003) found that the traditional age/crime distribution also applied to their sample of serious and persistent offenders and that both participation and incidence rates declined with age.

The distributions of RCL and RNO reflect age/crime tendencies of active offenders. Some authors have argued that the relationship between age and crime reveals changes in prevalence (participation) rather than incidence (frequency) of offending. In other words, the number of active offenders peaks in late adolescence and declines thereafter, but individuals who remain active in offending tend to do so at a relatively stable rate across various periods of the life-course (Blumstein, Cohen, and Farrington, 1988a,b; Farrington, 1986). Our results showed that distributions of RCL generally displayed a greater degree of linearity than those of RNO, particularly in relation to offense number.

In their follow-up of Glueck men up to age 70, Sampson and Laub (2003:584) argued that "life-course-persistent offenders are difficult, if not impossible, to identify prospectively using a wide variety of childhood and adolescent risk factors." It was interesting to observe that age of onset predicted RCL and RNO independently of age on offense for the CSDD males.

In the present analyses, risk scores were significantly but not highly predictive of RCL and RNO. This finding underlines the difficulty of making predictions based on information available in official records and supports the need for the use of self-reports of offending and other features of social background as predictors of future criminal behavior.

## Take-Home Messages

1 There was a general decline in RCL and RNO with age.
2 Over and above age on conviction, age of onset predicted RCL and RNO.
3 The type of offense and the number of co-offenders did not predict RCL and RNO.
4 Risk scores showed that the predictive power of these variables for RCL and RNO was significant but not very high.
5 Results showed that the highest RCL and RNO were observed in early adolescence, but it would obviously be undesirable to incapacitate young offenders for over 10 years.

## Unanswered Questions

1 Because estimates of RCL and RNO are likely to be an underestimation of the actual RCL and RNO, what are the effects of truncation and false desistance on career length and residual career length?
2 One of the limitations of the analyses conducted in this study relates to the fact that termination is measured as the last convicted offense. Because officially recorded offenses comprise only a small proportion of all committed offenses, results here can only be extended to official criminal careers, rather than actual criminal careers. Do self-reported measures of offending yield similar conclusions?

3 Our findings are based on samples of repeat offenders – that is, we measured criminal persistence among offenders who committed crime at rates high enough to register. Are the CSDD results similar or different with respect to a more representative sample?

4 Also, because most convicted offenses were nonviolent, can these findings be generalized to violent offenders?

5 What does the relationship between adult career length and mean aggregate lambda, or arrests per year over the duration of the "active" career, look like (Blumstein, 2005)? Are termination rates higher in adolescence compared to adulthood, and do termination rates vary across crime types?

# CHAPTER TWELVE

# A Summary and an Agenda for
# Future Research

This final chapter integrates the main findings of the book and summarizes the "take-home" messages from the various chapters. Based on these findings, we then highlight five key priorities for future criminal career research. We readily forewarn readers that we outline a very ambitious agenda and ask difficult research questions, but we believe that the data brought to bear on those questions will open new doors for theoretical, empirical (both quantitative and qualitative), and policy research. We conclude by outlining the next 40 years of the CSDD.

Before we present these findings, we would like to take stock of the motivation behind this book. Quite frankly, we were struck by the level of agreement about some key criminal career facts that many criminologists share (e.g., Farrington, 2003). At the same time, many other observations made by criminal career researchers over the past several decades have resulted in contentious exchanges on key questions that remain contentious and/or understudied (see Sampson and Laub, 2005a,b). In particular, we identified a number of issues that we sought to address using data from the CSDD, a longitudinal study of 411 South London males followed to age 40. Although we cannot hope to answer every question in excruciating detail, we do believe that, when taken together, the results presented in this book provide a very comprehensive, descriptive portrait of the criminal careers of these men. Now, what did we ask and what did we learn about these contentious criminal career issues?

## Summary of Main Findings

For ease of presentation, we organize the results of our study around the key criminal career topics examined in this effort (see Table 12.1). Regarding prevalence and frequency, we observed that prevalence peaks at age 17 and that through age 40 almost 40 percent of the South London males had incurred at least one conviction. And while the aggregate, or raw, conviction frequency closely tracked aggregate prevalence, $\lambda$ estimates for total convictions peaked at age 16 and slowly declined after age 20. Interestingly, $\lambda$ estimates for violence were a bit more stable, peaking in the late teens and remaining fairly flat through age 40. There was also remarkable continuity in offending, especially in adjacent age ranges, suggesting that there is important relative stability in offending above and beyond the environmental factors that were present in offenders' lives.[1]

Turning our attention to the relationship between onset age and frequency, we found that while the average age at first conviction was 18, both the mode and hazard peaked at age 14, a finding consistent with many American longitudinal data sets. As would be expected, we discovered that age at first conviction, especially early onset, was associated with many more convictions, a higher probability of violence, a lengthier criminal career, and involvement in many different types of offenses. Also, individual offending frequency was quite high in the years immediately after onset. At the same time, at the individual level the relationship between onset age and $\lambda$ was not as linear as expected, with individuals who onset between 17 and 20 exhibiting the highest average $\lambda$.

Another key criminal career parameter is specialization. Focusing on whether the South London males exhibited a marked tendency to specialize in violence, we found no evidence of this. It appears that in the CSDD violence is a function of frequency. As offenders roll the dice more often and commit more crimes, their chances of a violent offense increase. In fact, offense frequency was the strongest predictor of violence in the CSDD data.

One criminal career question that has received little attention is the nature of onset sequences, or the patterning of onset across distinct offense types. We employed self-report and official records and examined onset sequences through the lens of both retrospective and prospective data. Our analysis on this question indicated that average prospective onset tended to occur earlier than average retrospective onset. We also found that agreement rates between prospective and retrospective reports were lowest for minor offenses, while agreement rates between

---

[1] Of course, this does not imply that offenders did not change. Many, if not most, males who were delinquent as a juvenile were leading successful, crime-free lives by age 40.

Table 12.1. *Summary of Major Findings*

---

*On Prevalence and Frequency*

1 Prevalence peaks at age 17 in the CSDD conviction data.

2 Cumulative prevalence increases rapidly during the mid to late teenage years, stabilizing to almost 40 percent by age 40 in the CSDD conviction data.

3 The aggregate offending rate closely tracked prevalence in the CSDD conviction data.

4 Lambda estimates for total convictions increased to a peak at age 16, ranged above 1.2 in the first 20 years, only to begin a slow and steady decline between ages 20 and 40.

5 Lambda estimates for violence increased to a peak between ages 16 and 20, slowly declined in early adulthood, and remained flat and stable through age 40.

6 There was remarkable continuity in offending among the South London males. Although continuity was most pronounced in adjacent age ranges, it was also observed when comparing offending in the two longest age ranges (10–15 and 36–40).

*On Onset Age and Frequency*

1 While age 18 was the mean onset age in the CSDD data, both the mode and the hazard indicated that age 14 was the peak age of onset, while the median age at first conviction was 16.

2 Those individuals who exhibited an early onset ($<14$ years of age) tended to accumulate many more convictions over the life-course than those who exhibited a later onset ($\geq14$ years of age).

3 Individual offending frequency was quite high in the years immediately following onset and remained fairly stable immediately thereafter.

4 Violence was more likely among those individuals who exhibited an early onset, but the total number of convictions incurred by the males was a better predictor of violence than was onset age.

5 Onset age was significantly associated with career length, total convictions, and the variety index. That is, those individuals who exhibited an early onset were more likely to have longer criminal careers, accumulate more offenses, and be convicted of many more different types of offenses than their late-onset counterparts. However, the relationship between onset age and $\lambda$ at the individual level did not necessarily indicate a linear trend, as those individuals who onset between 17 and 20 evinced the highest mean $\lambda$.

*On Specialization in Violence*

1 Convictions in the CSDD indicate no evidence of specialization in violence for the Cambridge males.

2 Offending frequency is the strongest predictor of whether an individual is a violent offender.

Table 12.1. (*Cont.*)

---

*On Onset Sequences*

1 For those who admitted both, average prospective onset tended to occur earlier than average retrospective onset. This suggests that retrospectively offenders had a tendency to overestimate the age at which they committed their first offense.

2 Results indicated that the agreement rate between prospective and retrospective reports was lowest for minor offenses (vandalism, shoplifting, and theft from vehicles) and highest for theft of vehicles. Agreement rates between prospective and official ages of onset were highest for serious forms of offending. This result suggests that official onset may not be appropriate for minor offenses, due to the criminal justice system's tolerance and low priority given to these crimes.

3 In comparisons with official records, most self-reported offenses never led to a conviction, which is consistent with results from past studies.

4 Also in agreement with past research, the official onset of offending tended to occur much later than the self-reported onset. Furthermore, there appeared to be a positive association between the seriousness of the offense and agreement rates between self-reported and official ages of onset.

5 Many respondents tended to deny acts that they had reported at an earlier age; this was particularly true for minor types of offending.

*On Co-offending*

1 Much like the aggregate age/crime curve, the age/co-offending curve peaks in the late teenage years.

2 The incidence of co-offending decreases with age primarily because individual offenders change and become less likely to offend with others rather than because of selective attrition of co-offenders or persistence of those who offend primarily alone.

3 Co-offending appears more common for some crimes (burglary, robbery) than others.

*On Chronicity*

1 A small group of individuals is responsible for a good proportion of the offending activity.

2 The five-plus designation appears more arbitrary than a true reflection of the persister population in the CSDD. An inspection of recidivism probabilities indicates that a four-plus conviction is a better depiction of chronicity because the recidivism probability is reaching a fairly stable level, averaging 84.5 percent between the 4th and 10th convictions.

3 Chronics differ from all other offender groups (one-timers, below-chronics who incur two or three convictions) on various criminal career dimensions, including onset age and violence.

Table 12.1. (*Cont.*)

*On Trajectories of Offending*

1 Five distinct trajectories were identified in the CSDD data through age 40.
2 These five groups evinced distinct offending patterns, both in terms of onset, persistence, and desistance between ages 10 and 40.
3 The groups varied, as expected, on several criminal career dimensions.
4 More information post age 32 allowed for a clearer depiction of the natural history of offending into middle adulthood.
5 Important environmental and individual risk factors not only distinguished between non-offenders and offenders but discriminated between membership in different offender trajectories.

*On Career Duration and Residual Career Length*

1 Among the offenders in the CSDD sample with two or more convictions by age 40, the average career length was over 10 years.
2 Onset age is strongly related to career length. Individuals who experience an early onset have longer criminal careers.
3 Individuals with a later age at last conviction were more likely to have longer criminal careers.
4 Career length is predictive of an individual's total number of convictions. Those with longer careers had, on average, many more offenses throughout their careers.
5 Career length was also associated with the presence of at least one incarceration stint – that is, individuals who were incarcerated at least once by age 40 had longer criminal careers than those who were not incarcerated at all.
6 On average, the time interval between the first and second conviction was about 3.27 years. With increasing conviction frequency, the average time intervals decreased.
7 There was a general decline in residual career length (RCL) and residual number of offenses (RNO) with age.
8 Over and above age on conviction, age of onset predicted RCL and RNO.
9 The type of offense and the number of co-offenders did not predict RCL and RNO.
10 Risk scores showed that the predictive power of these variables for RCL and RNO was significant but not very high.
11 Results show that the highest RCL and RNO are observed in early adolescence, but it would obviously be undesirable to incapacitate young offenders for more than 10 years.

prospective and official ages of onset were highest for serious forms of offending. As would be expected, we also discovered that most self-reported offenses never led to a conviction and that official onset of offending tended to occur much later than self-reported onset. And while there appeared to be a positive association between the seriousness of the offense and agreement rates between self-reported and official ages of onset, we did find that many respondents tended to deny acts that they had reported at an earlier age. This was especially true for minor types of offending. These results demonstrate the limitations of retrospective data and support the importance of prospective longitudinal studies. Retrospective data cannot substitute for prospective reports of offending. More specifically, retrospective accounts seem to be particularly inappropriate for research requiring detailed information on offending (e.g., about age of onset), as offenders are unlikely to remember these specificities after long periods of time. Because many parameters used in criminal career research require precise information (age of onset, frequency, age of desistance, etc.), retrospective data may not be best suited for this type of research.

Another important parameter in the criminal career is co-offending; but due to data limitations in most longitudinal studies, very little information has been gleaned on this issue. Fortunately, the CSDD contains information on co-offending and co-offenders, affording us the ability to examine this issue in great detail. Here, we found that, much like the aggregate age/crime curve, the age/co-offending curve peaks in the late teenage years. Also, the incidence of co-offending decreases with age, primarily because individual offenders change and become less likely to offend with others rather than because of selective attrition of co-offenders or persistence of those who offend primarily alone. Finally, we also found that co-offending appears more common for some crimes, like burglary and robbery, than other crimes, like disqualified driving and sex offenses against a female.

A longstanding interest of criminal career researchers is the issue of chronicity and the identification of chronic offenders. Similar to most other longitudinal data sets around the world, we found, a small group of individuals was responsible for a high proportion of the conviction activity. At the same time, we found that the five-plus chronic-offender designation developed by Wolfgang et al. appears to be more arbitrary than a true reflection of the persister population in the data. Our analysis of the recidivism probabilities indicated that a four-plus designation was more useful because at that conviction number and above, the recidivism probability was similar for most individuals, averaging 84.5 percent. As would be expected, chronic offenders also differed in anticipated ways from other offenders, averaging an earlier onset age and a higher probability of violence.

A recent methodological development, the use of trajectories, has provided criminal career researchers with the ability to chart out distinct offender trajectories over the life-course. We applied this methodology to the CSDD data and identified five distinct trajectories of offending, each of which evinced distinct offending patterns in terms of shape and levels of offending and which varied, as expected, on several criminal career dimensions. One group in particular, the eight high-rate chronics, had the highest, most stable offending activity of all offenders in the data. Important environmental and individual risk factors discriminated between members in the five distinct trajectory groups, but these results were not as clear-cut as developmental criminologists probably would like, a finding that replicates the substantive conclusions reached by Laub and Sampson (2003:110).[2]

Finally, we turned our attention to the issue of career duration and residual career length. The issue of residual career length is especially important in the policy arena because information on the amount of time remaining in criminal careers can be useful in making decisions regarding incarceration length. Our analysis of the repeat offenders in the CSDD data indicated that the average career length was more than 10 years. Career length was also associated with several other criminal career parameters, as one would expect. For example, individuals who experienced an early onset tended to have longer criminal careers. Those with lengthy careers had, on average, many more offenses over the course of their careers and were also more likely to experience incarceration. Regarding residual career length (RCL) and residual number of offenses (RNO), we found a general decline of both with age. As expected, age of onset predicted both RCL and RNO, but the type of offense and the number of co-offenders did not. Additionally, risk scores showed that the predictive power of official criminal justice variables for RCL and RNO were significant but not very high. Finally, we found that the highest RCL and RNO were observed in early adolescence.

## Implications for Theory and Policy

Because the purpose of our study was descriptive in nature, we were not specifically focused on testing theoretical predictions or answering key

---

[2] As these authors note: "[W]e found no statistically significant differences in the means across group membership. These findings, along with the results of the graphical analyses, suggest that life-course-persistent offenders are difficult, if not impossible, to identify prospectively using a wide variety of childhood and adolescent risk factors." Their high-rate chronic group was comprised of 15 individuals (or about 3 percent of the delinquent sample).

theoretical debates, such as the issue of general/typological theories, the debate between persistent heterogeneity/state dependence, or the utility of offender groups (see the discussion more generally in Sampson and Laub, 2005a,b). At the same time, the results of our study do provide some information and context for developmental and life-course (DLC) theories.

For example, four particular findings stand out that bear import for DLC theories. First, our descriptive analyses regarding prevalence, frequency, $\lambda$, and chronicity indicate that a small subset of individuals harbor rather high criminal potential and evince extremely high rates of offending over a long period of time. Although this is certainly not a novel finding, it equates well with several criminological and DLC theories of crime: It shows that in every sample of individuals there is always a small subset of offenders who are responsible for much of the criminal activity.

Second, our detailed analysis of co-offending shows that the aggregate age/co-offending curve looks very much like the aggregate age/prevalence curve identified in prior criminological work. At the same time, the results indicate that the incidence of co-offending decreases with age primarily because individual offenders change and become less likely to offend with others rather than because of selective attrition of co-offenders or persistence of those who offend alone. Thus, as offenders age they become more likely to offend alone. With a few exceptions (Akers's social learning theory and Moffitt's developmental taxonomy), most criminological and DLC theories offer little by way of explaining co-offending. Analyses of the CSDD suggest that co-offending is important in certain segments of the criminal career but becomes less salient as individuals' careers progress. Theories should consider why this is the case and how it is relevant to their frameworks and explanations.

Third, our trajectory-based analyses offer important descriptive evidence with which to assess extant general and DLC theories. In contrast to Gottfredson and Hirschi's parsimonious explanation, our trajectories uncovered multiple groups of offenders, each of whom evinced distinct trajectories of offending, in terms of shape and levels, between ages 10 and 40. Additionally, membership in these offending classes was associated with differential risk on a number of factors considered at ages 8–10. In support of the more complicated DLC theories of Moffitt and Patterson, there appeared to be two groups of most interest to their frameworks: an adolescence-peaked group and a high-rate chronic group. The shape and level of offending of these two groups appeared to closely mirror the hypotheses put forth by those scholars.[3] At the same

---

[3] To be sure, this does not necessarily confirm the existence of "real" groups, or typologies of offenders in the real world. Researchers must be careful not to reify the existence of such

time, the trajectory analysis also uncovered several other groups that were not necessarily anticipated by those DLC theories, among them a low-rate chronic group that had low but stable rates of offending for much of the observation period (e.g., Moffitt, 2006). Thus, the trajectory evidence provides both support for and refutation of some key predictions made by two prominent DLC theories.[4]

Fourth, like some recent offender-based trajectory studies, our trajectory analyses indicated that by about age 40 most offenders had ceased offending – and even the most high-rate offenders, the eight high-rate chronics, had offending rates that were approaching zero. In line with Sampson and Laub's (2003) and Ezell and Cohen's (2005) recent findings using offender samples, these results appear to indicate that by middle adulthood most – if not all – offenders appear to desist from crime (but see Blokland et al., 2005). These results are in line with Gottfredson and Hirschi's expectation that even at the individual level of analysis, most offenders follow the aggregate age/crime curve to some extent and desist in early to middle adulthood. At the same time, they appear to contradict the expectation that a very small subset of offenders offend at very high rates for their entire lives (but see Piquero and Moffitt, 2005).

Turning our attention to policy, three findings stand out. First, in every cohort of individuals there is a small group of individuals who offend at fairly high, stable rates for lengthy periods of time and are responsible for a high proportion of the offenses of the larger cohort. At the same time, these individuals appear to desist by their late 30s, which suggests that lengthy incarceration periods into mid to late adulthood are unwarranted – at least for small segments of high-rate offenders from an unselected cohort of general-population individuals. Second, our analyses of the residual career lengths and residual number of offenses suggests that as offenders get older, their number of remaining years of active offending and their residual number of offenses both decline. This finding suggests increasing dropouts with increasing age. Thus – aside from the fact that residual careers shorten with age and the implications this has for sentencing decisions – the more general view that residual career length is an important piece of information for criminal justice decision makers cannot be taken for granted. Such information bears relevance for making sound decisions in a time when correctional resources are thin. Third, the analyses suggest that several variables collected in the CSDD

---

groups, especially when they are defined atheoretically (see, e.g., Laub and Sampson, 2003:289).

[4] Additionally, the specific risk factors assessed herein did not perfectly distinguish between the trajectory groups, but this may have been due to the small number of individuals in some of the groups (especially the high-rate chronic group, n = 8).

early in life are predictive of particular offending styles, but these variables appear to predict offenders better in general and not necessarily between trajectories. Four variables in particular are both causal and modifiable: low achievement, poor parental child rearing, impulsivity, and poverty. Early prevention that pays attention to these factors is likely to reduce not only the incidence of crime but also other problem behaviors correlated with crime, such as drinking, drug use, school failure, unemployment, and marital disharmony.

## Limitations

We embarked on a very ambitious research effort to provide a comprehensive descriptive analysis of the offending careers of 411 South London males. Although we believe this information will be useful to criminal career and DLC researchers, several limitations precluded us from answering every contentious question in great detail. Principally, the majority of analyses presented in this book were from official (conviction) records. And while such records provide an important glimpse into offending careers, it would be ideal for future research to consider complimentary official and self-report records. Granted, such data are both difficult and expensive to come by, but the use of both to answer similar questions is important to provide a more complete picture of criminal careers (see Elliott et al., 1987). Second, because of the nature of the sample (all male, mainly white), we were unable to examine the various criminal career issues for females or across racial/ethnic groups. Unfortunately, much of what we know about the longitudinal patterning of criminal activity over the life-course originates from white males. There exists very little information documenting the course of criminal careers across race (for exceptions, see Piquero et al., 2002b, 2005b; Tracy et al., 1990) or gender (for exceptions, see Broidy et al., 2003; Moffitt et al., 2001; Piquero et al., 2005a; White and Piquero, 2004). Data on such samples are especially important because they will provide a comparison for understanding the current state of criminal career information. Third, because of how the CSDD study originated, how the data collection process ensued, and the significant lack of funding and manpower, there was little predictive information collected over the course of the follow-up study. For example, although the early-life (ages 8–10) information was quite exhaustive, much has been learned about the etiology of offending since the 1960s, and important later predictors of criminality were not considered in the CSDD. Additionally, there was only limited information available about changes in key theoretical constructs over time – such as the turning points of marriage and employment – that can be used to predict changes within individuals in criminal activity. Analyses with those variables have shown that being employed as opposed to unemployed, getting married and staying married, and moving out of London are all associated with desistance (see Farrington and West, 1995). Finally, although there is some information on violence in the CSDD, violence was a very rare event among the South London males, a "problem" that has plagued other researchers using either birth cohort or panel studies (see, e.g., Laub and Sampson, 2003; Moffitt et al., 2001). Thus, we could not examine in specific detail questions related to the patterning and etiology of violence.

With these findings and limitations in hand, we next turn to an agenda for future research that is centered around five research priorities that we feel will advance the knowledge base of criminal careers.

## Research Priority 1: Intermittency

One of the more important observations in criminal career research that has not received much attention is the issue of intermittency (Barnett et al., 1989; Nagin and Land, 1993; Piquero, 2004). This aspect of the criminal career deals with the starts and stops in offending, not related to incarceration per se, that are exhibited within criminal careers. And although the idea that offenders are not constantly offending has been accepted for quite some time (Frazier, 1976; Glaser, 1964; Matza, 1964; Miesenhelder, 1977), very little empirical information has been brought forward. Because "a career in crime [is] a variable and varying process" (Meisenhelder, 1977:320), "[t]he view of criminality as a zig-zag path suggests that it may be more fruitful for rehabilitation objectives to shift the focus of criminological theories from the search for the processes that make for persistence in crime. What we need is the development and test of a theory on the conditions that promote change from crime to non-crime and back again" (Glaser, 1964:318). Various theoretical accounts can be considered as useful frameworks for understanding intermittency, including rational-choice theory, drift theory, informal social control theory, and general strain theory (see Piquero, 2004). As an example, consider informal social control theory: When controls are in place, offending is less likely, but when controls falter, offending becomes more likely, and these stops and starts could occur frequently in offenders' careers (Horney et al., 1995; Laub et al., 1998; Piquero et al., 2002a).

Because the empirical study of intermittency is in its infancy, many questions are open to investigation. For example, are the predictors of intermittency across offense types similar or different? How is inter-mittency within individuals exhibited over the life-course (i.e., across ages)? For example, during the adolescent time period, are intermittency periods rather short as adolescents quickly move in and out of various situations and acts, both illegal and legal? How do alcohol and drug use and abuse influence patterns of intermittency? Are there different intermittent periods among different groups of offenders defined by race and/or gender? Importantly, how can intermittency be defined and measured? These and other questions about intermittency will lead to important inquiries as criminologists attempt to better understand the constant zig-zagging that permeates criminal careers.

## Research Priority 2: Desistance

Closely related to the study of intermittency is desistance, or the end of an offender's career. Recognizing that researchers face difficulty in identifying the true end of a career (Laub and Sampson, 2001), largely because of right-hand censoring (i.e., people are followed only to a certain age, say 40), desistance remains one of the least understood aspects of the criminal career. One way that information on desistance and its correlates will be furthered is through the aging of longitudinal studies worldwide. To date, only three studies – the follow-up of the Glueck delinquent sample to age 70 (Sampson and Laub, 2003), Farrington et al.'s (1998) analysis of the mothers and fathers of the Cambridge Study males, and Blokland et al.'s (2005) analysis of the conviction records of samples of Dutch offenders followed through age 72 – provide the most expansive data available for which researchers can study desistance. As many of the world's most prominent longitudinal studies become "older," researchers will be better able to study the desistance process. Still, this is no set requirement because Bushway and his colleagues (2001) have developed an approach that allows researchers to measure desistance in a probabilistic fashion that will clearly help them study desistance without having to rely on data through death (see, e.g., Bushway et al., 2003).

Another approach to studying desistance is to engage in detailed case studies/life histories of former offenders. Prominent examples in the criminal career literature include the study of British offenders by Maruna (2001), the single case study of the "dying thief" by Steffensmeier and Ulmer (2005), and the life histories of 52 delinquent males by Laub and Sampson (2003). The latter study in particular is especially important because it originates from a sample of individuals who, mainly in their 60s, have had a chance to think about their lives in crime. While several of them are still offending in one form or another, others have stopped offending and could be said to have desisted. Information arising from these interviews is exceedingly rich, perhaps more so than most quantitative studies can offer.

## Research Priority 3: Health

One aspect of involvement in crime – especially frequent and serious criminal activity – that 'has escaped the imagination of many criminal career researchers is the effect of crime on health. Although researchers have long established a linkage between offending and poor health outcomes, little specific information is known. For example, what kinds of adverse health outcomes arise out of criminal activity? Are certain kinds of offenses related to certain kinds of health outcomes?

Two analyses of the offending/health linkage have been conducted with data from the CSDD data. In the first study, Farrington (1995) investigated the link between offending (measured by convictions and self-reports) and poor health (measured as illnesses, injuries, accidents, and hospital treatment) at different ages. A number of key findings emerged from his analysis. First, convicted males tended to have had serious illnesses and accidents by age 14; hospital treatment for injury, time off for injury, and a fighting injury by age 18; and a road accident injury by age 32. Second, he found that convictions and self-reported delinquency predicted later measures of physical health. For example, juvenile convictions (prior to age 17) predicted hospitalization for illnesses and injuries by age 18 and hospitalization by age 32. Similarly, self-reported delinquency at age 14 predicted hospitalization for an injury by age 18. Convictions between ages 17 and 25 also predicted both hospitalization and involvement in a road accident by age 32. Self-reported delinquency at age 18 predicted involvement in a road accident by age 32. Finally, when examining childhood predictors of injuries, Farrington observed that early-childhood risk factors (measured at ages 8/10) predicted hospitalization for injury by age 18, having four or more weeks off for injury by age 18, and hospitalization for injury by age 32. For example, low verbal IQ and hyperactivity were sturdy predictors of injuries. Many of the relationships regarding health outcomes predicted by offending held even after controlling for childhood risk factors. In a second analysis, Shepherd and colleagues (2004) examined the relations between childhood predictors of delinquency, teenage offending, and other delinquent behavior, injury, and illness at ages 16–18 and offending and health measures about 14 years later, at ages 27–32. Four key findings emerged from their analysis. First, childhood predictors of teenage offending predicted injury and cardiovascular and psychological illnesses at ages 27–32. Second, smoking more than 20 cigarettes per day at ages 18 was associated with a higher incidence of skin disease at age 32. Third, and unexpectedly, alcohol consumption at ages 16–18 predicted fewer illnesses overall and few infections at ages 27–32. Finally, evidence of conviction in the first 30 years of life was associated with a higher incidence of psychological/neurological disorders at age 27–32.

It would be important for researchers with longitudinal studies to add information on health outcomes to their instrumentation. It is likely that involvement in crime, aside from limiting educational, employment, and relational opportunities, also bodes poorly for one's physical health.

## Research Priority 4: Qualitative Narratives

Much of the knowledge base of criminal careers has come from the application of quantitative methodology to longitudinal records of criminal activity. And while much important information regarding the patterning of criminal careers has been documented, there are some things that quantitative data cannot assess. On this score, the richness of qualitative data, whether in the form of life histories or case studies, can enrich information gleaned from quantitative records.

Several prominent examples of qualitative data on criminal careers are available. Beginning with Shaw's (1930) classic interview with Stanley in *The Jack Roller* through today's seminal studies by Laub and Sampson (2003) with the Glueck delinquents and Steffensmeier and Ulmer's (2005) interview with the "dying thief," narrative information on criminal careers provides important glimpses into offenders' lives (see also Gadd and Farrall, 2004; Giordano et al., 2002; Maruna, 2001). Future efforts should strive to collect this rich vein of information regarding criminal careers, especially because much of it can provide useful insights into the kinds of data that should be collected in ensuing studies.

As an example, consider one of the key findings to emerge from Laub and Sampson's (2003) recent life histories of 52 delinquents from the original Glueck sample. One of the more important findings in that book arose – and likely could *only* arise – from the detailed qualitative interviews; that finding concerns the will, or the power of human agency, and its role in persistence/desistance. According to the interviews, some men who persisted in crime consciously chose to continue their involvement in crime and did not apologize or make excuses for their behavior. Similarly, many of the men who desisted from crime similarly displayed a variety of voluntary actions that facilitated the process of desistance (Laub and Sampson, 2003:280–281). These rich insights would undoubtedly be lost or at the very least be extremely difficult to pick up through quantitative methods.[5]

---

[5] Another insight gleaned from the in-depth interviews concerns the role of prison in offender's lives. For some of the Glueck men, prison worked to deter subsequent offending, but for others it had no effect or the opposite effect. Such contradictory messages would likely get evened out in a quantitative analysis, but in a qualitative study they provide a rich array of information that can be further expanded upon to better understand how individual characteristics influence the perception of punishment.

## Research Priority 5: Conditional Relationships: Race, Gender, and Neighborhoods

Because much research on criminal careers has utilized samples of white male subjects, there is a paucity of information on the criminal careers of women and racial/ethnic minorities. Unfortunately, most longitudinal data sets do not contain such information. As a consequence, this has resulted in criminologists knowing very little about how careers begin, continue, and end across gender and race/ethnicity.

This is not to suggest that criminologists know *nothing* about gender and race differences. For example, work on the Second (1958) Philadelphia Birth Cohort Study provided important descriptive information across race (white/black) and gender with regard to basic criminal career parameters (see Tracy et al., 1990; Tracy and Kempf-Leonard, 1996). Several studies have examined trajectories of offending across gender (see Broidy et al., 2003; D'Unger et al., 2002; Moffitt et al., 2001; Piquero et al., 2005a), and a few studies have examined race differences in careers, including Piquero et al.'s (2002b) analysis of race differences in the correlates of persistence/desistance among white and nonwhite California Youth Authority parolees and Elliott's (1994) examination of race differences in persistent violence using self-reported data from the National Youth Survey.

While these efforts are important, more information is needed on race and gender differences. For example, little is known about co-offending patterns and etiology across race and gender, and even less is known about career lengths – especially residual career lengths – across race and gender. Future research on these and related questions will provide much needed information on these issues, and we suspect that the data emerging from the three Causes and Correlates Studies will be especially fruitful here.

Another conditional relationship that has received little attention is the role of the environment, or neighborhood, in structuring criminal careers. Certain neighborhood contexts are likely to offer greater opportunities for criminal activity. For example, research by Anderson (1999) showed that on certain portions of Germantown Avenue in Philadelphia "old hands" mentored young kids by providing opportunities for criminal activity. Also, Lynam et al. (2000) used data from the Pittsburgh Youth Study to examine the relationship between impulsivity, neighborhood context, and juvenile offending. Their results showed that the effect of impulsivity on juvenile offending was stronger in poorer neighborhoods and that poorer neighborhoods did not have a direct effect on juvenile delinquency. Wikström and Loeber (2000) also used data from the Pittsburgh Youth Study to examine how risk and protective factors related to antisocial behavior across different neighborhood contexts. Their results showed that while most boys with high risk factors offended regardless of neighborhood context, neighborhood effects on crime were greatest among those individuals with the most protective factors.

And finally, recent work by Piquero, Moffitt, and Lawton (2005b) using multilevel data from the Baltimore portion of the National Collaborative Perinatal Project showed that while direct effects for individual and neighborhood risk were not present, a model incorporating individual-, family-, and neighborhood-level effects provided unique insight into chronic styles of offending. In particular, they found that the biosocial interaction between individual and familial risk was related to chronic offending only within African American, disadvantaged neighborhoods.

It is clear, then, that neighborhoods act as an important context when structuring roles and opportunities for individuals. These contexts may be implicated in the production of criminal activity and thus may be especially important when studying criminal careers.

## The Next 40 Years of the CSDD

The aforementioned research priorities should be considered in the context of a larger research program on criminal careers. Those priorities will be important across the range of longitudinal studies and researchers studying criminal careers more generally. The CSDD has provided important information on the longitudinal patterning of criminal careers and has influenced the thinking of the British government about crime policy. For example, between 1990 and 1992 it influenced Home Secretary Kenneth Baker and his junior minister John Patten, who drafted a Green Paper on early prevention in 1992 that drew on the CSDD Study's conclusion. In 1989, John Patten stated:

> This important study has been influential both in this country and in the United States. It bears out much of the Home Office's current thinking about juvenile crime. It is an excellent example of how academic work, funded by government, can help in policy-making. I will be examining Dr. Farrington's conclusions, and their pointers toward future action, very fully indeed.
>
> (Rock, 1994:153)

In documenting the development of early-prevention ideas in the Home Office in 1990–1992, Rock (1994:150) reported:

> There was one article [Farrington and West, 1990] that circulated about the [Home] Office at just that time, an article that had again made out the cause for using longitudinal studies to predict and control delinquency,

and for social prevention experiments to prevent the development of crime and antisocial behaviour. ... An official remarked of Farrington's influence: "There is a theory for a particular time and maybe what he is saying is just one of the things that particularly suit at the moment."

But all is not yet complete. The CSDD has been in existence for close to 40 years, and current efforts are underway to continue to expand the study in an effort to further probe various aspects of criminal careers.

In particular, an age-48 interview has recently been completed that seeks to expand the prior self-reported interview phase of the CSDD data collection effort (Farrington, 2003:172–174). A social interview was given to the males to assess their current and recent self-reported offending and their current success in different aspects of their lives (accommodations, employment, debts, illnesses and injuries, relationships, children, drinking, smoking, drug use, aggressive behavior and attitudes, and current personality). Questions were also asked about the use of health and social services, to permit an economic analysis of costs to society, and about problems of the men's children, such as lying, stealing, truancy, disobedience, bullying, and restlessness. Many of the questions to the males were the same as those that were given at ages 18 and 32; the same attitude questionnaire was given at ages 18, 32, and 48. The General Health Questionnaire was given at ages 32 and 48 and the Eysenck Personality Inventory at ages 16 and 48. The "Big Five" Personality Inventory was given at age 48.

The men were also given a medical interview using the Structural Clinical Interview 4 DSM (SCID) to assess their current mental health and their lifetime history of psychiatric disorders. Questions in both interviews, together with file data, make it possible to score each man on the Psychopathy Checklist. At the end of the medical interview, biological data were collected: saliva to measure testosterone, height, weight, waist circumference, pulse rate, blood pressure, and respiratory function. Questions on physical health and illnesses were also included, and medical records were collected.

In addition, the men's female partners were personally interviewed to collect information on household income, children, her child-rearing attitudes, relationships with the man, family violence, her physical and mental health, her antisocial behavior (including debts, offending, drinking, and drug use), his antisocial behavior, his personality (on the Big Five Inventory), characteristics of the neighborhood, and household victimization. At age 48, the partner completed the same General Health Questionnaire as the man, as well as the same child-rearing attitude questionnaire that his partner completed at his age-32 interview and his mother completed when he was age 12.

The main aims of the age-48 follow-up were to investigate offending in the 40s, characteristics of late-onset offenders, and how far men who had stopped getting convicted were still involved in antisocial behavior. In addition, the social interview will establish how former juvenile delinquents and chronic offenders are living successful lives in their 40s in such areas as accommodations, employment, relationships, drinking, smoking, and drug use, so that protective factors can be studied. The medical interview will establish the relationship between offending and adult mental health problems, including antisocial personality disorder. The partner interview will establish the prevalence of different types of family violence and how far it can be predicted by risk factors in childhood and adolescence.

In addition, children of the CSDD study males aged over 21 are being interviewed. This Third Generation Follow-Up aims to establish how far risk factors discovered years ago are still important in modern times and how far the relative importance of risk factors has changed. It will also provide unique data on the transmission of offending, antisocial behavior, and mental health problems between three generations and on why children from criminal families are particularly at risk of offending. Perhaps even more important, the new project should suggest reasons why children from criminogenic backgrounds do not become offenders.

Because of the extensive data on the study males, the Third Generation Follow-Up should provide detailed information about the importance of the father in relation to child antisocial behavior and offending. Many studies of family factors focus on the mother and neglect the father, because fathers are often more elusive than mothers. Also, this new project should make it possible to compare risk factors for antisocial behavior and offending for male children with those for female children. It is important to know whether the risk factors for offending are similar or different for males and females (see Moffitt et al., 2001).

To summarize, our motivation behind this book was to provide a comprehensive descriptive analysis of the criminal careers of the 411 males who have been followed as part of the Cambridge Study in Delinquent Development from age 10 through age 40. We have corroborated some key criminal career facts that have been evident in other longitudinal studies around the world, but at the same time we have uncovered some findings that are unique to the CSDD data, namely those involving co-offending patterns and residual career lengths. Although we could not answer all contentious criminal career questions – in fact, several that remain to be studied in the CSDD are escalation and seriousness – we have carefully studied the criminal careers of these men. In the vein of Wolfgang et al.'s (1972) classic study *Delinquency in a Birth Cohort*, we believe that such careful, descriptive studies are useful for establishing basic facts about the longitudinal patterning of crime, and we look forward to continued work with the CSDD on many of the above questions, as well as observing what other criminal career researchers uncover with their longitudinal data sets. As these studies grow older, they will allow for the study of questions that have heretofore escaped the research agenda. Through the aging of longitudinal data sets, the criminal career can be better understood.

# References

Andersson, Jan. 1990. "Continuity in Crime: Sex and Age Differences." *Journal of Quantitative Criminology* 6:85–100.

Ashford, J. B., and C. W. LeCroy. 1988. "Decision Making for Juvenile Offenders in Aftercare." *Juvenile and Family Court Journal* 39:47–54

Ashford, J. B., and C. W. LeCroy. 1988. "Predicting Recidivism: An Evaluation of the Wisconsin Juvenile Probation and Aftercare Risk Instrument." *Criminal Justice and Behavior* 15:141–151.

Auerhahn, Kathleen. 1999. "Selective Incapacitation and the Problem of Prediction." *Criminology* 37:703–734.

Ayers, Charles D., James Herbert Williams, J. David Hawkins, Peggy L. Peterson, Richard F. Catalano, and Robert D. Abbott. 1999. "Assessing Correlates of Onset, Escalation, De-Escalation, and Desistance of Delinquent Behavior." *Journal of Quantitative Criminology* 15:277–306.

Barnett, Arnold, Alfred Blumstein, and David P. Farrington. 1987. "Probabilistic Models of Youthful Criminal Careers." *Criminology* 25:83–107.

Barnett, Arnold, Alfred Blumstein, and David P. Farrington. 1989. "A Prospective Test of a Criminal Career Model." *Criminology* 27:373–388.

Blokland, Arjan A. J. 2005. *Crime over the Life Span: Trajectories of Criminal Behavior in Dutch Offenders*. NSCR: Netherlands.

Blokland, Arjan A. J., Daniel S. Nagin, and Paul Nieuwbeerta. 2005. "Life Span Offending Trajectories of a Dutch Conviction Cohort." *Criminology* 43:919–954.

Blokland, Arjan A. J., and Paul Nieuwbeerta. 2005. "The Effects of Life Circumstances on Longitudinal Trajectories of Offending." *Criminology* 43:1203–1240.

Blumstein, Alfred. 2005. "An Overview of the Symposium and Some Next Steps." *The Annals of the American Academy of Political and Social Science*,

*Developmental Criminology and Its Discontents: Trajectories of Crime from Childhood to Old Age* 602:242–258.

Blumstein, Alfred, and Jacqueline Cohen. 1979. "Estimation of Individual Crime Rates from Arrest Records." *Journal of Criminal Law and Criminology* 70:561–585.

Blumstein, Alfred, and Jacqueline Cohen. 1987. "Characterizing Criminal Careers." *Science* 237: 985–991.

Blumstein, Alfred, Jacqueline Cohen, Somnath Das, and Soumyo Moitra. 1988. "Specialization and Seriousness during Adult Criminal Careers." *Journal of Quantitative Criminology* 4:303–345.

Blumstein, Alfred, Jacqueline Cohen, and David P. Farrington. 1988a. "Criminal Career Research: Its Value for Criminology." *Criminology* 26:1–35.

Blumstein, Alfred, Jacqueline Cohen, and David P. Farrington. 1988b. "Longitudinal and Criminal Career Research: Further Clarifications." *Criminology* 26:57–74.

Blumstein, Alfred, Jacqueline Cohen, and Paul Hsieh. 1982. *The Duration of Adult Criminal Careers.* Final report submitted to National Institute of Justice, August 1982. Pittsburgh: School of Urban and Public Affairs, Carnegie Mellon University.

Blumstein, Alfred, Jacqueline Cohen, Susan Martin, and Michael Tonry, eds. 1983. *Research on Sentencing: The Search for Reform.* 2 vols. Panel on Sentencing, Committee on Research on Law Enforcement and the Administration of Justice, Commission on Behavioral and Social Sciences and Education, National Research Council. Washington, DC: National Academy Press.

Blumstein, Alfred, Jacqueline Cohen, Jeffrey A. Roth, and Christy A. Visher, eds. 1986. *Criminal Careers and "Career Criminals."* 2 vols. Panel on Research on Criminal Careers, Committee on Research on Law Enforcement and the Administration of Justice, Commission on Behavioral and Social Sciences and Education, National Research Council. Washington, D.C.: National Academy Press.

Blumstein, Alfred, David P. Farrington, and Soumyo Moitra. 1985. "Delinquency Careers: Innocents, Desisters, and Persisters." In *Crime and Justice: An Annual Review of Research*, vol. 6, edited by Michael Tonry and Norval Morris. Chicago: University of Chicago Press.

Blumstein, Alfred, and Elizabeth Graddy. 1982. "Prevalence and Recidivism in Index Arrests: A Feedback Model." *Law and Society Review* 16:265–290.

Blumstein, Alfred, and Soumyo Moitra. 1980. "The Identification of "Career Criminals" from "Chronic Offenders" in a Cohort." *Law and Policy Quarterly* 2:321–334.

Brame, Robert, Jeffrey Fagan, Alex R. Piquero, Carol A. Schubert, and Laurence Steinberg. 2004. "Criminal Careers of Serious Delinquents in Two Cities." *Youth Violence and Juvenile Justice* 2:256–272.

Breckinridge, Sophonsiba P., and Edith Abbott. 1917. *The Delinquent Child and the Home*. New York: Russell Sage Foundation.

Broidy, Lisa M., Daniel S. Nagin, Richard E. Tremblay, John E. Bates, Bobby Brame, Kenneth Dodge, David Fergusson, John Horwood, Rolf Loeber, Robard Laird, Donald Lynam, Terrie E. Moffitt, Gregory S. Petit, and Frank Vitaro. 2003. "Developmental Trajectories of Childhood Disruptive Behaviors and Adolescent Delinquency: A Six Site, Cross-National Study." *Developmental Psychology* 39:222–245.

Bursik, Robert J., Jr. 1980. "The Dynamics of Specialization in Juvenile Offenses." *Social Forces* 58:851–864.

Bushway, Shawn D., Alex R. Piquero, Lisa M. Broidy, Elizabeth Cauffman, and Paul Mazerolle. 2001. "An Empirical Framework for Studying Desistance as a Process." *Criminology* 39:491–515.

Bushway, Shawn D., Terence P. Thornberry, and Marvin D. Krohn. 2003. "Desistance as a Developmental Process: A Comparison of Static and Dynamic Approaches." *Journal of Quantitative Criminology* 19:129–153.

Canela-Cacho, José A., Alfred Blumstein, and Jacqueline Cohen. 1997. "Relationship Between the Offending Frequency ($\lambda$) of Imprisoned and Free Offenders." *Criminology* 35:133–176.

Capaldi, Deborah N., and Gerald R. Patterson. 1996. "Can Violent Offenders Be Distinguished from Frequent Offenders: Prediction from Childhood to Adolescence." *Journal of Research in Crime and Delinquency* 33:206–231.

Carney, Francis J. 1967. "Predicting Recidivism in a Medium Security Correctional Institution." *Journal of Criminal Law, Criminology and Police Science* 58:338–348.

Caspi, Avshalom, Darryl Bem, and Glen H. Elder. 1987. "Moving Against the World: Life-Course Patterns of Explosive Children." *Developmental Psychology* 23:308–313.

Caulkins, Jonathan P. 2001. "How Large Should the Strike Zone Be in "Three Strikes and You're Out" Sentencing Laws?" *Journal of Quantitative Criminology* 17:227–246.

Chaiken, Jan M., and Marcia Chaiken. 1982. *Varieties of Criminal Behavior*. Rand Report R-2814-NIJ. Santa Monica, CA: Rand.

Christensen, Ronald. 1967. "Projected Percentage of U.S. Population with Criminal Arrest and Conviction Records." In *Task Force Report: Science and Technology*. Report to the President's Commission on Law Enforcement and the Administration of Justice, prepared by the Institute for Defense Analysis. Washington, DC: U.S. Government Printing Office.

Chung, Ick-Joong, Karl G. Hill, J. David Hawkins, Lewayne D. Gilchrist, and Daniel S. Nagin. 2002. "Childhood Predictors of Offense Trajectories." *Journal of Research in Crime and Delinquency* 39:60–92.

Cohen, Jacqueline. 1986. "Research on Criminal Careers: Individual Frequency Rates and Offense Seriousness." In Alfred Blumstein, Jacqueline Cohen, Jeffrey A. Roth, and Christy A. Visher, eds., *Criminal Careers and "Career Criminals," Volume II.* Washington, DC: National Academy Press.

Cohen, Jacqueline, and José A. Canela-Cacho. 1994. "Incarceration and Violent Crime: 1965–1988." In Albert J. Reiss, Jr., and Jeffrey A. Roth, eds., *Understanding and Preventing Violence, Vol. 4: Consequences and Control.* Panel on the Understanding and Control of Violent Behavior, Committee on Law and Justice, Commission on Behavioral and Social Sciences and Education, National Research Council. Washington, DC: National Academy Press.

Conway, Kevin P., and Joan McCord. 2002. "A Longitudinal Examination of the Relation Between Co-Offending with Violent Accomplices and Violent Crime." *Aggressive Behavior* 28:97–108.

D'Unger, Amy V., Kenneth C. Land, and Patricia L. McCall. 2002. "Sex Differences in Age Patterns of Delinquent/Criminal Careers: Results from Poisson Latent Class Analyses of the Philadelphia Cohort Study." *Journal of Quantitative Criminology* 18:349–375.

D'Unger, Amy V., Kenneth C. Land, Patricia L. McCall, and Daniel S. Nagin. 1998. "How Many Latent Classes of Delinquent/Criminal Careers? Results from Mixed Poisson Regression Analyses." *American Journal of Sociology* 103:1593–1630.

Eggleston, Elaine, John H. Laub, and Robert J. Sampson. 2004. "Methodological Sensitivities to Latent Class Analysis of Long-Term Criminal Trajectories." *Journal of Quantitative Criminology* 20:1–42.

Elder, Glen H., Jr. 1985. "Perspectives on the Life Course." In Glen H. Elder, Jr., ed., *Life Course Dynamics.* Ithaca, NY: Cornell University Press.

Elliott, Delbert S. 1994. "1993 Presidential Address: Serious Violent Offenders: Onset, Developmental Course, and Termination." *Criminology* 32:1–22.

Elliott, Delbert S., Suzanne S. Ageton, David H. Huizinga, Brian A. Knowles, and Rachelle J. Canter. 1983. *The Prevalence and Incidence of Delinquent Behavior: 1976–1980.* Boulder, CO: Behavioral Research Institute.

Elliott, Delbert S., David H. Huizinga, and Scott Menard. 1989. *Multiple Problem Youth: Delinquency, Substance Use, and Mental Health Problems.* New York: Springer-Verlag.

Elliott, Delbert S., David H. Huizinga, and Barbara Morse. 1987. "Self-Reported Violent Offending: A Descriptive Analysis of Juvenile Violent Offenders and Their Offending Careers." *Journal of Interpersonal Violence* 1:472–514.

Ezell, Michael E., and Lawrence E. Cohen. 2005. *Desisting from Crime: Continuity and Change in Long-Term Crime Patterns of Serious Chronic Offenders*. Oxford: Oxford University Press.

Farrington, David P. 1973. "Self-Reports of Deviant Behavior: Predictive and Stable?" *Journal of Criminal Law and Criminology* 64:99–110.

Farrington, David P. 1986. "Age and Crime." In Michael Tonry and Norval Morris, eds., *Crime and Justice: An Annual Review of Research*, vol. 7. Chicago: University of Chicago Press.

Farrington, David P. 1989. "Self-Reported and Official Offending from Adolescence to Adulthood." In Malcolm Klein, ed., *Cross-National Research in Self-Reported Crime and Delinquency* Dordrecht, The Netherlands: Kluwer.

Farrington, David P. 1990. "Implications of Criminal Career Research for the Prevention of Offending." *Journal of Adolescence* 13:93–113.

Farrington, David P. 1991. "Childhood Aggression and Adult Violence: Early Precursors and Later Life Outcomes." In D. J. Pepler and K. H. Rubin, eds., *The Development and Treatment of Childhood Aggression*. Hillsdale, NJ: Lawrence Erlbaum.

Farrington, David P. 1995. "Crime and Physical Health: Illnesses, Injuries, Accidents, and Offending in the Cambridge Study." *Criminal Behaviour and Mental Health* 5:261–278.

Farrington, David P. 1998. "Predictors, Causes and Correlates of Male Youth Violence. In Michael Tonry and Mark H. Moore, eds., *Crime and Justice: An Annual Review of Research, Youth Violence*. Chicago: University of Chicago Press.

Farrington, David P. 2000. "Explaining and Preventing Crime: The Globalization of Knowledge – The American Society of Criminology 1999 Presidential Address." *Criminology* 38:1–24.

Farrington, David P. 2003a. "Developmental and Life Course Criminology: Key Theoretical and Empirical Issues – The 2002 Sutherland Award Address." *Criminology* 41:221–255.

Farrington, David P. 2003b. "Key Results from the First Forty Years of the Cambridge Study in Delinquent Development." In Terence P. Thornberry and Marvin D. Krohn, eds., *Taking Stock of Delinquency: An Overview of Findings from Contemporary Longitudinal Studies*. Boston: Kluwer.

Farrington, David P. 2005. "Introduction to Integrated Developmental and Life-Course Theories of Offending." In David P. Farrington, ed., *Integrated Developmental and Life-Course Theories of Offending, Advances in Criminological Theory*, vol. 14. New Brunswick, NJ: Transaction.

Farrington, David P., and J. David Hawkins. 1991. "Predicting Participation, Early Onset, and Later Persistence in Officially Recorded Offending." *Criminal Behaviour and Mental Health* 1:1–33.

Farrington, David P., Darrick Jolliffe, J. David Hawkins, Richard F. Catalano, Karl G. Hill, and Rick Kosterman. 2003. "Comparing Delinquency Careers in Court Records and Self-Reports." *Criminology* 41:933–958.

Farrington, David P., Sandra Lambert, and Donald J. West. 1998. "Criminal Careers of Two Generations of Family Members in the Cambridge Study in Delinquent Development." *Studies on Crime and Crime Prevention* 7:85–106.

Farrington, David P., and Rolf Loeber. 1998. "Major Aims of This Book." In Rolf Loeber and David P. Farrington, eds., *Serious and Violent Juvenile Offenders: Risk Factors and Successful Interventions*. Thousand Oaks, CA: Sage.

Farrington, David P., and Rolf Loeber. 1999. "Transatlantic Replicability of Risk Factors in the Development of Delinquency." In P. Cohen, C. Slomkowski, and L. N. Robins, eds., *Historical and Geographical Influences on Psychopathology*. Mahwah, NJ: Lawrence Erlbaum.

Farrington, David P., Rolf Loeber, Delbert S. Elliott, J. David Hawkins, Denise Kandel, Malcolm Klein, Joan McCord, David Rowe, and Richard Tremblay. 1990. "Advancing Knowledge About the Onset of Delinquency and Crime." In Bernard Lahey and A. Kazdin, eds., *Advances in Clinical and Child Psychology*. New York: Plenum.

Farrington, David P., Rolf Loeber, Magda Stouthamer-Loeber, Welmoet B. Van Kammen, and Laura Schmidt. 1996. "Self-Reported Delinquency and a Combined Delinquency Seriousness Scale Based on Boys, Mothers, and Teachers: Concurrent and Predictive Validity for African-Americans and Caucasians." *Criminology* 34:493–518.

Farrington, David P., and Barbara Maughan. 1999. "Criminal Careers of Two London Cohorts." *Criminal Behaviour and Mental Health* 9:91–106.

Farrington, David P., Howard N. Snyder, and Terrence A. Finnegan. 1988. "Specialization in Juvenile Court Careers." *Criminology* 26:461–487.

Farrington, David P., and Donald J. West. 1995. "Effects of Marriage, Separation, and Children on Offending by Adult Males." In Z. S. Blau and J. Hagan, eds., *Current Perspectives on Aging and the Life Cycle, Volume 4: Delinquency and Disrepute in the Life Course: Contextual and Dynamic Analyses*. Greenwich, CT: JAI Press.

Farrington, David P., and Per-Olof H. Wikström. 1994. "Criminal Careers in London and Stockholm: A Cross-National Comparative Study." In Elmar G. M. Weitekamp and Hans-Jürgen Kerner, eds., *Cross-National Longitudinal Research on Human Development and Criminal Behavior*. Dordrecht, The Netherlands: Kluwer.

Fox, James Alan, and Paul E. Tracy. 1988. "A Measure of Skewness in Offense Distributions." *Journal of Quantitative Criminology* 4:259–273.

Frazier, Charles E. 1976. *Theoretical Approaches to Deviance: An Evaluation*. New York: Bobbs-Merrill.

Gadd, David, and Stephen Farrall. 2004. "Criminal Careers, Desistance and Subjectivity: Interpreting Men's Narratives of Change." *Theoretical Criminology* 8:123–156.

Giordano, Peggy C., Stephen A. Cernkovich, and Jennifer L. Rudolph. 2002. "Gender, Crime, and Desistance: Toward a Theory of Cognitive Transformation." *American Journal of Sociology* 107:990–1064.

Glaser, Daniel. 1964. *The Effectiveness of a Prison and Parole System*. New York: Bobbs-Merrill.

Glueck, Sheldon, and Eleanor Glueck. 1950. *Unraveling Juvenile Delinquency*. Cambridge, MA: Harvard University Press.

Gottfredson, Michael R., and Travis Hirschi. 1986. "The True Value of Lambda Would Appear to Be Zero." *Criminology* 24:213–234.

Gottfredson, Michael R., and Travis Hirschi. 1987. "The Methodological Adequacy of Longitudinal Research on Crime." *Criminology* 25:581–614.

Gottfredson, Michael R., and Travis Hirschi. 1988. "Science, Public Policy, and the Career Paradigm." *Criminology* 26:37–55.

Gottfredson, Michael R., and Travis Hirschi. 1990. *A General Theory of Crime*. Stanford, CA: Stanford University Press.

Gottfredson, Michael R., and Travis Hirschi. 1995. "Control Theory and Life-Course Perspective." *Studies on Crime and Crime Prevention* 4:131–142.

Greenberg, David F. 1975. "The Incapacitative Effect of Imprisonment: Some Estimates." *Law and Society Review* 9:541–580.

Greenberg, David F. 1991. "Modeling Criminal Careers." *Criminology* 25:17–46.

Greene, Michael A. 1977. *The Incapacitative Effect of Imprisonment on Policies of Crime*. Unpublished Ph.D. thesis, School of Urban and Public Affairs, Carnegie Mellon University, Pittsburgh. Ann Arbor, MI: University Microfilms.

Greenwood, Peter W., and Allan Abrahamse. 1982. *Selective Incapacitation* Rand Report R-2815-NIJ. Santa Monica, CA: Rand.

Greenwood, Peter W., and Susan Turner. 1987. *Selective Incapacitation Revisited: Why the High-Rate Offenders Are Hard to Predict*. Rand Report R-3397-NIJ. Santa Monica, CA: Rand.

Guttridge, Patricia, William. F. Gabrielli, Jr., Sarnoff Mednick, and Katherine T. Van Dusen. 1983. "Criminal Violence in a Birth Cohort." In Katherine T. Van Dusen and Sarnoff Mednick, eds., *Prospective Studies of Crime and Delinquency*. Boston: Kluwer-Nijhoff.

Haapanen, Rudy. 1990. *Selective Incapacitation and the Serious Offender: A Longitudinal Study of Criminal Career Patterns*. New York: Springer-Verlag.

Hamparian, Donna, Richard Schuster, Simon Dinitz, and John Conrad. 1978. *The Violent Few: A Study of Dangerous Juvenile Offenders*. Lexington, MA: D. C. Heath.

Hawkins, J. David, and Richard F. Catalano, Jr. 1992. *Communities That Care: Action for Drug Abuse Prevention*. San Francisco: Jossey-Bass.

Haynie, Dana L. 2001. "Delinquent Peers Revisited: Does Network Structure Matter?" *American Journal of Sociology* 106:1013–1057.

Henry, Bill, Terrie E. Moffitt, Avshalom Caspi, John Langley, and Phil A. Silva. 1994. "On the "Remembrance of Things Past": A Longitudinal Evaluation of the Retrospective Method." *Psychological Assessment* 6:92–101.

Hindelang, Michael, Travis Hirschi, and Joseph Weis. 1981. *Measuring Delinquency*. Beverly Hills, CA: Sage.

Hirschi, Travis, and Michael R. Gottfredson. 1983. "Age and the Explanation of Crime." *American Journal of Sociology* 89:552–584.

Horney, Julie, D. Wayne Osgood, and Ineke Haen Marshall. 1995. "Criminal Careers in the Short-Term: Intra-Individual Variability in Crime and Its Relation to Local Life Circumstances." *American Sociological Review* 60:655–673.

Horwitz, Allan V., and Michael Wasserman. 1980. "Some Misleading Conceptions About Sentencing Research in the Juvenile Court." *Criminology* 18:411–424.

Huizinga, David H., Finn-Aage Esbensen, and Anne Wylie Weiher. 1991. "Are There Multiple Paths to Delinquency?" *Journal of Criminal Law and Criminology* 82:83–118.

Huizinga, David H., Anne Wylie Weiher, Rachele Espiritu, and Finn-Aage Esbensen. 2003. "Delinquency and Crime: Some Highlights from the Denver Youth Study." In Terence P. Thornberry and Marvin D. Krohn, eds., *Taking Stock of Delinquency: An Overview of Findings from Contemporary Longitudinal Studies*. New York: Kluwer/Plenum.

Jolliffe, Darrick, David P. Farrington, J. David Hawkins, Richard F. Catalano, Karl G. Hill, and Rick Kosterman. 2003. "Predictive, Concurrent, Prospective and Retrospective Validity of Self-Reported Delinquency." *Criminal Behaviour and Mental Health* 13:179–197.

Jones, Bobby L., Daniel S. Nagin, and Kathryn Roeder. 2001. "A SAS Procedure Based on Mixture Models for Estimating Developmental Trajectories." *Sociological Methods and Research* 29:374–393.

Kazemian, Lila, and David P. Farrington. 2005. "Comparing the Validity of Prospective, Retrospective, and Official Onset for Different Offending Categories." *Journal of Quantitative Criminology* 21:127–147.

Kazemian, Lila, and David P. Farrington. 2006. "Exploring Residual Career Length and Residual Number of Offenses for Two Generations of Repeat Offenders." *Journal of Research in Crime and Delinquency* 43: 89–113.

Kelley, Barbara Tatem, David H. Huizinga, Terence P. Thornberry, and Rolf Loeber. 1997. *Epidemiology of Serious Violence*. Office of Juvenile Justice Bulletin. Washington, DC: U.S. Department of Justice, Office of Juvenile Justice and Delinquency Prevention.

Krohn, Marvin D., Terence P. Thornberry, Craig Rivera, and Marc Le Blanc. 2001. "Later Delinquency Careers." In Rolf Loeber and David P. Farrington, eds., *Child Delinquents: Development, Intervention, and Service Needs*. Thousand Oaks, CA: Sage.

Kurlychek, Megan, Robert Brame, and Shawn Bushway. 2006. "Scarlet Letters and Recidivism: Does an Old Criminal Record Predict Future Offending?" *Criminology and Public Policy*, forthcoming.

Laub, John H. 2004. "The Life Course of Criminology in the United States: The American Society of Criminology 2003 Presidential Address." *Criminology* 42:1–26.

Laub, John H., Daniel S. Nagin, and Robert J. Sampson. 1998. "Good Marriages and Trajectories of Change in Criminal Offending." *American Sociological Review* 63:225–238.

Laub, John H., and Robert J. Sampson. 1993. "Turning Points in the Life Course: Why Change Matters to the Study of Crime." *Criminology* 31:301–325.

Laub, John H., and Robert J. Sampson. 2001. "Understanding Desistance from Crime." In Michael Tonry, ed., *Crime and Justice: A Review of Research*, vol. 28. Chicago: University of Chicago Press.

Laub, John H., and Robert J. Sampson. 2003. *Shared Beginnings, Divergent Lives: Delinquent Boys to Age 70*. Cambridge, MA: Harvard University Press.

Lauritsen, Janet. 1998. "The Age-Crime Debate: Assessing the Limits of Longitudinal Self-Report Data." *Social Forces* 77:127–155.

Le Blanc, Marc. 1997. "Socialization or Propensity: A Test of an Integrative Control Theory with Adjudicated Boys." *Studies on Crime and Crime Prevention* 6:200–224.

Le Blanc, Marc. 2002. "The Offending Cycle, Escalation, and De-Escalation in Delinquent Behavior: A Challenge for Criminology." *International Journal of Comparative and Applied Criminal Justice* 26:53–84.

Le Blanc, Marc, Gilles. Cote, and Rolf Loeber. 1991. "Temporal Paths in Delinquency: Stability, Regression and Progression Analyzed with Panel Data from an Adolescent and a Delinquent Sample." *Canadian Journal of Criminology* 33:23–44.

Le Blanc, Marc, and Marcel Fréchette. 1989. *Male Criminal Activity from Childhood Through Youth: Multilevel and Developmental Perspectives*. New York: Springer-Verlag.

Le Blanc, Marc, and Rolf Loeber. 1998. "Developmental Criminology Updated." In Michael Tonry, ed., *Crime and Justice: A Review of Research*, vol. 23. Chicago: University of Chicago Press.

Loeber, Rolf, and David P. Farrington, eds. 1998. *Serious and Violent Juvenile Offenders: Risk Factors and Successful Interventions*. Thousand Oaks, CA: Sage.

Loeber, Rolf, David P. Farrington, Magda Stouthamer-Loeber, Terrie E. Moffitt, and Avshalom Caspi. 1998. "The Development of Male Offending: Key Findings from the First Decade of the Pittsburgh Youth Study." *Studies on Crime and Crime Prevention* 7:141–172.

Loeber, Rolf, David P. Farrington, Magda Stouthamer-Loeber, Terrie E. Moffitt, Avshalom Caspi, Helene Raskin White, Evelyn H. Wei, and Jennifer M. Beyers. 2003. "The Development of Male Offending: Key Findings from Fourteen Years of the Pittsburgh Youth Study." In Terence P. Thornberry and Marvin D. Krohn, eds., *Taking Stock of Delinquency: An Overview of Findings from Contemporary Longitudinal Studies*. New York: Kluwer/Plenum.

Loeber, Rolf, and Dale Hay. 1994. "Key Issues in the Development of Aggression and Violence from Childhood to Early Adulthood." *Annual Review of Psychology* 48:371–410.

Loeber, Rolf, and Marc Le Blanc. 1990. "Toward a Developmental Criminology." In Michael Tonry and Norval Morris, eds., *Crime and Justice: A Review of Research*, vol. 12. Chicago: University of Chicago Press.

Loeber, Rolf, and Howard N. Snyder. 1990. "Rate of Offending in Juvenile Careers: Findings of Constancy and Change in Lambda." *Criminology* 28:97–110.

Loeber, Rolf, Evelyn Wei, Magda Stouthamer-Loeber, David H. Huizinga, and Terence P. Thornberry. 1999. "Behavioral Antecedents to Serious and Violent Offending: Joint Analyses from the Denver Youth Survey, Pittsburgh Youth Study, and the Rochester Youth Development Study." *Studies on Crime and Crime Prevention* 8:245–264.

Lynam, Donald R., Avshalom Caspi, Terrie E. Moffitt, P. O. Wikström, Rolf Loeber, and Scott P. Novak. 2000. "The Interaction Between Impulsivity and Neighborhood Context on Offending: The Effects of Impulsivity Are Stronger in Poorer Neighborhoods." *Journal of Abnormal Psychology* 109:563–574.

Lynam, Donald R., Terrie E. Moffitt, and Alex R. Piquero. 2004. "Specialization and the Propensity to Violence: Support from Self-Reports but Not Official Records." *Journal of Contemporary Criminal Justice* 20:215–228.

Maltz, Michael D., Andrew C. Gordon, David McDowall, and Richard McCleary. 1980. "An Artifact in Pre-Test-Post-Test Designs: How It Can Mistakingly Make Delinquency Programs Look Effective." *Evaluation Review* 4:225–240.

Maruna, Shadd. 2001. *Making Good: How Ex-Convicts Reform and Rebuild Their Lives*. Washington, DC: American Psychological Association.

Matza, David. 1964. *Delinquency and Drift*. New York: John Wiley & Sons.

Maxfield, Michael G., Barbara L. Weiler, and Cathy S. Widom. 2000. "Comparing Self-Reports and Official Records of Arrests." *Journal of Quantitative Criminology* 16: 87–110.

Meisenhelder, Thomas. 1977. "An Exploratory Study of Exiting from Criminal Careers." *Criminology* 15:319–334.

Menard, Scott, and Delbert S. Elliott. 1990. "Longitudinal and Cross-Sectional Data Collection and Analysis in the Study of Crime and Delinquency." *Justice Quarterly* 7:11–55.

Moffitt, Terrie E. 1993. "'Life-Course-Persistent' and 'Adolescence-Limited' Antisocial Behavior: A Developmental Taxonomy." *Psychological Review* 100:674–701.

Moffitt, Terrie E. 1994. "Natural Histories of Delinquency." In Elmar G. M. Weitekamp and Hans-Jurgen Kerner, eds., *Cross-National Longitudinal Research on Human Development and Criminal Behavior*. Dordrecht, The Netherlands: Kluwer Academic.

Moffitt, Terrie E. 2006. "Life-Course-Persistent Versus Adolescence-Limited Antisocial Behavior." In D. Cicchetti and D. Cohen, eds., *Developmental Psychopathology*, 2nd ed. New York: Wiley.

Moffitt, Terrie E., Avshalom Caspi, Michael Rutter, and Phil A. Silva. 2001. *Sex Differences in Antisocial Behaviour: Conduct Disorder, Delinquency, and Violence in the Dunedin Longitudinal Study*. Cambridge: Cambridge University Press.

Murray, Charles A., and Louis A. Cox. 1979. *Beyond Probation*. Beverly Hills, CA: Sage.

Nagin, Daniel S. 1999. "Analyzing Developmental Trajectories: A Semi-Parametric, Group-Based Approach." *Psychological Methods* 4:139–177.

Nagin, Daniel S. 2005. *Group-Based Modeling of Development*. Cambridge, MA: Harvard University Press.

Nagin, Daniel S., and David P. Farrington. 1992a. "The Onset and Persistence of Offending." *Criminology* 30:501–523.

Nagin, Daniel S., and David P. Farrington. 1992b. "The Stability of Criminal Potential from Childhood to Adulthood." *Criminology* 30:235–260.

Nagin, Daniel S., David P. Farrington, and Terrie E. Moffitt. 1995. "Life-Course Trajectories of Different Types of Offenders." *Criminology* 33:111–139.

Nagin, Daniel S., and Kenneth C. Land. 1993. "Age, Criminal Careers, and Population Heterogeneity: Specification and Estimation of a Nonparametric, Mixed Poisson Model." *Criminology* 31:327–362.

Nagin, Daniel S., and Raymond Paternoster. 1991. "On the Relationship of Past and Future Participation in Delinquency." *Criminology* 29:163–190.

Nagin, Daniel S., and Raymond Paternoster. 2000. "Population Heterogeneity and State Dependence: State of the Evidence and Directions for Future Research." *Journal of Quantitative Criminology* 16:117–144.

Nagin, Daniel S., and Richard E. Tremblay. 1999. "Trajectories of Boys' Physical Aggression, Opposition, and Hyperactivity on the Path to Physically Violent and Nonviolent Juvenile Delinquency." *Child Development* 70:1181–1196.

Nagin, Daniel S., and Richard E. Tremblay. 2005. "Developmental Trajectory Groups: Fact or a Useful Statistical Fiction?" *Criminology* 43:873–904.

Nevares, Dora, Marvin E. Wolfgang, and Paul E. Tracy. 1990. *Delinquency in Puerto Rico: The 1970 Birth Cohort Study.* New York: Greenwood Press.

Osgood, D. Wayne. 2005. "Making Sense of Crime and the Life Course." *The Annals of the American Academy of Political and Social Science, Developmental Criminology and Its Discontents: Trajectories of Crime from Childhood to Old Age* 602:196–211.

Parker, Tony. 1983. *The People of Providence.* London: Hutchinson.

Paternoster, Raymond, Charles W. Dean, Alex Piquero, Paul Mazerolle, and Robert Brame. 1997. "Generality, Continuity, and Change in Offending." *Journal of Quantitative Criminology* 13:231–266.

Patterson, Gerald R. 1993. "Orderly Change in a Stable World: The Antisocial Trait as a Chimera." *Journal of Consulting and Clinical Psychology* 61:911–919.

Patterson, Gerald R., L. Crosby, and S. Vuchinich. 1992. "Predicting Risk for Early Police Contact." *Journal of Quantitative Criminology* 8:335–355.

Patterson, Gerald R., Barbara DeBaryshe, and Elizabeth Ramsey. 1989. "A Developmental Perspective on Antisocial Behavior." *American Psychologist* 44:329–335.

Patterson, Gerald R., and Karen Yoerger. 1999. "Intraindividual Growth in Covert Antisocial Behaviour: A Necessary Precursor to Chronic Juvenile and Adult Arrests?" *Criminal Behaviour and Mental Health* 9:24–38.

Petersilia, Joan. 1980. "Criminal Career Research: A Review of Recent Evidence." In Norval Morris and Michael Tonry, eds., *Crime and Justice: An Annual Review of Research,* vol. 2. Chicago: University of Chicago Press.

Petersilia, Joan, Peter W. Greenwood, and Marvin Lavin. 1978. *Criminal Careers of Habitual Felons.* Washington, DC: National Institute of Law Enforcement and Criminal Justice, Law Enforcement Assistance Administration, U.S. Government Printing Office.

Peterson, Mark A., and Harriet B. Braiker. 1980. *Doing Crime: A Survey of California Prison Inmates.* Report R-2200-DOJ. Santa Monica, CA: Rand Corp.

Piquero, Alex R. 2000a. "Frequency, Specialization, and Violence in Offending Careers." *Journal of Research in Crime and Delinquency* 37:392–418.

Piquero, Alex R. 2000b. "Assessing the Relationships Between Gender, Chronicity, Seriousness, and Offense Skewness in Criminal Offending." *Journal of Criminal Justice* 28:103–116.

Piquero, Alex R. 2004. "Somewhere Between Persistence and Desistance: The Intermittency of Criminal Careers." In Shadd Maruna and Russ Immarigeon, eds., *After Crime and Punishment: Pathways to Offender Reintegration*. Cullompton, Devon: Willan Publishing.

Piquero, Alex R. 2005. "Taking Stock of Developmental Trajectories of Criminal Activity over the Life Course." In Akiva Liberman, ed., *The Yield of Recent Longitudinal Research on Crime and Delinquency*. Dordrecht, Netherlands: Springer.

Piquero, Alex R., Alfred Blumstein, Robert Brame, Rudy Haapanen, Edward P. Mulvey, and Daniel S. Nagin. 2001. "Assessing the Impact of Exposure Time and Incapacitation on Longitudinal Trajectories of Criminal Offending." *Journal of Adolescent Research* 16:54–74.

Piquero, Alex R., Robert Brame, and Donald Lynam. 2004. "Studying the Factors Related to Career Length" *Crime and Delinquency* 50:412–435.

Piquero, Alex R., Robert Brame, Paul Mazerolle, and Rudy Haapanen. 2002a. "Crime in Emerging Adulthood." *Criminology* 40:137–170.

Piquero, Alex R., Robert Brame, and Terrie E. Moffitt. 2005a. "Extending the Study of Continuity and Change: Gender Differences in the Linkage Between Adolescent and Adult Offending." *Journal of Quantitative Criminology* 21:219–243.

Piquero, Alex R., and Stephen L. Buka. 2002. "Linking Juvenile and Adult Patterns of Criminal Activity in the Providence Cohort of the National Collaborative Perinatal Project." *Journal of Criminal Justice* 30:1–14.

Piquero, Alex R., David P. Farrington, and Alfred Blumstein. 2003. "The Criminal Career Paradigm." In Michael Tonry, ed., *Crime and Justice: A Review of Research*, Vol. 30. Chicago: University of Chicago Press.

Piquero, Alex R., John MacDonald, and Karen F. Parker. 2002b. "Race, Local Life Circumstances, and Crime." *Social Science Quarterly* 83: 654–670

Piquero, Alex R., and Paul Mazerolle, eds. 2001. *Life-Course Criminology: Contemporary and Classic Readings*. Belmont, CA: Wadsworth.

Piquero, Alex R., and Terrie E. Moffitt. 2005. "Explaining the Facts of Crime: How the Developmental Taxonomy Replies to Farrington's Invitation." In David P. Farrington, ed., *Integrated Developmental and Life-Course Theories of Offending, Advances in Criminological Theory*, Vol. 14. New Brunswick, NJ: Transaction.

Piquero, Alex R., Terrie E. Moffitt, and Brian Lawton. 2005b. "Race and Crime: The Contribution of Individual, Familial, and Neighborhood Level Risk Factors to Life-Course-Persistent Offending." In Darnell Hawkins and Kimberly Kempf-Leonard, eds., *Our Children, Their Children: Race, Crime, and the Juvenile Justice System*. Chicago: University of Chicago Press.

Piquero, Alex R., Raymond Paternoster, Paul Mazerolle, Robert Brame, and Charles W. Dean. 1999. "Onset Age and Offense Specialization." *Journal of Research in Crime and Delinquency* 36:275–299.

Pulkkinen, Lea. 1988. "Delinquent Development: Theoretical and Empirical Considerations." In Michael Rutter, ed., *Studies of Psychosocial Risk: The Power of Longitudinal Data*. Cambridge: Cambridge University Press.

Quetelet, Adolphe. 1984 (1831). *Research on the Propensity for Crime at Different Ages*. Cincinnati, OH: Anderson Publishing.

Reiss, Albert J., Jr. 1986. "Co-Offender Influences on Criminal Careers." In Alfred Blumstein, Jacqueline Cohen, Jeffrey A. Roth, and Christy A. Visher, eds., *Criminal Careers and "Career Criminals."* Washington, DC: National Academy Press.

Reiss, Albert J., Jr., and David P. Farrington. 1991. "Advancing Knowledge about Co-Offending: Results from a Prospective Longitudinal Survey of London Males." *Journal of Criminal Law and Criminology* 82:360–395.

Robins, Lee N. 1966. *Deviant Children Grown Up*. Baltimore: Williams and Wilkins.

Robins, Lee N. 1978. "Sturdy Childhood Predictors of Adult Antisocial Behavior: Replications from Longitudinal Studies." *Psychological Medicine* 8:611–622.

Roeder, Kathryn, Kevin G. Lynch, and Daniel S. Nagin. 1999. "Modeling Uncertainty in Latent Class Membership: A Case Study in Criminology." *Journal of the American Statistical Association* 94:766–776.

Rojek, Dean G., and Maynard L. Erickson. 1982. "Delinquent Careers: A Test of the Career Escalation Model." *Criminology* 20:5–28.

Rowe, David C., D. Wayne Osgood, and W. Alan Nicewander. 1990. "A Latent Trait Approach to Unifying Criminal Careers." *Criminology* 28:237–270.

Sampson, Robert J., and John H. Laub. 1992. "Crime and Deviance in the Life Course." *Annual Review of Sociology* 18:63–84.

Sampson, Robert J., and John H. Laub. 1993. *Crime in the Making: Pathways and Turning Points Through Life*. Cambridge, MA: Harvard University Press.

Sampson, Robert J., and John H. Laub. 1997. "A Life-Course Theory of Cumulative Disadvantage and the Stability of Delinquency." In Terence P. Thornberry, ed., *Developmental Theories of Crime and Delinquency: Advances in Criminological Theory*, Vol. 7. New Brunswick, NJ: Transaction.

232 REFERENCES

Sampson, Robert J, and John H. Laub. 2003. "Life-Course Desisters? Trajectories of Crime Among Delinquent Boys Followed to Age 70." *Criminology* 41:555–592.

Sampson, Robert J., and John H. Laub. 2005a. "Preface." *The Annals of the American Academy of Political and Social Science, Developmental Criminology and Its Discontents: Trajectories of Crime from Childhood to Old Age* 602:6–11.

Sampson, Robert J., and John H. Laub. 2005b. "Seductions of Method: Rejoinder to Nagin and Tremblay's Developmental Trajectory Groups: Fact or Fiction." *Criminology* 43:905–915.

Sarnecki, Jerzy. 1990. "Delinquent Networks in Sweden." *Journal of Quantitative Criminology* 6:31–51.

Sarnecki, Jerzy. 2001. *Delinquent Networks: Youth Co-Offending in Stockholm.* Cambridge: Cambridge University Press.

Scarpitti, Frank R., and Richard M. Stephenson. 1971. "Juvenile Court Dispositions: Factors in the Decision-Making Process." *Crime and Delinquency* 17:142–151.

Schmertmann, Carl P., Adansi A. Amankwaa, and Robert D. Long. 1998. "Three Strikes and You're Out: Demographic Analysis of Mandatory Prison Sentencing." *Demography* 35:445–463.

Schumacher, Michael, and Gwen. Kurz, 1999. *The 8% Solution: Preventing Serious, Repeat Juvenile Crime.* Thousand Oaks, CA: Sage Publications.

Schwarz, Gideon. 1978. "Estimating Dimensions of a Model." *Annals of Statistics* 6:461–464.

Shannon, Lyle. 1982. *Assessing the Relationship of Adult Criminal Careers to Juvenile Careers.* Washington, DC: U.S. Department of Justice, Office of Juvenile Justice and Delinquency Prevention.

Shannon, Lyle. 1988. *Criminal Career Continuity: Its Social Context.* New York: Human Sciences Press.

Shaw, Clifford R. 1930. *The Jack-Roller: A Delinquent Boy's Own Story.* Chicago: University of Chicago Press.

Shepherd, Jonathan, David P. Farrington, and John Potts. 2004. "Impact of Antisocial Lifestyle on Health." *Journal of Public Health Medicine* 26:347–352.

Shinnar, Shlomo, and Reuel Shinnar. 1975. "The Effects of the Criminal Justice System on the Control of Crime: A Quantitative Approach." *Law and Society Review* 9:581–611.

Silver, Eric, William R. Smith, and Steven Banks. 2000. "Constructing Actuarial Devices for Predicting Recidivism: A Comparison of Methods." *Criminal Justice and Behavior* 27: 733–764.

Simons, Ronald L., Christine Johnson, Rand D. Conger, and Glen H. Elder, Jr. 1998. "A Test of Latent Trait Versus Life-Course Perspectives on the Stability of Adolescent Antisocial Behavior." *Criminology* 36:217–243.

Simons, Ronald L., Chyi-In Wu, Rand D. Conger, and Frederick O. Lorenz. 1994. "Two Routes to Delinquency: Differences Between Early and Late Starters in the Impact of Parenting and Deviant Peers." *Criminology* 32:247–276.

Smith, D. Randall, and William R. Smith. 1984. "Patterns of Delinquent Careers: An Assessment of Three Perspectives." *Social Science Research* 13:129–158.

Spelman, William. 1994. *Criminal Incapacitation*. New York: Plenum.

Stattin, Håkan, David Magnusson, and Howard Reichel. 1989. "Criminal Activity at Different Ages: A Study Based on a Swedish Longitudinal Research Population." *British Journal of Criminology* 29:368–385.

Steffensmeier, Darrell, Emilie Andersen Allan, Miles D. Harer, and Cathy Streifel. 1989. "Age and the Distribution of Crime." *American Journal of Sociology* 94:803–831.

Steffensmeier, Darrell, and Jeffery T. Ulmer. 2005. *Confessions of a Dying Thief: Understanding Criminal Careers and Illegal Enterprise*. Somerset, NJ: Aldine-Transaction.

Stolzenberg, Lisa, and Stewart J. D'Alessio. 1997. "'Three Strikes and You're Out': The Impact of California's New Mandatory Sentencing Law on Serious Crime Rates." *Crime and Delinquency* 43:457–469.

Stouthamer-Loeber, Magda, Evelyn Wei, Rolf Loeber, and Ann S. Masten. 2004. "Desistance from Persistent Serious Delinquency in the Transition to Adulthood." *Development and Psychopathology* 16:897–918.

Svensson, Robert. 2002. "Strategic Offenses in the Criminal Career Context." *British Journal of Criminology* 42: 395–411.

Tarling, Roger. 1993. *Analyzing Offending: Data, Models and Interpretations*. London: Her Majesty's Stationery Office.

Thornberry, Terence P. 1989. "Panel Effects and the Use of Self-Reported Measures of Delinquency in Longitudinal Studies." In Malcolm W. Klein, ed., *Cross-National Research in Self-Reported Crime and Delinquency*. Dordrecht, The Netherlands: Kluwer Academic.

Thornberry, Terence P. 1997. "Introduction: Some Advantages of Developmental and Life-Course Perspectives for the Study of Crime and Delinquency." In Terence P. Thornberry, ed., *Developmental Theories of Crime and Delinquency: Advances in Criminology Theory*, Vol. 7. New Brunswick, NJ: Transaction Publishers.

Thornberry, Terence P., and Marvin D. Krohn. 2001. "The Development of Delinquency: An Interactional Perspective." In Susan O. White, ed., *Handbook of Youth and Justice*. New York: Plenum.

Thornberry, Terence P., Alan J. Lizotte, Marvin D. Krohn, Carolyn A. Smith, and Pamela K. Porter. 2003. "Causes and Consequences of Delinquency: Findings from the Rochester Youth Development Study."

In Terence P. Thornberry and Marvin D. Krohn, eds., *Taking Stock of Delinquency: An Overview of Findings from Contemporary Longitudinal Studies.* New York: Kluwer/Plenum.

Tibbetts, Stephen G., and Alex R. Piquero. 1999. "The Influence of Gender, Low Birth Weight, and Disadvantaged Environment in Predicting Early Onset of Offending: A Test of Moffitt's Interactional Hypothesis." *Criminology* 37:843–878.

Tittle, Charles R., and Harold G. Grasmick. 1997. "Criminal Behavior and Age." *Journal of Criminal Law and Criminology* 81:309–342.

Tolan, Patrick H., and Deborah Gorman-Smith. 1998. "Development of Serious and Violent Offending Careers." In Rolf Loeber and David P. Farrington, eds., *Serious and Violent Juvenile Offenders: Risk Factors and Successful Interventions.* Thousand Oaks, CA: Sage.

Tolan, Patrick H., and Peter Thomas. 1995. "The Implications of Age of Onset for Delinquency Risk. II. Longitudinal Data." *Journal of Abnormal Child Psychology* 23:157–181.

Tracy, Paul E., and Kimberly Kempf-Leonard. 1996. *Continuity and Discontinuity in Criminal Careers.* New York: Plenum.

Tracy, Paul E., Marvin E. Wolfgang, and Robert M. Figlio. 1990. *Delinquency Careers in Two Birth Cohorts.* New York: Plenum.

Tremblay, Richard E., Christa Japel, Daniel Perusse, Pierre McDuff, Michel Boivin, Mark Zoccolillo, and Jacques Montplaisir. 1999. "The Search for the Age of 'Onset' of Physical Aggression: Rousseau and Bandura Revisited." *Criminal Behaviour and Mental Health* 9:8–23.

Tremblay, Richard E., Frank Vitaro, Daniel S. Nagin, Linda Pagani, and Jean R. Segúin. 2003. "The Montreal Longitudinal and Experimental Study: Rediscovering the Power of Descriptions." In Terence P. Thornberry and Marvin D. Krohn, eds., *Taking Stock of Delinquency: An Overview of Findings from Contemporary Longitudinal Studies.* New York: Kluwer/Plenum.

Visher, Christy A. 1986. "The Rand Inmate Survey: A Re-Analysis." In Alfred Blumstein, Jacqueline Cohen, Jeffrey A. Roth, and Christy A. Visher, eds., *Criminal Careers and "Career Criminals,"* vol. 2. Washington, DC: National Academy Press.

Visher, Christy A. 1987. "Incapacitation and Crime Control: Does a 'Lock 'Em Up' Strategy Reduce Crime?" *Justice Quarterly* 4:513–543.

Visher, Christy A. 2000. "Career Criminals and Crime Control." In Joseph F. Sheley, ed., *Criminology: A Contemporary Handbook*, 3rd ed. Belmont, CA: Wadsworth.

Visher, Christy A., and Jeffrey A. Roth. 1986. "Participation in Criminal Careers." In Alfred Blumstein, Jacqueline Cohen, Jeffrey A. Roth, and

Christy A. Visher, eds., *Criminal Careers and "Career Criminals,"* vol. 1. Washington, DC: National Academy Press.

Warr, Mark. 2002. *Companions in Crime: The Social Aspects of Criminal Conduct.* Cambridge: Cambridge University Press.

West, Donald J. 1969. *Present Conduct and Future Delinquency.* London: Heinemann.

West, Donald J. 1982. *Delinquency: Its Roots, Causes, and Prospects.* London: Heinemann.

West, Donald J., and David P. Farrington. 1973. *Who Becomes Delinquent?* London: Heinemann.

West, Donald J., and David P. Farrington. 1977. *The Delinquent Way of Life.* London: Heinemann.

Western, Bruce, Jeffrey R. Kling, and David F. Weiman. 2001. "The Labor Market Consequences of Incarceration." *Crime and Delinquency* 47:410–427.

White, Norman, and Alex R. Piquero. 2004. "An Empirical Test of Silverthorn and Frick's Challenge to Moffitt's Developmental Taxonomy." *Criminal Behaviour and Mental Health* 14:291–309.

Wikström, Per-Olof H. 1985. *Everyday Violence in Contemporary Sweden: Situational and Ecological Aspects.* Stockholm: National Council for Crime Prevention, Research Division.

Wikström, Per-Olof H. 1990. "Age and Crime in a Stockholm Cohort." *Journal of Quantitative Criminology* 6:61–83.

Wikström, Per-Olof H., Ronald V. Clarke, and Joan McCord. 1995. *Integrating Crime Prevention Strategies: Propensity and Opportunity.* Stockholm: Fritzes.

Wikström, Per-Olof H., and Rolf Loeber. 2000. "Do Disadvantaged Neighborhoods Cause Well-Adjusted Children to Become Adolescent Delinquents?" *Criminology* 38:1201–1233.

Wilson, James Q., and Richard J. Herrnstein. 1985. *Crime and Human Nature.* New York: Simon & Schuster.

Wolfgang, Marvin E., Robert M. Figlio, and Thorsten Sellin. 1972. *Delinquency in a Birth Cohort.* Chicago: University of Chicago Press.

Wolfgang, Marvin E., Terence P. Thornberry, and Robert M. Figlio. 1987. *From Boy to Man, from Delinquency to Crime.* Chicago: University of Chicago Press.

Zimring, Franklin E., Sam Kamin, and Gordon Hawkins. 1999. *Crime and Punishment in California: The Impact of Three Strikes and You're Out.* Berkeley: Institute of Governmental Studies Press, University of California.

# Index

**Other books in the series** (*continued from page iii*)